Relics Of A Woma

MW01230187

This book belongs to:

_____

Relics

Of A

Woman

by

Gwendolyn Hampton

GREETINGS EVERYONE:
PLEASE ENJOY THIS RENDITION OF THE CHRONICLES OF THE SEASONS AND EPISODES OF MY SIXTY YEAR LIFE SAGA.

FOR ALL INTENTS AND PURPOSES, SIXTY (60) YEARS IS A LONG TIME TO LIVE ON THIS PLANET. HOWEVER, THE TRUTH THAT COUNTED FOR ME WAS HOW I LIVED MY LIFE FROM ZERO TO SIXTY. THEN WHEN I CONSIDERED ALL THINGS, I REALIZED THAT AGE WAS TRULY JUST A NUMBER.

IN *RELICS OF A WOMAN (ROAW)*, I GET THE HONOR OF SHARING MY TESTIMONY WITH OTHERS: MOST ESPECIALLY WOMEN. ALSO, I AM BLESSED TO GIVE MOTIVATION TO EVERYONE TO LIVE THEIR BEST LIFE EACH AND EVERY MOMENT: SIXTY (60) YEARS IS NOT GUARANTEED.

OFTEN, I FOUND MYSELF GUILTY OF COMMITTING FELONY FOOLISHNESS IN MY LIFE AND WAS REMANDED TO SELF-IMPOSED PRISONS OF DRAMA AND TRAUMA. MANY TIMES, WITH NO ESCAPE IN SIGHT, AND NO PLEA BARGAIN ON THE HORIZON, I ENDURED IN SILENCE. THUS, I PRAY THAT YOU WILL ACCEPT MY STORY AS A *CAUTIONARY TALE*. I ENCOURAGE YOU TO TAKE HEED TO THE MISTAKES I'VE MADE AND CHALLENGES I'VE FACED.

BY EXAMINING THE EVIDENCE AND EXHIBITS OF MY PAST THROUGH *ROAW*, I HAVE STOPPED ASKING QUESTIONS OF *GOD* AND STARTED LIVING FOR *HIM*. ALL THE FRAGMENTS OF MANY DREAMS, FEIGNED HOPES, AND UNDENIABLE DEFEATS HAVE PUSHED ME TO NOW FIGHT FOR **MY** OWN LIFE.

AND SO, I NOW INVITE YOU TO SIT ON THE JURY BENCH AND WITNESS THE UNRAVELING OF A WOMAN. YOU SHALL OBSERVE THE STEPS TO REDISCOVERY THAT HAVE LEAD TO PUTTING THE PIECES OF MY LIFE BACK TOGETHER. AND, YOU SHALL SEE HOW, THROUGH *GOD*, I WAS ABLE TO OVERCOME EVERYTHING.

GODBLESS!!! LOVE ALWAYS
GWENDOLYN HAMPTON

P.S. "THIS AIN'T A LESSON IN WORLD ENGLISH LITERATURE." SMILE ☺

CONTENTS

Disclaimer: DON'T TRY THIS AT HOME

The expressions, views, and opinions in *Relics Of A Woman* are those of the Author. All persons and incidents contained herein are for the sole purposes of sharing stories for the context of this book. It is with regret the Author apologizes if anyone consider these stories as offensive or intentionally harmful. There is no intended likeness or coincidence to any person or incident other than those represented in *Relics Of A Woman*.

DEDICATION

Relics Of A Woman is dedicated to my *Heavenly Father GOD*, who is the True Author and Finisher of this great masterpiece. May the words on these pages fulfill *His* purposes as intended when *He* conceived this book in *me*.

And it is with honor and respect that I devote this commission to my parents *Mr. & Mrs. Wilson and Margie Bradford*.

ACKNOWLEGEMENTS

THERE IS NO WAY I COULD EVER ACKNOWLEDGE EVERYONE THAT HAD A PART IN THE SUCCESS OF **RELICS OF A WOMAN**, SO I WILL SAY **THANK YOU** TO EVERYONE FOR THEIR WORDS OF ENCOURAGEMENT AND SMILES OF SUPPORT. TO THOSE THAT DOUBTED MY EVER COMPLETING THIS MISSION, I ALSO SAY **THANK YOU** BECAUSE YOUR DOUBT PUSHED ME, AND I DIDN'T WANT YOU TO BE RIGHT.

SARAH BURTON, KIMBERLY PEDRO, AND LINDORA BAKER I APPRECIATE YOUR EFFORTS TO HELP.

Special thanks to Linda Sullivan, Fran Green, Gloria Taylor, and Neverlyn Townsel for taking time out of their busy schedule to read **Relics Of A Woman (ROAW)** with critical eyes in context and grammar. Their feedback was invaluable in the completion of **ROAW**

Gwendolyn Hampton

SEASON I

YOUNG AND RECKLESS

EPISODE I: THERE ONCE WAS A TIME

On December 16, 1959, in Shreveport, Louisiana, Mr. Bradford anxiously awaited the nurse as he paced the floor. The ebb and flow of the panic he was feeling inside seemed to threaten a volcanic eruption. Grabbing the nearest seat to him, all he could see in his mind's eye was himself, bolting to the men's restroom, and falling to his knees in the stall praying. *LORD, please take care of my wife and baby. Father, if something happens to Margie, I don't know what I'll do. Our sons need their Mother, and I need her too.*

"Mr. Bradford, it's a girl. And don't worry, your wife and daughter are fine", the nurse said. Quickly, the panic subsided, and he couldn't stop smiling as he thanked the nurse. With overflowing joy, Mr. Bradford thought *A daughter, A daughter. Just what I wanted. And Thank You GOD! Margie's okay!* Still smiling, he imagined what his household would look like with his four boys, Kenneth (Kenny), Jerry, Terry, and Gregory (Greg) and now a daughter.

My parents named me, their beautiful bundle of joy *Gwendolyn Sue*. Admittedly, the name *Gwendolyn* was a mouthful, and it didn't take long for my family to shorten it to *Gwen*.

I enjoyed my place as the baby of the family for almost three years. This was when I became a big sister to the cutest baby girl named Patrice.

It was an exciting time for me, getting ready for first grade. At age six, I was full of anticipation, thinking about how much fun it would be to follow in my brother's footsteps. Even as a shy introvert, getting in on the popularity of this rowdy crowd would have been a dream come true for me.

On the first day of school, I was proud and felt really important when the teacher escorted our class of first-graders to the first room, on the first wing of Eighty-First Street Elementary School. It didn't take long to find out that hanging out with my brothers was not an option; The Bradford bravado these little men had created was well-known and not a place for a girl, much less a little sister. My understanding of life was limited, so quickly adjusting myself to this reality, I got busy finding my place.

The years were good and fun at Eighty-First until we got word that we'd have to transfer to Atkins Elementary. The school system had integrated the black and white schools together. As excited as I was about going to a new school, I hated the fact that I wouldn't finish my elementary days at my beloved Eight-First Street Elementary School.

My parents worked very hard to provide a stable environment for us. Never wanting for anything our family traveled by car, train, and plane. As a family, we had so many fond memories, especially during the holidays when there would be true joy in the house. Our street went wild one Christmas after our parents bought all six of us a bike. As the Bradford Clan took to the streets, everyone, even the elders came out grinning to see. Then there was the Christmas we all got roller skates. As a family we'd have good times shelling pecans, then eating them with peppermints by the heater watching Carol Burnett.

Dad and Mom would be so proud of us whenever we entertained family and friends. Sometimes, my sister and I, all dolled up with pretty dresses, white lace socks, and patent leather Mary Jane shoes would strut our stuff, showcasing our dance skills to songs like *Tighten up*.

Our neighborhood, Cedar Grove (The Hood), was considered a stepchild to the more affluent subdivision across the street called Eden Gardens, and the much more affluent subdivision down the way called Spring Lake. In spite of everything, we were taught to have pride in our circumstances, and our community. Mr. and Mrs. Bradford held a prominent place in the community as they helped to raise so many kids who needed support, especially in a place like Cedar Grove.

As for me, I played with all the kids in my neighborhood. Corner to corner my block brimmed with sisters (Cynth, Cookie, Lolo, Jackie, Ne-Naw, Lavon, Rosie, and Lil Momma) and brothers (Mel, Ray, Quintin, James, Joe Wayne, and Jimmy), of other mothers, and husbands, wives, and single parents (Ms. Mamie, Mr. Johnnie, Ms. Kizzie, The Browns, The Williams, The Mosley's, The Jenkins) who became my unofficial aunties and uncles. Not to mentions the Elders (Momma Sarah, Ms. Emma and PawPaw, also Mr. Jackson and Momma Georgia) who were the keepers of traditional ways and who also had permission from my parents to reprimand as needed. They would make sure my parents would get the word of any wayward behavior of mine, and this would mean a second reprimand when I got home, often in the form of a whupping. The names I mention are just some of the ones that were an integral part of my childhood.

Sometimes it was hard to defend myself as an overweight kid, and meanness could be the order of the day with taunting names from my brothers like ***"Pudgy"*** and ***"Baby Blimp"***.

In the sixth grade, my classmate Pam started bullying me. I did my best to ignore her because I was excited about entering junior high school the next year. She wouldn't stop. One day after school, I was stopped by a mob on the way home. Front and center was Pam, and she said to me "I'm gonna whup your ass!"

Hearing my Mom's words in my head, I told her, "I'm not going to fight you on the school grounds." Stricken with fear, I swiftly walked off campus, heading for the railroad tracks. I'd never had a fight with anyone outside of my siblings, and I didn't want this to be my first. I didn't want to fight Pam but with each step, my anger began to mount. By the time I reached the first track, I was in a full-blown fury.

Tired of Pam bluffing me, and knowing I hadn't done anything to her, I turned to say something. Surprised, she shocked me with a **"sucka"** punch that perfectly connected with my face. Then, books flew everywhere as I released the anger of pent up emotions. Pam was in trouble as I pummeled her. In an effort to help, her sister even tried to get a piece of me, only to be stopped by some guys. We were still fighting by the time I reached home, and the mob had switched sides and was cheering for me. When my sister Pat ended up fighting Pam's other sister, the crowd went crazy. It was, after all, how some kids in the neighborhood fought; as a family, and nothing less. Later, when I asked Pat about the fight, she simply said, "You brought the fight to 73rd."

This incident really opened my eyes. I got to see how my sister felt when I *tried* to bully her. We didn't always get along, and she never gave in to my bullying, instead we'd fight to the end. It was a blessing my brothers and I didn't fight like my sister and me because I never could win a fight with them.

Our fighting came to a head when Mom snapped one day. We were fighting in the backseat then the car came to a screeching halt. Looking us dead in the eye, Mother screamed, "Get out!". We didn't move because we couldn't believe she meant it. Then she screamed it again, "Get out!". This time we knew she was serious, and immediately got out. Stunned as she drove away, we looked at each other thinking about how we'd behaved, and the long walk home.

Then there was the time we fought while playing in the backyard. We were sitting on the BBQ pit laughing and talking when things went bad. We started arguing, and then things got really bad when we started throwing punches. My sister knocked me off the

BBQ pit, and I landed on the ground with such a force that I floundered to breathe. Running for dear life, my sister never looked back as she ran nonstop the four blocks to our Grandmothers'. My little sister earned my respect that day, and any thoughts I had that she was a chump was squashed. This incident brought us closer, and we rarely fought afterward.

My mother had always shown amazing strength and patience, but when she went to night school to get her GED, my admiration soared. She had a husband, six kids in school and worked a full-time job. How she managed to get her high school diploma was beyond me.

Eden Gardens Junior High School was an awakening to me. Age twelve was my first consciousness of who I was. I found myself looking at boys differently when I started having strange new stirrings inside. Feeling ashamed when I became attracted to one of my brothers' friends, I tried to figure out what was going on. Confused and afraid to ask questions, I just concluded that this was a normal part of growing up.

Watching television was a joy and a hobby for me. Every day I would rush home to watch the soap opera *Dark Shadows* on TV. My favorite shows were *Star Trek, The Twilight Zone, Alfred Hitchcock, The Wild, Wild West and The Lola Falana Show*. Lola Falana was amazingly beautiful, and I even wished there had been some way to connect with her. She sang a song that inspired me tremendously. Softly she would bellow, "You can be, anything and everything you want to be. You can go, anywhere, and everywhere you want to go. **GOD** made us to be what we want to be." This song became an anthem for me many days when I was in doubt, or fearful.

In my adolescence, I was bookworm, not street smart, and had only a little bit of common sense. My self-esteem was practically non-existent and I didn't think I had much going for myself. I spent too many days being depressed. Many times though, I'd find peace sitting under the tree in our front yard. There, I would daydream about my future. I loved to dance, and under that tree, I would jam to the latest songs on my transistor radio. When the DJ would slow the music down with songs like *Betcha By Golly Wow*, I would settle down. Then, I would meditate on having a family one day, writing a book, running a business and being rich. Under my tree, I was invincible and was sure I could be anything I wanted to be.

Things weren't like that in real life however, I was a seventh grader in love with an older man. He was a handsome eighth-grade athlete in my class. Embarrassed and unsure, I just didn't know how to handle my feelings toward him. No one except my sister and Lolo knew how mixed-up I was over that boy. Fear overruled any chance I had with him; actually, I had never talked to him. In my mind, I decided he had rejected me, and the perceived rejection from this guy was heart-wrenching. Many moons passed with dreams of what could have been, but nothing ever came of my fantasies.

There was a bright spot however while sitting in class one day. My friend LaDonna, started singing, "**GOD** gave me a song that the Angels cannot sing. I been washed in the blood, of the crucified one, I've been redeemed. The LORD has been so good to me, he opened doors I could not see...". LaDonna wrote the words down for me when she saw how touched I was by the song, helping me memorize the words and the melody. This beautiful song became my go-to comfort many nights.

Something magical happened in Mrs. Howard's home economics class in the eighth grade when I discovered my talent as a seamstress. This talent was unearthed in a big way when the intrigue of sewing pushed me to a frenzy. Saturday mornings were the designated time for trips to the fabric store. Anxious to get home, I would race through the pattern books and fabrics making my selections. Cutting out patterns was time-consuming, but once I sat down at my sewing machine something amazing would happen. Time would fly, and I would finish the outfit for church the following morning. My mom was so impressed that she even bought me an expensive Sears Kenmore sewing machine.

Our parents taught us all they knew about puberty. When the stirrings inside of me turned to fantasizing about sex, I found myself wanting to know more. Though afraid to have sex, I did find ways to experiment. On the sly, I engaged in shameless intimate touching with others also caught in the same web of puberty. Hide-and-go-seek even got a new name: hide-and-go-get it. Ashamed of myself for those pre-sexual encounters, I prayed that **GOD** would not punish us for our curiosity.

My sister Pat would follow me as we trod millions of miles in our *hood*. The traffic groves in the street trekking from house to house was always worth it, especially when it came to a good game of Monopoly. Most times, I would have no problem with my sister following me, but when I wanted to take girlfriend strolls around the way, I would send her home, she didn't like it, but she would go home anyway. It was always nice to know that my friend's sisters and brothers loved us, and we all got along.

The spiritual base for our household was reinforced with attendance to Mt. Olive Baptist Church. Songs like, *Precious LORD, Amazing Grace, and At the Cross* confirmed to me that church was where I wanted to be. The Preacher at Revival said, "If you want to be saved, you have to believe that **GOD** created you, and he sent **JESUS** to Earth to save you. Believing in **Christ** is what makes you a Christian." Quickly making my way to the front, I sat on the front pew, or the Mourning Bench as it was called. I wanted to be saved, and be a Christian.

The day I was baptized, nothing seemed different when I came out of the baptismal pool. I'd been expecting something cosmic to happen, and though nothing ever did, I was confident that I had done the right thing. Being involved in church activities was how I discovered my love for the choir. No one, not even the director, told me I couldn't, "sang". And I would be terribly hurt during rehearsals when I would hear kids snickering and laughing at me behind my back because I couldn't carry a tune. Sure my voice would never change, I decided to quit the choir. But, I wasn't going to quit until after the youth performed my favorite song, *JESUS CHRIST IS THE WAY*.

As a Christian, I was conflicted by the fact that I still enjoyed rhythm and blues music. Lolo's mom impressed me as a single woman raising kids, working full-time, and taking care of her elderly mother. It never occurred to me that she had soul vibes; I only knew her to be an Usher at their church. One day through their open window, I heard a song playing. The tune seemed to lull my senses, and the lyrics were alluring; "Hello baby, I bet you never thought I would call. Well, my heart just went in with this dime...Remember what I told you to forget." I thought, *Alright Ms. Mamie*. The song was *Remember what I told you to forget*, and right then, I knew I had to have that record. And that day, Ms. Mamie became the coolest mom to me, next to my own.

Dr. Martin Luther King Jr's individual fight for civil/social justice had ended just a few years ago with his death, but the struggle was far from over. His assassination on April 4, 1968, was a tragic blow to Black America. I was only eight-years-old at the time, but I understood that everyone was praying for a change. The day Dr. King died was also my parent's anniversary and Greg, my youngest brother's birthday.

Black America was still fighting for human rights, even after years of oppression, dating back to slavery. We lived in a racially charged, violent, and prejudiced country and black lives were in danger daily. When I began to evaluate my life, all kinds of questions plagued me; *Why had I been OBLIVIOUS to the fact that my father and brothers had targets on their backs every time they walked out the door? Why wasn't I MAD? Where was PEACE?*

Black love and black power movements were started to encourage the civil rights fight. The news told of the volatile world around us. Never being afraid of the world I lived in attested to the fact that my parents had done an amazing job incubating me from these harsh realities. "War! What is it good for? Absolutely nothing", and "Diamond in the back, sunroof top, digging in the scene with the gangster lean, Oh Ho" was on so many turntables.

When The Jackson 5 sang "ABC", many evils were soothed. Even so, the undercurrent rage in some of the young men in the neighborhood was swelling. On the radio, "Young black male shot while trying to rob a motorcycle shop. The man is in serious condition at the hospital". This was a terrible incident, especially since the young man was my oldest brother.

When I enrolled at Captain Shreve High School, I was determined to break out of my self-imposed prison, and get off the rollercoaster ride of self-doubt and fear.

My passion for sewing blossomed, and I wanted to learn more. Enrolling in the Fashion Merchandising course at the Caddo Career Center, I fully delved into the curriculum of sewing, tailoring, design, and alterations. Perfecting my skills, I had the honor of teaching my mother how to sew, and her friends even hired me for sewing projects. Sewing was a blessing as it fulfilled many lonely spots in my life I kept hidden from others as a great place to hide.

My junior year in high school was challenging. In an attempt to console me, Mom planned the perfect day. We went to see the premiere of the movie *Mahogany* starring Diana Ross. The movie was excellent, but when Diana Ross dripped hot wax over her naked torso, I couldn't imagine being an adult woman doing that. I could only marvel.

After the movie, we stopped by the record shop. Mom bought me the record *Mahogany* from the soundtrack. I was really, really happy. Once we arrived home, I played the record over, and over, and over again. "Do you know where you're going to? Do you like the things that life has showen you? Where are you going to? Do you know?"

Before long the atmosphere changed and my listening and singing exploded into crying. My mom was truly taken aback when she couldn't figure out what happened. As if to herself, she asked, "Weren't we just smiling, laughing, and having a good time?" Our day had turned ugly, and I just couldn't explain why I was so emotional. I guessed it was the beauty of the love Diana Ross's character had for her man, her determination, and her passion for fashion.

My first job was that of a seamstress at the hospital where Dad worked. Making baby sheets was among my duties, and this seemed quite fitting when I began baby-sitting for several families. I learned so much from these kids, and their happy curiosity had me struggling to remember, *When was I ever THIS happy about life*? Being responsible for these kids forced me into an unknown maturity, and the mistakes I made as a babysitter, taught me how to care for children. When the jobs were over, I was proud of the wonderful opportunities I'd been given.

EPISODE II: SAILING IN THE SKY

My senior year was oh so bittersweet, as I went from cruising to crashing to cruising.

Jerry, my brother, was a senior at Howard University, working at The Smithsonian Institute. I received an awesome belated 17th birthday and early graduation gift from him. At a symposium he scored a copy of the newly released novel, Roots, autographed to me by the author Alex Haley, {Gwen-best! Alex Haley}.

When my prom date stood me up I was devastated, all dressed up with nowhere to go. My despair overwhelmed thoughts of enjoying the evening, so I stayed home. A part of me died in my tears. Later, drained from it all, I felt like I had cried a river.

The fun I had at our senior party truly made up for missing the prom. Our theme was *Sailing in 77*. Dressed in sailor garb, with our rock and roll jazz oxfords on, our senior group partied throughout the night.

The roller coaster ride didn't stop at the prom. One day, feeling grown and sexy, I accepted a ride from this really cute guy. We went to a park on the other side of town. Already there was a group of his friends, no one I knew. Before long, I started to feel uneasy. Fear struck my heart when the hairs on my body stood up, and I started shaking. I knew I was in danger when the guy got a weird look in his eye, and his friends started looking at me like I was a steak.

Trying to talk, I was only able to choke out, "What's going on?" When he ignored me, I started crying and screaming **LOUD**. Suddenly, he threw me in the car, drove near my home, opened the door and said: "**Get out!**" Shaken, I couldn't understand what had happened, but I was overwhelmed with thankfulness when my feet hit the ground running.

Not only was I ashamed, but I had broken two cardinal rules: Never leave home without permission and never leave without coins in your pocket. **GOD** was true to me that day because not only had I flounced out of the house without permission, but I didn't have one red cent with me. Grace and mercy were the only reasons why I didn't need a coin to make *The Call* for help that day.

Fearing my brothers might put out an APB on this guy and seek *"gangsta"* retribution, I kept the secret of that frightening day to myself. Holding it close to my heart, I swore to never get in the car with a stranger again: No matter how cute he was. I had nightmares thinking about the plans those boys must have had for me. It was a blessing that graduation plans kept me busy, and I was able to put that terror behind me.

Our parents were very proud when all my brothers graduated from high school. But their pride doubled when Jerry and I were scheduled to graduate the same month. He would be graduating from Howard University and me from Captain Shreve High School.

Time crept slowly as Graduation Day approached, and I was scared to death of being exposed as a fake because I didn't know what I wanted to be when I grew up. When May 30th, 1977 finally came, I realized that I wasn't the only graduating senior afraid. That feeling of fear went away though when I crossed the stage. With my diploma in hand, I started to feel happy about my future. It was a great day. Next up was college, and before I would ever step a foot on a college campus, I swore to enjoy my summer vacation.

EPISODE III: REAL LOVE

My friend and roommate Michelle and I were hanging out freshman year at Southern University Shreveport-Bossier (SUSBO) when HE walked through the door. All I could do was stare when Michelle grabbed this man an introduced him to me as her cousin.

From that day forward, this man and I were practically inseparable. As boyfriend and girlfriend, we had fun riding horses and cruising around in his pink pickup. He was a mechanic, and he taught me some basics of car care. It was shameful, but nice though the times we'd steam up the truck windows instead, being grown. I was happy, and even my brothers' teasing, "You believe the sunrise and set on this man" couldn't dampen my love.

After completing the two-year curriculum at SUSBO, I then enrolled at Louisiana State University Shreveport (LSUS), a predominantly white university. The Black college culture I had just left did not prepare me for the differences in schools. I was stunned by my invisibility on campus: nobody seemed to care for me as I felt like any face in any crowd. By the end of the semester at LSUS, I was discouraged. Unsure what was real about the world I was being educated to enter into, I then decided to quit school.

During my time off, I worked hard at odd jobs. Not only did I take in more sewing projects, but I delivered phone books and even became a Crew Leader for the Census Bureau. These were fun times, but I knew the lifestyle I wanted to live would require a college education.

A year passed before I decided to go back to school. Confident in my decision to return to school, I was elated when my boyfriend supported my decision. We even celebrated when the acceptance letter from Southern University Baton Rouge (SUBR) arrived. Our conversation turned serious though when I shared with my boyfriend the fear I had of losing him. In an attempt to calm me, he said "The four-hour drive is nothing. I'll make time to visit you." Unsatisfied with his answer, I spoiled the moment by suggesting we get married. "Don't we represent marriage already?" I asked. In my heart, I just knew I'd be a wonderful wife and mother. His simple "No" broke my heart that day, and left me wondering, ***Had I smothered him?***

EPISODE IV: SCHOOL DAZE

After everything was said and done, I left for Baton Rouge a single woman. The devastation from breaking up with my boyfriend left me thinking to myself, ***No one will ever want me, because I am FAT; and not PHAT (pretty hot and tempting).*** I knew I had to change my way of thinking, but I just didn't know how. I didn't have any friends in Baton Rouge, so I didn't have a shoulder to cry on. No one knew that my calls some nights were to my ex, asking him to reconsider. *Take It on the Run* by REO Speedwagon became my crying song during the lonely hours.

In addition to the emotional pains I was going through, the time came when I had to deal with my living arrangements. This was my first time living in a dormitory and was shocked by how some of the freshmen girls behaved. I understood the idea of freedom from Mom and Dad, but when they started partying it was more than I could stomach. Never in my life had I awaken to vomit in the bathroom sink. I was ashamed for them.

When Jerry was accepted to the Thurgood Marshall School of Law at Texas Southern University (TSU) in Houston, I made plans to get out of Baton Rouge. A timely response from TSU meant that I could start in the fall, the same semester as my brother. A summer vacation at home that summer had me feeling all mixed up though. Hanging out with an older thug guy from the neighborhood, I found myself doing things that were out of character, things that could have led to my death. Fearing I might get caught up, and knowing the consequences of such a life as his, I quickly withdrew from him. Haunted by my actions, I couldn't wait for school to start.

Lack of self-love and poor self-esteem was evident as my weight ballooned that summer. Every day I would start my diet, but by lunch, I had failed: Heeding the calls of burgers and fries.

Everything was so confusing to me. I existed in a world where I believed in **GOD** and knew that ***JESUS WAS MY SAVIOR***. Even knowing the words, *I can do all things through Christ which strengthens me*, did little to help. No matter how hard I tried, I could not get those words to correlate with Gwendolyn. ***LORD, please help me, have mercy on me***, was my mantra as I left for school.

My brother, his girlfriend Barbara, and I headed off to the big city. Barbara had come along to help as we transitioned to our new city, an apartment. I didn't have any friends yet in Houston, but I did have a favorite cousin that lived there. I was ready for a change, and on my own away at school, I was sure I would make good choices.

EPISODE V: BIG CITY GIRL

Skyscrapers, miles of interstate, and the time it took to get from point A to point B was an awesome backdrop for a new beginning in Houston. Texas Southern University (TSU) was this sprawling space that released a serenity in me like I'd never known. Crisscrossing the campus was therapeutic, and meeting people from all over the world was really cool.

One day, sitting on a bench taking in the bustling scenery, a man stopped in front of me. I must have looked weird sitting there, because he asked, "Do you need some help?". At first, I couldn't make out his words because his accent was hard to discern. We spent the afternoon talking. He was from Lagos, Nigeria, and I was interested as he talked about the African culture, living in London, and his family. He especially captured my heart when he told me, "A fine woman like you (*he meant pleasingly plump*) would be held in high esteem in my country." I really liked him; even his native name Innocence was intriguing. After a while, we started dating, and our relationship was full of laughter, wonder, and mutual respect.

Jerry and I had a nice apartment, but it just wasn't spacious enough for a whole lot of privacy. Barbara and I shared many laughs and crossed eyes between us when Jerry would lock himself in the closet to study. When I found out that these two had gotten married, I couldn't help but feel like a fifth wheel. Sharing this angst with my boyfriend, he suggested I move in with him. Not in a hurry to make this major decision, I thought it was good time for a road trip home. My family and neighbors were fascinated by the African man with the strange accent that I brought home.

When we returned to Houston, I decided to move in with him. My instincts said, ***This is a bad idea***. I should have listened. The very first morning, he didn't even squeeze the toothpaste right. It didn't take long before his true jealous nature showed up and we were clashing hard. I knew there would be cultural differences that might cause problems, but I was unprepared to deal with a controlling, possessive man. We were living in a dangerous bubble, and I refused to stay in the intolerable situation. When my cousin agreed that I could stay with her, I made plans for what felt like an escape, to leave.

When moving day came, my ex-boyfriend decided to contest my choice. We got into a massive fight in the parking lot. If his friend had not stepped in to stop us, I'm sure something terrible would have happened. When I finally got in the car, I looked over and saw my sandal on the ground. I really liked that pair of sandals and refused to leave the one on the pavement. Still steaming mad, I proudly stepped out and retrieved my sandal. Immediately, I peeled out of the apartment complex: You would have sworn I was being chased by the Tasmanian devil himself. Speeding down I-45, I was thankful for my siblings who taught me to hold my own in a fight.

Mad at myself later, I decided to call my brother. I had refused to cry, but when I saw Jerry my composure quickly eroded. Ugly, and tear-faced, I babbled my story. Jerry then quietly told me "Gwen you gotta take off your rose-colored glasses. Men are like this; when they know where your buttons are, they will push, and push, and push. You have got to stop the madness." Still searching for answers, I even called Mom. Vaguely telling her what was going on, she said, "You need to find peace. Nothing in this world is like peace."

A part-time class schedule allowed me to explore different types of work. Time served as a door to door encyclopedia salesperson was different, but not my cup of tea. Working as a promoter's assistant for city festivals, I was introduced to the works of Ntozake Shange. Ravishing through her novel, *For Colored Girls Who Have Considered Suicide When the Rainbow Is Enuf*, I was profoundly affected. In my head, playing like a broken record, all I could hear

17

was Ms. Shange say, ***The Rainbow Is Enuf***. As crucial and poignant as these words were, they brought me no closer to putting my pieces together right. My pride swelled however when I made extra money cutting and styling hair for several teachers, and office workers at school during their lunch breaks.

A family is a blessing from above. My cousin Brenda was very supportive in giving me a place to stay and a chance to breathe. She even helped me get a full-time job working nights where she worked.

One lazy morning, I was listening to the radio. Teddy Pendergrass was softly singing "This one's for you wherever you are." Brenda then urgently knocked on the door. She came with the news that my oldest brother Kenneth was dead. He had moved to Los Angeles, and now he had been murdered in a pool hall. I had no more details.

My head exploded as I wished like heck that the knock had never happened. All I could think about was Mom and Dad, and my brother's two sons Jamil and Kenneth. The weeks ahead were hard. The funeral was very interesting, as I observed how family and friends grieved in many different ways. Kenneth loved hard and was given strong love in return. The mothers of his sons flew in from L.A. for the funeral. There was even another woman bound for the front row that was deeply affected by his passing. Though others in my family had passed, this day I felt as though I had gained an ***Angel Wing***.

As we laid my brother to rest, knowing I would never forget him, I thanked ***GOD*** for sweet memories. Laughingly, I remembered how mean Kenny could be. It wasn't easy to forget the day he hit me so hard that I heard bells all that day (funny now but not then). Even better, however, were the Christmas memories of him leading our six-pack down the street on our bikes, or the six of us flying down the street roller skating.

The fact that Kenny was no longer alive pushed me, and I got up the nerves to get my own apartment. I could hardly contain myself when I meet my next door neighbor. His name was Elvis, and he was a **very** handsome young man.

Being independent felt wonderful, and I was living good and enjoying my life. On Saturdays I would hide out in my apartment indulging in westerns like *The Lone Ranger* and *Have Gun Will Travel*. During the week I spent time working out at the gym or sweating it out in an aerobics class when I wasn't working.

I was enjoying the "college experience" like never before, even attending some of the parties and basketball games at TSU and the University of Houston (UH). UH's basketball team, nicknamed *Phi Slama Jama,* had some smoking hot players. Clyde Drexler and Hakeem Olajuwon were my favorite players.

Clusters of friends kept me busy.

My friend Dora was a Nigerian transfer, and we sat together on the city bus on our way to school. I couldn't believe it when a fast-talking salesman convinced her to buy a cheap "As Is" old Ford Pinto with a stick shift. She didn't even know how to drive a stick, but the salesman had convinced her that the low price was worth it because she could learn to drive it easily. I was no help because I couldn't drive a stick either. We were a blessed pair as we'd take off to school sputtering down the frontage roads, jumping on and off the interstate in that old Pinto.

Sisters Evelyn and Londa, young single mothers down the way, taught me a lot about being responsible. Then when Hurricane Alicia ripped through Houston, Mary, her sister Shirley, our friend Glenda and I hid out in Mary's apartment. When it was safe, we gathered our meat to make sure nothing spoiled, and we had a big cookout on the balcony.

I worked hard to complete core classes by the end of the first semester of senior year. My last semester in college was spent enjoying fun-filled classes like swimming, and tennis. I prayed Kenny was proud of me as graduation day approached.

My friend Ben picked me up for a ride in his taxi the day before graduation commencement services. Down, down, down the interstate, we went until the signs read, Galveston. As the sunset unfolded into a beautiful evening, I realized the depth of Ben's feelings for me. He was in love with me and I could only think, *This is a fine time now to be showing me your feelings*. Then, I decided not to even address the issue: I didn't want to get into that discussion. The next day, my parents and *GOD*brother Jerry were coming down, and **I WAS GOING HOME**. I did, however, enjoy a small picnic with my friend Ben. In the warm breeze on the sandy beach, we watched waves roll in and out as the moon, and stars caressed the night on Galveston Island.

When I walked across that stage on May 23rd, 1984, and raised my fist, all I could do was smile. My brother received his Juris Prudence degree that day. We were proud of each other, but our parents were doubly delighted, this time Jerry and I had graduated at the same place during the same time. Mom presented me with a graduation gift, and I never laughed so hard. She had bought me a copy of the song from the movie *Mahogany*, the song I'd heartily cried to years before; "Do you know where you're going to? Do you like the things that life is showing you? Do you know?" Never in the history of time was there a song so befitting an occasion. Mom had nailed it, and I laughed as I thought, *Seven years is a long time to go to school and not have Dr. in front of my name*. Leaving my brother and his wife behind, I took a deep breath, relaxed in my seat, and enjoyed the ride home.

EPISODE VI: NO! NO!! NO!!!

1984 was supposed to be my year. After graduation, I got a job as Assistant Manager at a plus size women's dress shop that I enjoyed.

I'd heard that "Church was a good place to meet a man", so I set out to meet one.

When we caught each other's eye that Sunday, those words made me smile. Slyly, I peered at him, only to find him looking at me. Like a slow simmer, our relationship brewed to a constant boil. I was twenty-five, and he was forty-one. This sixteen-year age gap brought our May/December romance into the congregation's limelight. He was a father of two daughters, and many were concerned that my childless status should be protected and saved for someone with no kids. I didn't have a problem with his daughters or his age, but what I should have had a problem with though was a forty-one-year-old man living with his parents. No one ever mentioned that fact.

I was young, energetic, and fresh out of college when he asked me to marry him. I said "Yes," thinking this was what I wanted. Impressed with his military stance, it seemed that he would be a hard-working provider. He was not very affectionate, but I made him my prime catch, knowing I would never be his trophy wife.

Getting ready for our small wedding raised my stress to one hundred. The night before was filled with last minute details. After dinner at his mother's house, my fiancé went out, while I stayed to finalize everything. Since my parents lived on the next street, we agreed that it would be safe for me to walk home.

Thinking about getting married had me really nervous, and feeling a certain closeness to my fiancé. So before leaving for home, I decided to hang out in his room. After all, this would have been his last night there. Milling around, I looked up at his calendar. Something was very fishy so I took the calendar off the wall and inspected it closely, frantically flipping the pages, I looked at the months. Staring me in the face, listed on this calendar, was names, times, and locations of dates he'd had with other women. All of which occurred during the times he'd been seeing me, calling me his fiancé.

Blinded by tears, I searched for the exit as I quickly said goodbye to my soon to be in-laws. Running home, I found a quiet spot to think things out. Rationalizing, I convinced myself that there was a good explanation as to what the information on the calendar meant. Then, the constant, deafening sound of the word *NOOOOOOO*! in my mind scared me. Unable to ignore the noise, I admitted the truth to myself: ***This man is a cheat***.

Sunrise found me still awake, with the unanswered question, ***What are you going to do?*** still looming heavily on me. Too far in to back out, later at church, I said: "I DO". We had planned a honeymoon close to home. The three-hour trip to Hot Springs gave me every chance to expose my husband, but I didn't. Even though I knew the very nature of our relationship, the beautiful weather, and the stunning resort gave me hope for our survival. Our honeymoon was not the romantic escapade every girl dreamed of. And I realized how wrong I was, basing our marriage on lies, both his and mine because I held that secret.

EPISODE VII: I BELIEVE I CAN FLY

A promotion to Store Manager motivated me to dream bigger.

Waiting on customers one day an idea started rising in my belly, ***What if I could have my own store?*** I quietly began researching how to start a dress shop for full-figure women and teens. It didn't take long before I believed I had everything needed to be a formidable competitor to my employer. After all, I was a young plus-size model with a degree in business marketing and management, and I had experience in the field. Not trusting my husband enough to share my vision, I put my dad on the spot when I laid out business plans. My parents had recently signed to help me purchase a brand new car, so I really stuck it to Dad when I asked him to partner with me in a business venture we would call, ***Stouts 'n Style***. Pressured by me,

Dad finally said, "Yes", and with his support, I was determined to create a brilliant business.

Stouts 'n Style opened her doors with pomp and circumstance as a premiere dress boutique for full figure women. I was a twenty-seven-year-old business owner, and this was my proudest moment. Daily congratulations greeted me for weeks as I plowed into my work. Every morning I would pop in the cassette player music by Phil and Brenda Nichols. Their songs **GOD'S** *Woman*, and *It Is Well* would motivate me to work hard and be my best. Following a daily order, I'd then gather my courage to open my doors by playing *If I Be Lifted*. After all, that was all I wanted to do was glorify and lift **JESUS** up. I would be comforted as the song continued "I'll draw all men unto me". These words, in particular, eased my fear of rejection and alleviated the stress of counting customers.

Stouts 'N Style became a saving grace for me as I delved deeper into business. I would hire my friends Mary, Linda, and Vayion as temps during busy seasons or if I had to travel to Atlanta or Dallas for a buying trip. Their help was always invaluable as my best friends, confidantes, and sounding boards. Being unable to hire them full-time was always an issue for me.

My husband and I found it easy to fall into a routine of church and work. I couldn't help but ask myself, *What happened to you woman? It wasn't that long ago when you were filled with such joy and promise. When did you get to be an old maid?* Sadly, I still held the secret of my husband's pre-marital actions, but I was too busy for bitterness to set in.

EPISODE VIII: I'S MARRIED NOW

The phone rang.

"Hey Honey," my husband said.

"Hey, what's up?" I said.

"I'm on my way to Dallas to referee a game." He said.

"What are you talking about?" I asked.

"I got assigned to a game in Dallas. I'll be back tomorrow." He said.

"OK, I'll see you then", I said. Since he didn't have a set game schedule, I wasn't alarmed when he told me about this unscheduled trip to Dallas. A trip so far away was odd though. When I hung up, smiling, I found myself relishing the thought of being alone.

As I reviewed the bills the next month, I noticed something very strange. Looking at the phone bill, a date stood out like a neon light. Grabbing the calendar, I checked the date again. Listed on the phone bill was a motel room charge from Waskom, Texas a 15-minute drive away. This charge was on the same day my husband was supposed to be in Dallas, Texas, which was 166 miles away. My thoughts started raging. *This man called me from WASKOM! You mean to tell me he was laid up in bed with another woman while I was here at home waiting for him?* I blew a gasket, and couldn't wait for him to get home.

When my husband walked in the door, I blasted him with the phone bill and accused him of cheating. He didn't even deny my accusations. Then, I mentioned the calendar at his mothers' house, all the names, and places. His blasé attitude toward this situation made me feel terrible, used, and unappreciated. We agreed to part company, and it wasn't long before he left me. Not long after that, I kicked dust myself. Moving out of the apartment, I gave all the furniture away.

EPISODE IX: AGAIN???

I moved into a nice townhouse with new furnishings and a dependable car. Feeling armed and ready, I recommitted to *Stouts 'n*

Style. I was surprised that I had forgotten so much about my marriage in such a short time. As hard as I tried, I couldn't even remember who I had given the marriage bed to.

Looking and feeling particularly fine one day, I truly expected something wonderful would happen to me. So when He walked into the business, my interest was immediately peaked. His professional dress and suave mannerisms captured my attention. Since it was slow that day, I gave him a chance to share the business opportunity He called financial services which included insurance sales, money management, and recruiting.

After his spill, He gave me his number. Then He said, "If you have any further questions, call me. If a woman answers the phone, it's just my roommate. If I'm not there just leave a message." Curious, I made the call, and the decision to work part-time in his business. It wasn't long before I found out that roommate meant wife, and I had to respect that.

As my Upline Manager, this man trained me in the phases of the financial services business. I got really excited by some early successes and when I passed my insurance exam the first time around I knew I had stumbled upon something good. Eventually, my part-time venture became a full-time obsession. I became lost in this man's dream and when I was no longer able to see my dream, I second guessed where my love and loyalty was.

Stouts 'n Style suffered as a burden on me. As I evaluated my business, I started thinking that maybe I was beating a dead horse. As a young business, I had already committed a deadly error by giving in-house credit to several regulars. I was hurt when one of those same ladies said to me later "I was going to stop by, but I was on my way to the mall." Torn, I struggled with lack of passion for *Stouts 'n Style* and slow sales. Years passed, and as the only permanent employee, window washing, floor sweeping, sales, buying, bookkeeping, you name it, began to wear me down.

Finally, I made the tough call to close the doors of **Stouts 'n Style.** The look of disappointment on my father's face was more than I could bear. I felt like the failure of the century, and it wasn't long before decisions were being made for me. When my rent got too far behind, I had to move. I sold my furniture to make car payments, but I couldn't catch up, so my car was repossessed. Lonely and afraid, I hid out at my parents, **again**.

Still holding on, I convinced myself that this second-hand financial services business was right for me, and was given an opportunity to learn from the best in the financial services field. Ms. Altha was the *millionairess* who offered me a hands-up in the business. Not only did I move in with her family in Houston, but I also got to work closely with her. I started believing I was establishing myself financially, but after a while, the only checks I was seeing was Ms. Altha's. Shocked by all those zeroes, I finally admitted I was not that good at or committed to that business either. I didn't have the fire or desire needed for commissioned sales anymore either. When my income became null and void, I found myself spending money I didn't have, begging and borrowing.

I was very ashamed when I called my parents to ask if I could come home, **again**. My Upline manager and I picked back up, but I struggled in the business. When he uprooted his family and moved back to their home up north I was devastated. Feeling abandoned, the shame I endured from this episode was so intense. Suicidal thoughts came calling as I started to believe I was losing my mind.

EPISODE X: REALLY

December 1993. After licking my wounds, I was finally able to hold my head up again.

Brother Jerry, and his family had moved from Houston to Dallas, and he offered me a chance to start over. I moved to Dallas with what little dignity I had left. Their family hospitality, and nurturing was just what I needed.

One day, while meditating on a sunset I had an epiphany. *No matter where you go Gwen, no matter how far you run, you will still have to take me with you. Thus, I was my problem and my solution.* I prayed constantly for divine direction and order. Taking deep breaths, I would cry out, "*LORD* please help me, and have mercy on me. I CAN turn things around. *LORD*, I need your guidance. I CAN take care of myself."

Things changed when I found a good paying job in retail management. My life was good. Like a recovered addict, fresh from rehab, everything was new again. While spending time with my nephews, I found a great sense of humor. One day at work, I cracked up when I discovered I had worn mix-matched shoes. My staff and I enjoyed the day, laughing hard as comments were made.

Ringing in the New Year, 1994, things were going good, and I was enjoying the change. Super Bowl Sunday came, and we all were relaxing, waiting for the game to come on. Upstairs, I heard the most beautiful song ever floating up from downstairs. Running down, I asked my brother what the song was. He said, "Donnie Hathaway, *You were meant for me.*" *Sold, I'll take it,* was all I could think.

Later, during the game the phone rang, and it was for me. Surprised to find my estranged husband on the other line I couldn't speak. After a long moment of silence, I finally said, "What's up?" He wanted another chance. Shocked, I suggested we stay in touch.

After a few months of conversation, I decided to go back to him, praying things would be different between us. A seamless job transfer happened when a position came open at a store in the Shreveport area. I was able to move back home without losing any benefits.

Though our relationship still was not my romantic dream, I made do. My thoughts turned to pure joy when I got pregnant. I knew having a baby would help me endure anything, even this marriage, and I would finally have a love of my own.

But it wasn't meant to be.

That day, I was bleeding.

That day, I had a miscarriage.

Happiness turned into a despair I just didn't know how to handle.

As my world crashed, feelings dissipated into resentment toward my husband. I soon had no desire or reason to continue in the marriage. It was evident that this man couldn't fulfill what was missing inside of me.

I left him and moved in with my parents, **again**.

EPISODE XI: RUNNING WOMAN

Moving back in with my parents was not what the doctor ordered.

Mom and Dad were lovingly cordial, but they were under stress. The dynamics of the family had changed. Greg, my youngest brother was now chasing his dreams as a truck driver, and my sister Pat was making plans to join him in Dallas. Until then, she and her beautiful little boy were there with our parents. Terry, Jerry's twin, was a Marine now stationed in Okinawa, Japan. His daughter, Sherry, aka Baby Girl, was there with my parents. They had agreed to take care of her, helping to relieve some pressure off my sister-in-law Annie, who was caring for their other daughter Kerrie, during their separation. Feeling distressed for reasons of my own, and realizing there were too many grown folks under one roof, I thought up a plan.

Ms. Charlsie, my grandmother, agreed that I could live with her. This would have been a good idea if my grandmother's disciplined and orderly ways hadn't collided with my chaotic, unprincipled failures. As I sowed my wild oats, angry at the world, my grandmother put her foot down. She told me, "If you want to stay out all night, running around buck wild, then you can go live somewhere else." So, as defiant as ever, I left.

Running from pillar to post, friend to friend, I found myself just anywhere. My last stop ended up in the country, in my friend Mary's front yard. She and her daughter welcomed me. With all my belongings in tow, I lived out of the trunk of the car. The short drive from the country was somewhat therapeutic. Most days I lived like a zombie, but I didn't have any idea I looked like one too.

My manager stopped me one day at work, wondering if I was okay. "You don't look good," he said. Then he followed by asking me, "Have you been drinking?" "NO" I answered. Leaving in a huff, I headed straight to the bathroom. I looked like crap. Then it hit me, the full implication of what the Manager meant, implying *I'd been drinking, then coming to work.* Before leaving that day, I headed back to the bathroom to take a long hard look in the mirror. Still looking and feeling pretty rough, I started toward the country.

It was a beautiful day outside, and tears flooded my eyes as the clouds lifted inside of me. Then I was immersed in a place where it was raining inside of me. In that strange moment, I knew I was being cleansed and purified. When I got to the house, Mary, alarmed by my appearance screamed, "What happened?" After recounting the details of my day, we could only pray and rejoice in the goodness of *GOD.*

The next morning, I began my search for an inexpensive place to live. I settled on a small dingy place across from the cemetery, and down from the nursing home that I called *my hut-hut*. This was not a happy place, but I was happy

Things were changing for the better when I was given credit at

29

the furniture store. I ordered a love seat, an armoire, and a bed. Realizing I failed to order a mattress only made me laugh. Figuring I could get one later, I was just thankful for what I had coming. When the delivery man gave me the invoice it listed a mattress set, I had already been charged for it, and I couldn't believe my eyes when they set my bed up, with my beautiful new mattress set.

"Thank you **GOD** for knowing my needs," I cried out. My respect and confidence was slowly developing: I was getting over my past guilt's. A siesta from love revealed a clearer picture of where I wanted to go, what I wanted to be, and how I could get there.

SEASON II

ALL MY CHILDREN

EPISODE I: ALL THE RIGHT INTENTIONS

To kick off 1995, I decided to go back to school. I was excited about the Master's Degree in International Business and Finance at Grambling State University. Just the sound of the words *International Business and Finance* made me fall in love with the idea of getting my Master's Degree. I especially liked seeing myself as a confident businesswoman with her portfolio.

To celebrate going back to school, I decided to attend the first ever Essence Music Festival in New Orleans. Essence magazine was celebrating their 25th anniversary, and this was supposed to be the event of the summer. Everything was in order with my ticket and room reservations and I was super thrilled about my New Orleans excursion. My joy was overflowing and I believed this was the ticket to another fresh start.

The Sunday before I was scheduled to leave for New Orleans, I decided to attend a church I've never been to. No one had invited me to that church, but my spirit had insisted that I go. On the way, Stevie Wonder belted out a song on the radio that stalled me. Suddenly saddened by the words, I pulled over. "For your love I would do anything, just to see the smile upon your face", Stevie sang.

Memories started to flood my mind about past relationships and my miscarriage. My biological clock was exploding, and I couldn't stop thinking about my great-aunt Roxie. From what I understood, she lived a very nice life in Chicago. Recently though, her husband of fifty years had died, and she was now widowed with no kids. When the time came that she was unable to care for herself, the family decided to move her to Shreveport where lived with her sister, my grandmother, Ms. Charlsie. It was as if Queen Elizabeth had moved in with Mother Earth, what a sight. When Roxie died, her funeral was the saddest thing to me. Left to mourn were sisters, nieces, and nephews. Not a child who had lost their mother's love. It was then I decided I wanted kids, no matter if I was thirty-five years old.

Shaking myself from a trance, I had to compose myself and get to church. Checking out the congregation as I took my seat, I spotted something familiar. ***What the heck?*** I thought.

Sitting in front of me a few pews up was my ex-husband sitting very close to some woman. When church was over, I ran out of there, unable to even recall the sermon.

During that week I was preoccupied, and my thoughts were all over the place. I kept my spirits up with thoughts of my upcoming mini-vacation in New Orleans. The sights and sounds of the music festival I would be enjoying kept me motivated. That Thursday after work I headed over to visit Mom and Dad. Slowly, I drove down their street. Then just a few houses before I got there, Jimmy bounded out of his father's house, popped over to the car and asked," Would you drop me off at my brother's house?"

EPISODE II: WHO WOULDA THUNK IT

Why? Why? Why? Why didn't I just drop him off at his brothers' house? Why didn't I keep driving? What was a girl to do when a man looked so fine and smelled so good?

Jimmy and I talked the night away, and our conversation ran the gamut. Though a childhood friend, I really didn't know him. I was surprised, and interested to hear him talk about his hopes and dreams. Looking at the thug life he led, it was hard to believe he even had one dream. The idea that I could make a difference in his life filled my mind. That night, out the window went my trip to the music festival in New Orleans and going back to school. The rest became history.

Things moved swiftly as we got to know each other. Shortly after our first night together, Jimmy moved into ***my hut-hut.*** Then on September 16th, 1995, we stood before Pastor Ellis looking like twins in our green silk shirts, and black denim jeans saying "I Do". I wanted things to work out for us because we were both underdogs that deserved a break. Also, we were childless, and each other's ticket to parenthood. We had hopes for a better future, and lots of fun playing, laughing and dancing to Michael Jackson, Stevie Wonder and The Isley Brothers.

I will never forget the morning I stopped by my parents to break the news of our marriage. Over coffee, I laid the foundation with conversation about this and that. My parents didn't think it odd when I then started small talk about how Jimmy was doing positive things and working now. They always had hope for a positive change in his life because they had witnessed the delinquent ways of his past.

Going in for the kill, I blurted out to my parents that I had married him.

Mom screamed, "You did what?!"

They were so hurt knowing my past, and Jimmy's. It was as though I had slashed, dashed, trampled, and stomped their hopes for my life. In tears with no defense against my parents, I ran back to my husband and told him what had happened. The reassurances he made to me was enough to dry up my tears.

EPISODE III: BABY BLUES

This was a fast-paced marriage, so it was no wonder we got pregnant just as fast. Jimmy and I both wanted kids: we just never really talked about having them. I was happy and somewhat afraid, but I wanted our baby. When I thought about Aunt Roxie again, I became fearless.

I was working full-time, and very pregnant, when we started dreaming about having our own business. My husband wasn't making much money at the small restaurant where he worked, and he had a lot of idle time on his hand. He was; A jack of all trades, and a master of some. His skills included cement finishing, carpentry, plumbing, lawn care, even tinkering with cars at times as a shade tree mechanic. Though his unused skills were a good starting point, we decided a venture that didn't require much money would be best. When we finalized plans for **Jimmy's Car Detail Shop**, Jimmy immediately quit his job and became an entrepreneur. He couldn't spell the word entrepreneur, but he sure liked the sound of it.

Hidden realities started slipping in as my stomach grew. The stresses of being a business owner and my pending delivery seemed to push my husband near the edge. Not only was he working at the detail shop daily, but he was also making routine runs to the old neighborhood. For me, visits to the old neighborhood became unusual. Smiles had been replaced with looks of contempt, and embarrassing jeers and jabs were made. Someone even referred to me as "The good girl gone bad". Though hurt by these actions, I accepted the idea that I couldn't stop someone else's thoughts or reactions. Besides, I had more pressing situations at home to deal with.

I'd heard a lot of pregnant women talk about how bad labor pains hurt. When I started having them, I understood the truth of labor pains: **They were hell**. Nothing compared to the cramps I'd experienced during my cycle. I immediately called the doctor when the pains started. She told me to relax, and that these painful spasms were just the beginning. I had to wait hours before she agreed with me: It was time to go to the hospital. Later, the anesthesiologist had the audacity to ask me if I wanted an epidural. "Yes" came out before the question mark was at the end of his question: I couldn't imagine a woman saying no to this pain relief.

Then, I wished I had said no when the anesthesiologist started with his first try to stick me in my back. Determined, he continued to stick me five times with the longest needle I had ever seen. Explaining, "You have small slots in your vertebrae. These are the spaces I have to inject the medicine into your spinal cord. I have to find a space big enough for my needle to get the medicine to you." I knew he tried to explain what he was doing in simple terms. But when he'd tell me to sit still while he explored my back, poking me with that huge needle and a major labor pain would hit, it would take my husband and a nurse to hold me. I had never seen Jimmy so afraid; nor myself.

When the time came, my husband and I bonded over our marvel of creation. Our son was the most beautiful sight I'd ever seen. And I couldn't help notice he had the ripest most kissable lips I'd ever seen. Even the nurses commented on how beautiful his lips were. We named our son *Jimmy Jr*.

We outgrew *my hut-hut* real fast. My Dad was now a real estate investor, and he rented us a nice DIY house that was perfect. The dirt and clutter inside was frightening, but the vision beyond was strong encouragement to get it clean. Our baby was three-months-old when we moved in.

The cracks in our marriage started widening, and I spent lots of time wondering, *Where's my husband?* Feeling like a single mother, the post-partum depression I was experiencing intensified. After a while, I had to put those feelings aside, because the end of my maternity leave was fast approaching, and it would be back to work.

Back at work, I had a rude awakening. I had no idea how hard life could be. Consumed in a routine of drop the baby off to daycare, work, pick the baby up, and wonder *"Where's my husband?"* the cycle seemed endless, but I had great friends who rallied to help. Jackie, a friend from work practically kidnapped Jimmy Jr, even sporting the name *Jimmy Jr's Nanny.*

EPISODE IV: KNOCK, KNOCK, WHO'S THERE?

The atmosphere this night was uneasy. I had been up and down all night with the baby when my husband brought the noise home.

It was 2:00 am, and he'd finally found his way home after a night of carousing. Plopping on the couch he said, "Baby can you fix me something to eat?" Begrudgingly, I fixed him a sandwich then headed off to bed.

Looking over at the clock, I wondered who was knocking at the door, and ringing the doorbell at 4:00 a.m. ***Knock, knock*** came again, only louder this time. I got up to answer the door, "Who is it?" "Police ma'am, we need you to open the door". Fear struck as I swung the door open. "Ma'am we are here to arrest your husband, he's being charged with rape," the policeman said. Wide-eyed and unable to move I stammered out "What do you mean?" "Your husband has been accused of rape, and we're here to arrest him. Is he here?" he reiterated. Dumbfounded, I say "Yes." "We need to see him," the policeman firmly said.

Finally, able to move, I went to wake my husband from his drunken stupor. The policeman told him the charge and that he was identified by the tattoo on his arm. While his rights were being read, he adamantly denied any wrongdoing.

Jimmy had been arrested for rape. I became furious every time I thought about the details of what had happened earlier. Replaying in my mind I just keep repeating, ***He had been with another woman, come home to us, and had the audacity to ask me for something to eat***. Feeling like a fool, I snuggled my baby close as I cried myself to sleep. Waking up early, I quickly dressed, dropped the baby off at daycare, and then raced to the jail. There was nothing I could do at the jail because I didn't have any money for bail. They put him on lockdown where days turned into months.

When our son started walking, my husband's request to see him became unrelenting. Finally agreeing I reluctantly took Jimmy Jr to see his father. A deep shame like never before consumed me as I trudged my handsome son down those halls of correction.

I became reclusive, hiding my shame from everyone. Then the call came, my husband had been released. After eight months, this nightmare ended when the woman recanted her story. She had gone to the authorities and told them that Jimmy hadn't raped her. No one would explain to me how this came about, and just like that, the nightmare was over. Our little family returned home, and my son was happy with the outpouring of love lavished on him by his father. This endearing sight softened my heart as pleas for forgiveness, and *I'm gonna do rights* rang in my ear.

EPISODE V: REST ASSURED

Allowing my husband to come home wasn't an easy decision to make.

I wanted my son to grow up with his father, and I believed Jimmy still had some good in him and deserved a chance to change. With so many mistakes under my belt, I was hardly one to cast judgment. And besides, I still cared for him. Never in all my experiences had I ever felt such closeness like I felt with this man. So I surmised that this must have been what real love was. Digging my heels in, I went to war for our family. Not long after this trying incident, I was pregnant again.

In June 1998, things took a turn for the worst. The notice came that our company was bankrupt and that all stores would be closing. I waited for my bosses to say something else like maybe our jobs would be outsourced to another company or something. But, instead, I was tasked with the responsibility of breaking this terrible news to the staff. I didn't want to be the messenger: How could I tell my staff, my friends, that they would no longer have a job? Then, I questioned what would this mean for my family; we had no savings, a two-year-old toddler, and a baby on the way.

Nothing prepared me for the despair I witnessed the day I broke the news of the store closing to the staff. As a crew, we all worked hard and had so many good and bad times, and I was *The Mother*

Hen who cared for, fussed and pushed them hard. Things were no different when it came to packing up the store, we all pulled together, and even though tears fell, we shared fun memories that had us all laughing.

A favorite story of mine was about an employee who was expecting and her baby's due date was near. One day at work, she told me her water had broken. Freaking out, and not knowing what to do, I told her to go to the bathroom. Then, in my mind like a flash, *I saw this woman going to the bathroom, sitting down, and having her baby in the toilet.* Quickly, I collected my senses as I burst into the bathroom. It wasn't long before we all got word from her husband that she was alright, and the baby was beautiful and healthy.

Priorities quickly shifted when my blood pressure rose. My baby and I were in danger and the doctor wanted to induce labor. The scheduled date was July 15th, and I begged the doctor if I could wait just two more days to have the baby, which would have been my Mother's birthday. A resounding "No" from the doctor helped me to understand the seriousness of our situation.

During delivery I found myself praying hard to **GOD** for direction. Looking into son *#2's Angel Eyes*, I suddenly felt **GOD** presence. He was so near that I was compelled to name my son, *Joshua Reassured*, pronounced *Rayshard*. Releasing myself to enjoy the moment with my husband, I found renewed purpose. Looking at my two, healthy, baby boys, really three when you counted my husband, was enough to put a smile on my face.

EPISODE VI: OH MY *GOD*

Time was running out, and I had to find a job quick because my unemployment benefits were running out. I enjoyed being at home with the kids, but a stay at home Mom was a job for Superwoman, and I wasn't her.

Looking for a job was a job in itself. Perusing through the classifieds in the newspaper one day, I spotted a job that greatly interested me. It was an assistant manager's job at the local glass factory outlet. **Bingo**, I thought, as I remembered the heartbreak from my last job. I really didn't want to manage a crew, but I knew I would make a great assistant.

November 1998, I was very happy and fortunate to get the job as Assistant Manager. From the start, the young manager seemed unwilling to share nothing more than the minimum requirements for my job. This was disheartening because I only wanted to be a great help. When the news came that day, it was a guarantee he would never know of my desire for his success. On his way to work one morning, our Manager was killed in a car accident. Sad as this was, the manager's position was now open. When I was selected as the first minority manager of the outlet, I was left with a bittersweet taste in my mouth. Even so, my family could use the extra income.

EPISODE VII: 9-11-1999

"Happy Birthday to you...", I sang into the phone. This was my father's 66th birthday and I was so grateful that he was still here with us and doing well. Then, a little while later, I got a strange burning sensation. Picking up a pen and a spiral notebook, I headed out the door. Opening the notebook, I looked up, then asked, "Now what?" Three words came to me. **Tell your story**.

Confused by these words, I asked, "Why me?" I didn't get an answer.

Then, as if watching a movie, I saw myself as a teenager, under the tree in my parent's front yard. Sitting in the cool grass, I was dreaming about what kind of book I would write.

The question **Why me?** began to invade my consciousness. I knew that everyone had a story and was going through something, but I still wanted an answer. Reality started setting in, as I prepared to ask *GOD* more questions.

Then the revelation came: *You have lived the life of a fool on so many occasions. You've learned so much by making so many mistakes, surely you can help someone.* I took a moment to pray for strength and guidance. When I was sure of what I was going to do, I took a deep breath, held my head high, and stopped asking, *Why me?*

Never in a million years would I have imagined the book of my childhood dreams would have been about me. *Relics Of A Woman (ROAW)* was the title given to the book. While meditating on *ROAW, THE LORD*

revealed to me that this book would also be used as a fundraiser.

Writing was so different from reading. My perspectives on life began to change as I found relief and escape in my words. I now had a place of peace, a place of my own, on the pages of my life. Writing was a time when I could think about everything and talk to *GOD* about it all. So many poignant events had happened to me, and I wondered *Will I be able to stop writing?*

My plate was full as a wife, and a mother of two beautiful sons, working a full-time job. It just didn't seem like I could fit another thing into my schedule. My blessings were many, and I didn't want to fight *GOD'S WILL*, so I decided to let the spirit flow, and let *GOD* do his work through me, through *Relics Of A Woman (ROAW)*.

Fears haunted me each time I picked up my pen and notebook. I was afraid of exposing myself because so much had been kept hidden. I was also terrified of being rejected. Doubts would come as I questioned the validity of my life to be hope to inspire someone else. The fears and doubts intensified as the consequences of poor choices stared me in the face through my words.

Even so, I stood on **GOD'S** promises. I fought to put a past filled with many regrets and heartbreaks behind me. Boldly, I stepped into a new life filled with promise. It was then I could finally tell myself, *It wasn't all bad. Girl, you have accomplished some phenomenal things. GOD still loves you, and he has never forgotten you or left you alone. Look at your two angels.*"

I'd met so many people whose personal stories divinely touched me, and I prayed, **LORD, with this commission, please let me do justice to my calling. Thy will be done, on earth, as it is in Heaven. LORD, please don't let my life be in vain. IN JESUS'S NAME.** *Relics Of A Woman (ROAW)* would be the seasons, and episodes of my life. And I knew one thing for sure, I wouldn't stop till **GOD** said when. I even realized that I couldn't tell it all, but anyone reading *ROAW* would get the message!

EPISODE VIII: PARTY LIKE IT'S 1999

December 1999 was the end of a century, and the beginning of a new millennium. Fear and paranoia were spreading like wildfire. Words like doom and dread were being thrown around like nobody's business. Some said the world would end, others said that banks and computers systems would go on the blink. As the New Year approached, CNN, Fox News, and other news sources consumed our daily breakfast, lunch, and dinner.

The singer, Prince, was a genius. His foresight in 1982 when he released the song "1999" was dead-on. He sang "When I woke up this morning I could have sworn it was judgment day." It was as if he'd had a premonition; one that foretold of a head-on collision between mass hysteria, and a faulty society afraid of the unknown.

I didn't want to fall into this dreadful way of thinking. After all, I had a lot to live for. The world made it to the year 2000.

Things were good at work. I was proud to announce to the team that we had reached *A MILLION DOLLARS IN SALES*. This was a milestone in the outlet's history because sales had never reached a million dollars. Many congrats came my way for being a great Manager, but the truth was, I had a phenomenal staff.

I found contentment in working hard, keeping order at home, and giving my husband encouragement.

EPISODE IX: A NEW MILLENNIUM

January 1, 2000! The turn of the century! I heard some old folks say "I didn't think I'd live to see it".

New Years' Day for my family was a day filled with gratitude and resolutions. Forging into the New Year, my husband and I were holding strong to the renewed commitments we'd made to each other and to our kids.

Valentine's Day found us happy as we could be. We enjoyed each other's company like newlyweds. Lately though, I hadn't given much thought to birth control. In poor judgment, I just assumed I wouldn't get pregnant at forty-years-old. Well, it wasn't long before I was pregnant with our third child.

I had a tiny fantasy this time around. In it *I had a daughter, and as Daddy's Little Girl, she would reel Daddy in for the family good*. But when I put the fantasy aside, I had to admit how scared I was. The thought that I might not make it through or our family would be destroyed was overwhelming. I tightened the hold on my *String to Heaven* and kept tying knots to hold on. A foreboding feeling of doom took hold of me, and I couldn't get past it. *What does this mean?* I asked myself.

When I went to visit my parents, I started getting strange looks again. It was like everyone had a secret, and they wouldn't tell me.

EPISODE X: TWO-FOR-ONE

I told the staff I'd be back after my doctor's appointment. They shared my excitement because I would be getting my first ultrasound at four months.

Waiting quietly on the nurse, I prayed for the health of our baby, and I prayed for me, my audacious 40-year-old self, who was trying **GOD** one more time. Surprised by the nurse, I jumped. Then I winced as she rubbed that cold lotion on my stomach. My anxiety rose as she quietly concentrated on the screen.

Suddenly she asked me a question. "How are you doing?"

"Fine" me.

"How's your blood pressure?" nurse.

"Fine" me.

"What do you see on the monitor?" nurse.

"A baby" me.

Then she rotated the probe and our conversation continued. "What do you see now?"

"The same baby you just showed me" me.

"No. That's another baby!" nurse.

Then it hit me: I was pregnant with twins. I paused. "Ma'am I know you are April fooling me!" I said this as a comic relief, because I couldn't believe what she'd just said. It was mid-June.

"Ma'am I would never do that to you!" nurse.

Confused and dazed, I asked myself, ***How could this be?*** I'd always heard twins skip a generation, and since my Mom had twins, her kids wouldn't. Well, another old wives' tale had been shot down.

The nurse readjusted the monitor so that I could get a better view. *This can't be real*, I thought as she described the genitals of the babies. *Two boys. Yes, two more boys*. Baby A and Baby B were the names she gave them. She even printed a photocopy of the screen and gave it to me.

I stared down at the photo and felt disappointment welling up inside of me. Not even a girl in the mix. Suddenly, I felt so all alone. Just the thought, *I would still be the only girl amongst all these men* made me even sadder. The visions of my finally having a baby girl disappeared as the tears fell. I couldn't stop thinking *Really? Is this really happening? Will I ever stand a chance in any fight with these men?*

When I got back to work, I broke down. My staff didn't know what was going on, but suddenly they were on alert, prepared to call 911. I talked fast, as I explained to them what had just happened.

Lately, affection from my husband had been in short supply, so when I got home, I bitterly told him what happened at my appointment. I was also upset that he hadn't gone with me, upset that I was alone when I heard the news that I was carrying not one but two boys. Unable to hide my disappointment, crying uncontrollably, I shouted, "All this and I can't even get a girl!"

Later, while I was talking to a friend of mine, she said, "Don't you know what that means? When a woman has a boy that means she's the one who did all the work?" Smugly, I nodded: I really did feel like I was the one who did all the work.

EPISODE XI: THE AFTERMATH

Everything was all wrong.

July 2000 I was going crazy.

It was 5:00 a.m. Five months pregnant and confused, I had to get out. Hauling my pregnant self out of bed, I grabbed my keys and headed out the door. By the time I came to my senses, I had taken a very long ride to the country down Jefferson Paige Road. Then I had to stop, there unmoving like a statue in the middle of the road stood the largest cow I'd ever seen. Like ringing the Liberty Bell, I pressed my horn loud and hard. That cow refused to move, looking at me as if to say; *You have gone far enough, go home.* Forced to turn around, I was in a full depression by the time I got to bed. As the months passed, I did my best to keep it together, but everyone was feeling my wrath. Fortunately, there were no complications from my foolishness. The doctor told me, "The babies are doing good, but your pressure is up. I'd like to see you in a few weeks." ***GOD'S GRACE AND FAVOR*** prevailed as I put my bad attitude aside, and walked a grateful walk.

EPISODE XII: HALLELUJAH

Sunshine has a way of appearing unexpectedly in the midst of a storm.

Dad and Mom had decided to sell us the house we were renting. Not long after the ink dried on our mortgage papers, my husband shared his ideas on how we could raise the value of our home. Conflicted when he said "We should remove the siding, and paint the house", I balked at the idea. What he said made no sense: the house looked fine. However, after elaborating on how beautiful the natural wood would be, and bombarding me with his carpenter's jargon, I gave in. I didn't have the strength for another fight, and I knew I wouldn't have won the fight anyway.

Matters got worse when we were had to make a transportation decision. The Lincoln Town Car we were driving couldn't accommodate all of us. We didn't hesitate when we had a chance to upgrade from our car to a van. It was perfect, and the whole family fit. I just don't know what was said to convince me that a $525 car note was feasible. We were already living on the fly without a family budget.

My blood pressure was too high at thirty-eight weeks. The doctor scheduled November 28, 2000, as the date to induce my labor. I thought to myself, *In three weeks I will be forty-one, and I have only gained twelve pounds carrying twins. I guess my fluffy body came in handy. I sure am an old Momma, and GOD is good to me.*

Doctors Mitchell and Montgomery performed a C-section on me. Baby A-*Jaleen Cortez* and Baby B-*Jeremy Cortez* made their dramatic appearances. I asked the doctors to tie my tubes and make sure they never met in the same zip code. I couldn't believe how blessed I was. Like my parents, I had four healthy sons, which included a set of twins.

Fear struck my heart when Jeremy got a respiratory infection right before Christmas. The pediatric specialist Dr. Holloway was called in to care for my baby. She stopped by the hospital on Christmas Eve with her family downstairs in the car, in the cold. I had been profusely thanking her when she stopped me and said, "I had to come. If something happened to your baby overnight, I could never forgive myself." Dr. Holloway became my *Christmas Angel*. Just a few days later, Jeremy was released, and my family was complete.

When the phone rang that day, I couldn't imagine the blessing I had waiting for me on the other end of the line. Mrs. Frazier wanted to come over and talk to Jimmy and me about how she could help out. Soon, Mrs. Frazier became *Granny* to our family as she cooked, cleaned and made sure the kids were taken care of. During this time though, my husband seemed downright resentful of the help I was getting from her. There were even times I apologized to Granny for his insolent behavior. I, however, appreciated the blessing she was to my household. And I was blessed with four healthy, handsome sons that completed me as only a child could do for their Mother.

SEASON III

HELTER*SKELTER-

2001

EPISODE I: CAN DO ENTERPRIZES?

February 2001 had come fast, and already my New Year's resolutions were down the drain.

I was so glad the **LORD** believed in me. As though to make my life crazier, once again *He* enticed me with an immense undertaking. Obediently, I grabbed my pen and paper and wrote the vision of *Can Do Enterprizes (CDE)* down.

Needing some time to digest this message, I was thankful it was the weekend. Pondered, I questioned the **LORD,** "Would you really trust me with such a major undertaking?" All I could see through the tears that filled my eyes was the fact that I was so unworthy of such a daunting task. Four boys, an absentee husband, an unforgiving past, and an uncertain future did not seem to fit the ideal leader profile for such a program. If anything, I would be the first in line.

I couldn't help myself when I said to the **LORD** "First, *You* have required me to share my life stories in *Relics Of A Woman,* and now *You've* given me a vision called, *Can Do Enterprizes.* And I'm supposed to be the leader?"

"What does this mean?" I asked of the **LORD**. Then he showed me a village, and the words came, *Can Do Enterprizes is to be a village, a foundation, and a community of help in times of need*.

Thinking about my own life, I knew a program like this could be very beneficial. The aspects of this vision would probably have saved me from being lost so much of my life. I saw it clearly, and the vision was so beautiful. *Can Do Enterprizes* represented hope for families from the ravages brought on by the torments of life. And it would be a place of refuge for spirits wounded by tribulations of word and deed. It was sad that I couldn't even share this vision with my husband: his mind was just not there.

So many brothers and sisters had lost their lives to a world intent on their destruction, this did not even count the kids affected. *What if there really was a way to turn it all around?* I wondered. Before long, I found myself fretting about *Can Do Enterprizes*. I whispered a small prayer, "*LORD*, you will have to work out the **HOW** of this vision. I gotta go now because the babies are crying."

EPISODE II: FAMILY MATTERS

April 2001. My six-month maternity leave was ending, and I wanted to do something special for our team at work.

Dinner at Copeland's gave me a chance to thank and congratulate each of them for a job well done in my absence. Pulling my assistant to the side, I told her about a conversation I'd had with Felicia, our second assistant and cashier Freda. As a gift to me, these ladies wanted to take the kids for a weekend before I was due back at work. I asked my assistant to check her upcoming schedules, and see if there was a time when she could coincide their floating off day with their weekend off, giving them available time to help me out. Not long after, the work schedule was set accordingly, and I was ecstatic when they picked the kids up.

The showering of love shown my first day back at work was overwhelming. Customers from all over the country kept the phone lines busy with congratulations. It was a beautiful day, but that all changed when the phone rang at 3:00 pm

The call was from the payroll department in Ohio. I had failed to fax timesheets in. Planting myself at my desk I rushed to complete them so the employees would get paid on time. It had been six months since I'd done payroll, and I actually made some mistakes in calculations. This meant I had to backtrack and correct errors on the timesheets of the ladies who had helped me out with the babies. Their floating days off had been entered wrong. Pressed for time, I used whiteout to correct my entries; experiencing a big sigh of relief when the last sheet was faxed.

When I was called to the office I couldn't believe my ears.

51

Felicia and I were charged with collusion to falsify documents, and the decision was made to fire both of us. It was deemed that we sought to commit a forgery when I used whiteout on the timesheets. **Whiteout!** I thought. As long as I'd been working I never knew you shouldn't use whiteout on documents. I guess I never had an occasion to use it for the wrong reason.

I fervently fought for my job, only to be met with the fact that I worked in Louisiana, a right-to-work state. In other words: *You have the right to work for us, and you can quit when you choose. We have the right to hire you, and dismiss you when we choose.* I didn't stand a fighting chance. Being released from my job was very hard, and it didn't help that my assistant now had my job.

EPISODE III: WHERE'S MY CHILD?

Losing my job sent a tremor through my family of epidemic proportions.

It seemed like this news was more than my husband could handle. Work at the detail shop had slowed down, and unbeknown to me, Jimmy had quit working at the shop weeks earlier. I found out that he was spending his days in the neighborhood while I was at work, and the kids were at daycare. Within a week, I even found out more about what the strange looks from the neighborhood were about.

Apparently, my husband had set up his *street business* in the blue dump house down the street from our parents. The disrespect he exhibited in doing this was unbelievable. Knowing this helped me to make sense out of some of Jimmy's recent behavior. It suddenly made sense why he had been so adamant about removing the siding on the house, *Sold to the highest bidder* (not only had he been a seller but a consistent user-house siding had funded his escapades) I concluded. This was just too much. I was sure our marriage wouldn't survive this lifestyle he had chosen.

Sitting down consoling my oldest son one night, I did my best to relieve his concerns. When Jimmy Jr spoke it was as though he was a Prophet and I froze when he said, "Momma, Daddy gone go to jail."

"What do you mean son?" I asked

"Daddy gone go to jail cause he ain't never home with us" my son replied.

I tried to help when I said, "Son that's not true. Everything's gonna be alright."

These were frightening words from a four-year-old child. When my husband got home I told him what our son said, but he brushed it off like nothing. The argument that followed was unsettling, ending with his words "I AM A MAN!" I had no words left.

I reminded myself that, not only did both our parents live in this neighborhood, but my grandmother still lived there also. And in spite of any shame, I was feeling, this was not going to stop me from visiting my family.

One day at my parents, the kids were having a good time outside until it got too hot for the babies. Going inside to cool off, everyone was counted for except Joshua. Knowing he liked to play hide-and-seek I went outside to get him. He was not there, and after many rounds, inside the house, outside the house, there still was no sign of my son. Panic-stricken, I jumped in the van, driving frantically through the streets. Joshua was nowhere to be found. I went back to the house again, only to find out he still wasn't there. I paced the floor like a caged animal, going outside every few minutes to see if he was there.

I then understood every parent's nightmare as I experienced the fear that something horrible had happened to my child. This thought was tearing me apart. While my parents watched the kids, I got back in the van, determined to find my son.

53

Turning the corner, a few blocks down, I saw someone walking. I then recognized my son. He was walking with his daddy. Blinded by anger I pulled over next to them and rolled the windows down. Jimmy explained, "I was walking down the street when I saw Joshua outside. I decided to take him to the store." It never crossed his mind to tell me what was going on. The words that came out of my mouth next were probably illegal, but Joshua was just smiling: all he knew was that he was out enjoying a walk with his dad. When my husband said "Let me in" I unlocked the van door. Expecting me to open the door he just stood there. When I refused to open up the door, he got indignant, like I had done something wrong to him. Impatient with his refusal to open the door, and not wanting to make a scene, I drove off.

By the time I reached my parents' house I was furious. Then it occurred to me that I might have just left my son with a madman. Quickly, I told Dad that I was going back to get my Joshua. Before I could get out the door though, neighbor kids were banging on the door.

"Gwen the police have your husband and baby at the corner." Their sing-song was so loud it rattled my senses. The corner they were talking about was the same corner I had turned just minutes before. And my parents' house sat just three houses down from there. Running I rushed to the corner: A chilling sight unfolded before me. I could see my husband being handcuffed. Running as fast as I could, I saw the police putting my crying son in their car. Hysterical, I yelled, "What's going on?!"

Dad had followed me and was standing by my side, fighting to calm me down. The officer explained that my husband was being arrested and gave no explanation as to why he had been stopped. But he did, however, say that in Jimmy's pocket was something illegal. I was also informed that child protection services had been dispatched for my child.

Barely composing myself I explained quickly, "He's my

husband, and that's our son, but we are not together. My kids and I had come over to visit my parents. They live right there. My husband had come down the street, and when he saw our son outside, he took him to the store without my knowledge."

I started crying while repeating my story. Eventually they allowed me to take custody of Joshua. On the way home I severely admonished myself, *What have I done? What have I done? If only I had reached over an opened the car door this wouldn't have happened. Why didn't I just open the door?*

Guilt and gloom flooded my soul. Then the chill down my spine was frightening as I heard my son's words replay in my mind, *Momma, Daddy gone go to jail.*

Out of the mouth of a BABE or PROPHET? I wondered.

EPISODE IV: ON MY OWN

May 2001-Anger was consuming me.

I was having trouble adding junior to Jimmy Jr's name when I called him. Jimmy Sr. had done little as a father, and calling my son junior left a bad taste in my mouth. He was nothing like his father, or even me for that matter. He was a level-headed child.

In the midst of all the confusion with my husband's arrest, I had forgotten that Jimmy Jr was graduating from ECE or Early Childhood Education in a few days.

Getting everyone ready for graduation that day was a miracle. When my auntie traveled with us, I thanked *GOD* for her. I was taken off guard when I unexpectedly started to cry. As the graduation march played, profuse tears came as the group of little graduates strutted out of the building.

To memorialize this historic occasion, my sons and I took pictures at Walmart. Gazing into my eyes on the picture later, I was amazed that I couldn't even recognize the pain I was feeling. ***Was I a good actress or what?*** I asked myself. It was a beautiful photograph.

I didn't know whether I was coming or going, as I faced an uncertain future. Bills were mounting, and my previous employer was fighting my unemployment. One day, however, I opened an envelope and I knew the **LORD** loved me because his mercy was abounding. The mailman had delivered an unsecured credit card with a $1500 limit. I couldn't believe this was real.

When my husband called later, excitedly I shared with him about *The Card*, and how I had been able to pay our bills, get diapers, and take care of the household. He got so upset and wanted to know why I hadn't used *The Card* to bail him out of jail. I tried to explain what I thought this blessing was about, taking care of four kids. It never occurred to me to bail him out, after all this was not his first rodeo with the legal system, and I just assumed he would do time. His sentence was forty months which meant he'd be in jail for three years and four months: I was shocked.

With no husband and no job, what was I supposed to do now as a forty-one year-old single mother of four boys? I asked myself. All of this for a girl who had been afraid to even have kids. My intellect never prepared me for what I was about to face. I didn't know how I was going to make it, but I knew that it was a good time to reconcile with my family and church.

I was so glad when school started in the fall. Finally, I could get some stability with a routine in place. One kid in elementary, and three in daycare seemed like a reasonable proposition that would allow me a chance to find a job. I was ready! Being a single stay-at-home mom was no joke, I had to bow down to the women living this life. My understanding of things I'd heard was nothing compared to what I was experiencing.

EPISODE V: 9-11-2001/HORROR STORY

Dad's birthday was today, so I made a mental note to either call or stop by when I finally got everyone off.

Before calling Dad, I turned on the TV, and saw some incredibly horrible scenes unfold. There'd been a terrorist attack on U.S. soil.

This was unreal. Two hijacked planes had exploded into The World Trade Centers. A third hijacked plane had crashed into the Pentagon. The death toll was staggering. Fear of the unknown was fueling the fears of everyone. "Is America headed to war?" was the question on everyone's lips.

All I wanted to do was pick up my sons, run, and find us a hiding place. Living within a stone's throw from a major air force installation surely meant we would have a hard time finding that hiding place.

I was so unprepared for any type of social emergency. This year so far has been mighty hazardous for me personally. It had only been about four months since I lost my job, my husband went to jail, and I became a single mother. I'd heard it so many times before, ***THE LORD won't put no more on you than you can bear***. I wanted to believe this, but lately though I'd been wondering about my strength. I even asked myself, ***Are you janky, or even a jinx maybe?*** I prayed for forgiveness for such thoughts, ***LORD you still show up and fortify me, please forgive me. Father, it's only you keeping me out of the looney bin, and still providing for my family.***

Unplugging myself from the TV, I made the call. "Happy Birthday Daddy," I said. You were doing well, but I knew it had to be hard when your birthday had just been marred by such horrific events.

57

President Bush and every other politician was trying to assuage the public hysteria by swearing vengeance on the terrorist perpetrators.

Oh Daddy, Daddy, I am so sorry…

EPISODE VI: POETIC JUSTICE

Things between my husband and I were strained.

As the months passed, I had to fight the feeling of being a walking dead woman. Fighting through a maze of confusion in my mind, I knew; if the option for a nervous breakdown had been open, I couldn't have taken it anyway because I didn't have the time.

My better half found it convenient to make collect calls from jail. This gave him a chance to insinuate blame on me for his predicament. He even accused me of failing him by not posting bail.

The Card I received in the mail had become a source of contention for us. To make matters worse I had maxed out *The Card* and even missed a few payments. My credit was compromised and it was hard to get back on track when my unemployment payments finally did begin.

All the responsibilities I faced each day were more than enough to deal with, so I vowed to not fight with my husband anymore, nor would I accept his calls.

I had to keep going for my beautiful brown angels, my sons. But, I was having a hard time being a loving mother. Short-tempered and impatient, my days went by in a blur. Diapers, tears, poop, and temper tantrums were enough to make a sister want to run. Thank *GOD* though, the smiles, kisses, and little things my sons did to make me know LOVE was more than enough to strengthen me to get up each day and do it again. I knew no one would fight for these four black boys like I would. Statistics said only one in four black males would make it in this world (my four brothers were victims to these statistics), while the other three would be doomed to incarceration, poverty, and even death. I rebuked those statistics and swore *I will fight the devil straight to hell for all of them, ALWAYS*.

My husband changed his strategy when he was unable to reach me by phone. His heartfelt letters and beautiful poetry that arrived in the mail regularly were not enough to convince me he wasn't just spouting someone else's jailhouse revelations. When I did sit down to write back, my words were not those of a loving wife. The boys were keeping me busy, their energies focused on playing and fighting. My house was cluttered, clean clothes were piled to the ceiling, and my disposition was not a pretty sight.

Jimmy was transferred to a detention center in Tallulah, La. and he was now two and a half hours away from the family. I couldn't believe the audacity when he wrote asking if I would bring the kids to see him during the Christmas holidays. This would mean I'd have to maneuver four kids and myself on a long trip in the cold.

Considering the negative changing behavior of Joshua since the arrest of his Dad, I thought this trip might help. It had been hard watching my three-year-old son change as he was becoming a terror. A two-and-a-half-hour road trip with four small kids would be worth the hope of change. And I was really tired, and sick of being mad all the time

When I loaded the van, we looked like we were headed to a vacation spot. Between the pit stops and barrage of questions from Jimmy Jr and Joshua, we made the trip to Tallulah. During the trip, I had spent a lot of time trying to prepare my two older ones for what I thought they might see. I had a sigh of relief when the visiting room was not as harsh as I had imagined.

My husband, however, was unrepentant, and his callous attitude toward everything burned me down to the soles of my feet. *What happened to all those lovey-dovey words he'd been writing?* I wandered. Even so, I kept control for the sake of my boys, all they knew was love. They were happy to see him, laughing and chatting like old friends. I couldn't believe the twinge of jealousy I felt while looking at him with the kids, so much so that I had to ask *GOD'S* forgiveness for the thoughts in my head. When the visit was over I was really ready to get on the road. I just wanted to get as far away from this man as I could. It was getting dark out, and I knew this would be the longest trip of my life.

Packing the boys up for the trip home, I couldn't hold back my tears. "What's wrong Mommy?" my sons asked.

All I could say was, "Everything's going to be alright. Mommy's okay!"

I had to compose myself because I was not the best night driver, and I had a long way to go with precious cargo. It was unbelievable when it started to snow on the way home. When my visibility got bad I could hardly see. Creeping along, I followed the traffic. The kids, meanwhile, were excited by the snow while I was having a panic attack.

On the front window, an unnerving pattern formed as the van moved slowly down the highway. The snow that fell on the windshield appeared to be a wide mouth dragon that was consuming little bits of me. Vivid memories of my life with this man played like a broken record in my mind.

Then there was calm when the snow stopped. Earlier, the snow must have blinded me because I could no longer see Jimmy in my mind. It was then I decided I could no longer be this man's wife. And I became more determined than ever to be a great mother.

SEASON IV

DAYS OF MY LIFE

EPISODE I: ROAD RAGE

I was close to breaking; the last nine months of unemployment and madness had me on edge.

My depression was temporarily muted when I got a job in February 2002. A pay reduction, and a 80-mile round trip daily commute to and from Vivian would be my trade for a career change. The perks of not more working nights, holidays off, and state benefits made my decision easy. After a very short deliberation, I accepted the job. The change from retail to state employment was compelling, and I was encouraged by the new challenges and opportunities this position presented.

I was surprised by my tearful outbursts on the drive to work my first day. It was a very long drive, and I had a lot of time to think. Pressed with thoughts like, ***Why did you made so many mistakes? For real, your husband IS in jail! If YOU had been smart when YOU were younger YOU would have saved YOUR money, been prepared for kids, a house, a car, and rainy days***. My thoughts vacillated from melancholy to red fury. Before I knew it I was at work. It was a blessing I had on tinted glasses because they helped to hide my puffy eyes as I entered the door.

When I found out I was the first minority to ever work in this small community office, I checked myself quick. Knowing this, I turned everything I knew about business up a notch. Again like my last job, I would have an opportunity to represent my heritage as a first, and I intended to do a superb job.

The drive home that evening was not much different from my drive earlier that morning. I did, however, have a better understanding of what I was going through. As the days passed my commute got less dramatic. I could finally listen to songs like *We Fall Down* and *Stand Still* without crying. For a long time, on the way home after the first fifteen miles were behind me, I'd break out and start singing the song *Twenty-Five Miles*. At the top of my voice, I'd sing, "I got twenty-five miles to go now..." then "I got fifteen miles to go now..." counting down each mile as the odometer rolled.

Making arrangements for doctors' appointments was imperative in the two-person office where I worked. When emergencies arose I would plead understanding from my manager. In the spring of 2002, Early Childhood Education (ECE) was not agreeing with Joshua; his behavior had become disruptive, and he was getting out of hand. Calls to my job about his antics soon turned to "Ms. Hampton, can you pick Joshua up?" which meant I would have to make the 80-mile trip twice a day. I thought I might lose my job because of this, but my manager was a *Blessing*.

My son Joshua had no idea how his actions were affecting the family. He was only three and thought the world revolved around him. His anger was hard to contain, even at home. I knew I had a situation on my hand.

One day at school while the teacher was reading, Joshua wouldn't sit still. Hoping to relax him, the teacher put Joshua in her lap; never imagining he would kick and beat her. This incident had me begging for another chance for my son. The School Board administration informed me that ECE was not a mandatory level in the public school system and that he would have to go back to daycare, even if it was the middle of the semester.

My guilt forced me to feed into his behavior; I spent so much time showing him how much I loved him, all at the expense of my other three sons. This was something else to occupy my mind down that long road to work. Visions of my future ahead filled me with uncertain thoughts.

EPISODE II: MY TRUTH

We had a promising start for the new school year of fall 2002.

Jimmy Jr was now six, and Joshua was four, and both of them

was excited about going back to school. Joshua would be repeating ECE. It was great news when he fell in love with his teacher. At daycare, the twins were almost getting too much love. They were popular, and everyone was surprised at their differences as twins. The workers even gave them nicknames, Yellow, for Jaleen's light complexion, and Smokey, for Jeremy's dark complexion. I did not want my kids to have nicknames, and though it took a while, the staff finally got the message and stopped calling them Yellow and Smokey. Work was also wonderful; I was learning so much. There were even times I got to run the office alone.

I filed for bankruptcy when the financial strain of being a single mother became overwhelming. Ashamed that I even had to go the bankruptcy route, I was however thankful for the relief.

The divorce judgment from my son's father was rendered on October 21, 2002. When asked if I would have a party, I said "No". Divorce was such an ugly beast and I wasn't happy that I now had two under my belt. In spite of everything, I just couldn't believe that **GOD** meant for me to live the words ***Till Death Do Us Part*** when my past two marriages had ***DIED***! I was sure that in the eyes of the church how I was thinking was considered blasphemy against **GOD**. However, it just didn't matter at that point what anyone thought, because I went to **GOD** and asked for forgiveness for my sins.

So then I tried my hand at poetry:

XXX'S

We all have one, two, three maybe more.

Sympathy, empathy we try to ignore

All the X's in our lives

We just weren't born with enough eyes

For all the X's in our lives

Be they X-convicts, X-husbands, or X-wives

This is for all the X's in our lives

As the New Year approached, I believed 2003 would be my best year yet. I wanted to be a conduit for good, and the desire for positive change in my life gave me reason for hope. I had been scarred, but not taken out of life.

EPISODE III: CHANGE

On January 1, 2003 we had so much fun ringing in the New Year. I laughed so hard when the boys threw those fire cracker poppers. Then they would scream loudly, as they watched the firework displays on our street. I had so much to be thankful for and was very proud of myself for having maintained our household thus far. As I prayed for my son's father, a moment of loneliness intruded on my joy. Pushing the feeling aside I continued to enjoy my sons.

March 6, 2003, I was totally exhausted. After a long day, I finally got the boys down to bed. And I even managed to get their clothes ready for the next day.

It had been at least six months since I'd had a bath, always jumping in and out of the shower. This night was going to be a treat deal for me though because I was going to take **A BATH**. When the quiet settled over the house, I immediately ran a tub full of very hot bubbly water. For a moment, I thought I scalded myself when I slid into the hot water. Enjoying the glow of the candles, and Yolanda Adams rocking *Open my Heart* and *The Battle Is Not Yours* I luxuriated with my Essence magazine. I was so tired when I sank under the waters. Not only was I physically tired, but I was tired of being an empty vessel in my life, tired of being malnutritioned, misdirected, and lost. Then my mind started to wonder.

This is nice! I thought as I started to feel a new love for myself. That night, I even gained a respect for all I had gone through. It had taken many years to get to this point, and I refused to count those years as wasted. Any blessings, energies or opportunities I'd given to no one that cared were to be counted as lessons that night.

Then, as if words to a song, these words appeared as a letter to **Gwendolyn**:

FORGIVE ME BODY

Forgive me body. Forgive me for the years I abused you when I took my life for granted. Forgive me for the abuse and torture I have put you through. Forgive me for not recognizing my own potential to accomplish. Thank you for carrying my overweight, undisciplined, self-centered self. Thank you for still being here for me, and giving me another chance. Just imagine, I did all of this thinking and acting as though you actually belonged to me to do with what I pleased. I am glad to know you didn't belong to me, but that we belonged to **GOD***. I know* **GOD** *abides in clean places so I am cleaning up my act. I need you to operate on my behalf before the* **LORD** *as I go through this gift, my life. Oh, body, thank you for being my vehicle for life, and I shall strive to always do my best for you through* **Christ***. Now I cast these cares onto* **THE BIG SHOULDERS OF THE LORD'S***. Love always, Gwen.* This was my prayer.

EPISODE IV: A MOTHER'S SORROW

When I heard this story March 15, 2003, the pain in my heart was tremendous.

A young man named Marquise had been killed by the police with eight gunshots. They said he brandished what appeared to be a gun: it was only a cell phone.

Community outrage was fierce, charging that the police had murdered this young man. There were many particulars to this story, but all I could think about was this young man's mother. My love and prayers for comfort went out to her. I had never met this lady, but as a mother of four boys I felt a strong kinship to her. Then, later finding out he was a husband gave me an even deeper kinship to this family.

I was really drawn into this story when I found out that Marquise was the nephew of a very good friend. I wrote a poem, and I asked my friend to deliver it to his sister, Marquise's Mother, along with a lovely dolphin wind chime. When the words to this poem appeared on paper, it was as though they had written themselves:

WHEN THE BELL TOLLS

When the bell tolls, and it tolls for me

Where will I be captive or free?

*When my **Master** says to me*

Tell Me about your life

Shall I mumble, grumble, and complain, tell all about the strife

*No, I think not, because all praises go to **Him***

*Gracious and merciful **GOD** you loved me still*

Even loving me when I was such a fool

Not knowing, but thinking I had been to school

Not just any school, but the school of life

With all its bumps and bruises

Thinking I needed to be someone's wife

Let me not forget the many blessings bestowed

*So patiently **You** waited **LORD** while I went through*

*Giving insight that **You** were always there too*

*For all the times I knew **You** were mine*

And until the time I shall stand and testify

You are the WHO the WHAT the WHEN the WHERE the WHY and the HOW

When the bell tolls and it tolls for me

*I shall kiss **Papa** and thank **Him** that I am free...**GOD BLESS***

EPISODE V: EASY? LIKE SUNDAY MORNING?

Fall of 2003 was alright with me.

The twins had been selected among the first group of kids to enroll in a zero-to-three-year-old ECE program, where the teachers would come out to the home. They were also enrolled at the Goldman school, where Ms. Theresa and Ms. Dewanna became major influences in our lives. Kindergarten didn't put an end to Joshua's defiant streak, but he did seem to enjoy his classes. Jimmy Jr was a great student and a big help with his brothers. Work was fulfilling as well. Though my divorce was finalized, I still had some lingering guilt. I didn't have any regrets though because I knew I had fought a good fight. I thanked **GOD** for providing for my family.

I was in trouble at hello, when someone called the office asking for directions. Preoccupied with a call earlier from the school about Joshua, I had a phone conversation with an unknown man that lingered into private territory. Though this was not the time for frivolity, the call was a welcome escape. Questioning myself as to my actions, I realized my intrigue had to do with the soothing sound of the man's voice on the phone, and the things he said, things I wanted to hear. When this man made it to the office later that day he was nothing like I expected. That was okay though because he didn't appear to be a monster.

I allowed this man named Edward into our world. My sons and I were enjoying the attention he was giving us, and he scored big brownie points when 2004 rolled in, making sure the boys had a huge fireworks celebration.

My dual personality always seemed to ensure that I would live in extremes, either as a **Sheep** or a **She-ro**. Edward had no real job, a piece of a car, and no home to call his own. I asked myself if I was being easy, or if there was a future for us. However, I just knew I could make a difference in this man's life. He was a very smart computer whiz with an intense desire to succeed, but he just didn't have any direction. And he was just humble and hungry enough to get under my skin. Working together we even got a great deal on a new used car. Making sure it was in both our names, I named our car *Taz*.

EPISODE VI: SABOTAGED

When I was promoted to Office Manager in March of 2004 things were looking good. Once again in unfamiliar territory, I was the first minority to ever hold this management position in this office.

Stresses were mounting at work. Previous unfelt prejudices now surfaced as complaints about me reached the Commissioner's office in Baton Rouge. Customers were complaining that "She don't do things like the other Manager." In my defense, I knew I was diligent and meticulous in my work. As a minority, I didn't want my work to be questioned in any way. It turned out that my customer service skills instead were being questioned.

I was terribly disturbed by these accusations because I'd never had a complaint from my superiors on any job about how I treated a customer. I couldn't believe the extent of the complaints against me, even local politicians got involved. I'd only held the manager's position for six months when my upper management scheduled a meeting with me in Colfax, La.; two hours away to discuss my future with the bureau. I sat there as they railed me about what was going on in the office. Feeling like I was being railroaded out of town, I listened as they tried to explain to me what the complaints were.

I was demoted, then given an ultimatum, either to continue working in Vivian or be transferred to Shreveport. I did not fight them, but before the meeting ended I gave each of my managers a short three-page letter explaining my position. I surprised myself by even writing the letter. And before I left for home, I explained to them that as a Mother of four young boys, an 80-mile daily trip was not an easy task. Then I defended the fact that I wouldn't waste my gas or put the stress on my car to take the long drive and not do an excellent job. The last point I made was the fact that I had never been reprimanded before by either of them for such actions as I was now being accused of should have spoken for my character. My anger was intense, and I was still angry by the time I got home.

Edward, and I were now dating. When I got home, he took a chance getting his head chopped off when he said, "This is a good thing."

All the screaming I did finally died down when I realized the sanity of his words. Even though I had been demoted, I didn't lose any benefits, not even my manager's pay. When I considered all things, giving up a daily 80-mile round trip to work, and the stresses of managerial duties would be more than alright with me. I thanked **GOD** for the change, and I thanked him for knowing better than me. This was an ideal transfer; not only was I nearer to my kids, but I also got some extra sleep.

In September of 2004, the people in the Shreveport office welcomed me as an old friend. I wanted to believe this new start would be just the inspiration I needed to get the extra pounds off. I had sabotaged myself earlier and needed help as my weight had ballooned to 225 lbs.(my highest weight ever).

EPISODE VII: STRANGE FEELINGS

When school began fall 2004, it was a joy knowing my kids were doing well. Joshua was now in the first grade. I made sure his teacher knew he could be a firecracker, and that she should get her bluff in early. Jimmy was in the 4th, and the twins were still in ECE. Also, Edward had started pushing for more in our relationship, and I found myself pushing away. I just wasn't ready.

At first, I couldn't explain the strange feelings I was having, then I identified the cause of my uneasiness when I realized my ex-husband was due to be released soon. Anxiety and doubt soon became full blown. When he knocked on the door that day, I instantly knew there was no turning back to what used to be. I allowed him to spend time with the kids, and they held onto him for dear life. It broke my heart when there was no one to shield me from the one question my sons shot at me when he left.

"Momma, when Daddy coming back home?"

"He's not," I said, then gave them a long list as to why this couldn't happen. It didn't matter what I said; they only came back with more "whys", and "buts".

The contempt I saw on my two older son's faces was really hard. I knew they didn't hate me, but they wanted Daddy back home. My boyfriend was no substitute for their Dad, and the best he could do was be like a big brother or friend to them at that point.

As time passed our household started looking normal. With four boys, there was always an adventure waiting to happen. At any moment a football, hockey, basketball game or wrestling match could erupt when the boys played, fussed or fought.

For a long time, I held out hope that their Dad would see past me and see that his sons needed him in their lives. This, however, was not the case. When he did a disappearing act, I couldn't explain to my kids where he was because I didn't know. I did, however, find out what he was thinking when I went to the old neighborhood. I was told, "You deserted him and he wants nothing to do with you". This hurt, but I put my feeling aside. I knew that for the past forty months I had been Mom/Dad to our sons, and no one was going to make me feel less as a parent. I held my ground, but I still felt isolated.

I virtually became a hermit. My family was never far away and Mom and Dad were always available when I needed them though. I also kept in touch with several good friends. When I called them I was able to unload some of my burdens, but when I would visit with them, to my surprise, I found out that these friends were having some serious family issues themselves. I would take these moments to get out of myself and give solid advice and encouragement. It wasn't long afterward that I would find myself lost in *mommyville* again, and soon, I was back on the grind.

Joshua was becoming more rebellious than ever. Calls from the teacher about his behavior became frequent. She was a wonderful teacher that really cared for Joshua, but she was unable to help him. He became the class instigator, disrupting the class on every hand when he was bored and didn't want to do his work. When the school year ended, with regret his teacher informed me that Joshua would be held back in first grade. She told me that repeating the first would give him some time to mature and that it was for the best. I resigned myself to the fact that maybe this was for the best while praying for direction and help for all my sons. Everyone else did well in school that year.

I was so proud of Jeremy: he was discovering **HIS GENIUS**. A conversation with him could leave you confused and shaking your head. He actually believed he was smarter than everyone in the house. I called him *Einstein in the making..*

EPISODE VIII: THE CALVARY-JUNE 2005

What a handsome man, was all I could think as he approached my desk.

While handling his business at the DMV, we made small talk. "What do you do?" I asked. "I have a martial arts school", he answered proudly. As he reached into his pocket for a card, I smiled remembering a dream I once had about being a karate girl. Then I thought about my four boys, and what the martial arts might mean to my family. I immediately blurted out, "This is what I have."

When he gave me his card, I handed him a picture of me and my sons. Since we had taken the family portrait years before after Jimmy Jr's ECE graduation, I had started the tradition of trying to take a yearly family portrait. The framed picture I showed him was our latest one. My sons were practically dressed alike and we all had on cool hats. Looking at the picture strangely, he smiled and said, "Bring your sons in for an evaluation." Not wanting to get in trouble at work I quickly finished, but before he left my desk I told him, "I'll bring my kids in soon." I was elated thinking *This could be the answer to my prayers*. My sons were now nine, seven and four and ½ two times.

Edward, my boyfriend tried hard to get in the mix, but after our first class session at Tae Kwon-Do (TKD), he got pushed way back, but I was hooked. While I watched the interaction between Master B aka Mr. B and the boys I knew I had made the right decision. As a retiree, Master B. had the time to invest, as a Marine Vet he understood the need for discipline, and as a 4th Degree Black belt, a business owner, and a former Team USA competitor, he would be an excellent instructor/mentor for my sons.

Unfortunately, I was only able to get the boys to class on the weekends. By the time Saturdays came around, Mr. B would earn his title all over again because the boys would have to be re-acclimated to his instructions, especially Joshua, who fought the instructor on every hand. This was the first time other than in school, or by me that Joshua had ever really been challenged about his behavior. He didn't like class, but that was his problem, not mine because he was going.

I'd get the chance to marvel at their strength and abilities while waiting for class to end. Sitting there I would say to myself, **You need to have your fat butt over there working out**. I wanted to be a part of everything, but I was afraid and embarrassed. And though my weight had blossomed to its peak, I still felt strong enough to do the class, even at forty-five-years-old. There were two other adults working out in the class, and I thought, **Why not me?** With encouragement from my sons and Mr. B, I stepped across that line. It was a life-changing moment when I latched on to Tae Kwon-Do. This class had become crucial to me, and though I was never financially sound, I made every effort to keep my family in the class.

I had a great incentive to do well in my new venture when Hurricane Katrina hit New Orleans with an unparalleled vengeance on August 29, 2005. The mass number of displaced persons in our city seeking shelter inspired me to do my best. At work, daily business for these people was heartbreaking. The images of New Orleans and other Gulf Coast states under water reminded me of what the world probably looked like as Noah sailed The Ark after The Flood in the Bible.

Then, less than a month later, Hurricane Rita attacked the area with another powerful force. Once again there was a swell of displaced persons needing shelter. Bordering states opened their doors to help during this regional disaster. Everyone at work was praying hard for our co-worker Rita who had been on a cruise during Hurricane Rita's torment. When she made it home safely, "Hallelujahs" reigned because Rita had survived Rita. I wanted to be better than ever, as these catastrophes ravaged many lives.

SEASON V

HERE COMES THE BRIDE

EPISODE I: RIGHT QUESTION/WRONG TIME

It was fun having Tae Kwon-Do (TKD) in common with my kids. I was feeling a confidence that made me so proud of myself.

Then, sorrow struck. In November 2005, they buried my Auntie Gloria. I had gained another **ANGEL WING**. All my aunties were my favorite, but this was a special lady with a regal aura that shone brightly. When I was younger she would say to me, "There's a little girl inside of you that wants to come out." These words were not meant to be malicious, but motivating as she witnessed my weight and self-esteem battles. Auntie would be so proud of me, now that I had lost ten pounds since joining Tae Kwon-Do.

Thoughts of my beloved, deceased grandmother, Big Momma surfaced after my aunt's death. Fond childhood memories of hanging out at her house made me smile. She had raised a big family, and my Dad and his siblings had the utmost respect for their Mother. We all loved Big Momma and loving her was easy.

Edward and I spent more time together when he started **Ed's Computers**. He even laid out plans to expand his business with my help. My dreams of owning a business resurfaced as my interest was piqued. I was proud of him, and even shared with him my vision of **Can Do Enterprizes**. It was nice having a man in my life to talk to me about business instead of vice versa.

Edward moved in when the flu took me off my feet. I became too weak to walk, and couldn't get in and out of the bed to take care of the kids. When I finally could eat something, I asked for some cheese and crackers. The kids returned with a little cheese and entire sleeve of crackers. I cracked up thinking, **Am I that greedy? Is this my normal portions?** The laugh was good for me as my body healed.

The men in my life made my birthday special. On December 16th, 2005, we all dressed up and drove to Marshall, TX. We shopped and had an amazing dinner afterward. That night, I had put together an odd combination that looked fabulous on. When we got home I grabbed a pad and sketched what I had worn. It had been a long time since I had drawn anything. Soon, I found myself smitten with designing, and my spare time was spent sketching. My kids were happy to see me involved in something other than fussing.

Buried dreams demanded my attention when feelings of possibility started growing. I even mapped out a plan for *Queenie's Closet*, another retail venture that would host *The Bradford Collection*. *The Bradford Collection* would be my debut designs named in honor of my parents. I started thinking a lot about the success of *Queenie's Closet*, and what it would mean to be successful. *My sons would be so proud, and the struggles would be over*, I thought.

A Christmas marriage proposal from Edward left me with mixed feelings. Waving red flags in Technicolor flooded my vision.

I was concerned that Edward had never been married, and this would be my third marriage. When I mentioned to him that he had not established a fatherly bond with my kids, he said he could handle the responsibility. Our house was a messy whirlwind, and the men of the house adamantly promised to do better. TKD had become a major factor in our lives, but Edward still had no interest in it at all. I even made a concession about him not having a place for us since my home was big enough. And I couldn't help but think about all the meanness I had exhibited toward him over the last two years, and he stayed. We held a family meeting where I said *"Yes"* to his proposal. Then I paraded my engagement ring (the one we bought) for about two weeks.

After much consideration, I told Edward I didn't want to get married. Then I gave him back the ring and the receipt and told him to return it. His devastation surprised me, as his pleadings surpassed any words, any man had ever spoken to me. His begging made me feel more like a woman. After all my relationship issues, finally, a man was there confessing his undying love as my **Guardian Angel**, promising to do, and be all that I could ever want. As a forty-six-year-old single Mother of four young sons, I then reevaluated what my love life might look like under these circumstances. Even though I still longed for a passionate love, I started to believe that maybe my window of opportunity had passed. I even started thinking **Maybe this man is my chosen challenge. Maybe with a lot of work, grace, and mercy a marriage to Edward could work**.

Then I re-accepted the ring, I was bent on being a **Good Wife**. **Shame on you Gwen** should have been my first name because what I was doing was so wrong. I knew I would manipulate this man to my benefit. Forgetting all the times I had told friends I would never remarry, I admitted to myself that I wanted someone else in on my trials and tribulations. Someone to wipe my tears when the going got tough, which was often the case. Then I would feel better when Edward would praise my strength, and as I listened to him talk about how different I was from other women, I would feel proud.

The final words to myself was, **He truly cares for me and my boys, and we care about him.**

We then held another family meeting where I once again explained to my children that I would be marrying Edward. I fell just short of begging when I told them their cooperation would be needed to make things work.

EPISODE II: "ido"

Saturday, January 21, 2006, was a beautiful day.

My friend Glenda, the Justice of the Peace, had agreed to marry us. Silently, standing before **GOD, and to GOD**, I confessed the error of my action. Then I looked over at Edward, with regret I knew this marriage wouldn't work. Feeling bad, I became concerned about of how this situation might affect him. Thinking about my past personal pains, I had to ask myself, *How could you perpetrate such a farce on someone else, even if we have plans to be in business?*

I even had the audacity to look at Glenda sideways for an instance, thinking, *Why didn't she require us to go through marriage counseling before marrying us?* I shut this thought down quickly though because she was happy for me and was more than glad to perform my wishes. But, I probably wouldn't have married Edward if all the cards had been laid on the table before someone else.

My sons seemed happy enough, and Edward truly believed things would work out between us.

We didn't fly away to a romantic destination for a once in a lifetime honeymoon. Instead, we got into a fight on the way home. There was no lovey-dovey that night. And when Sunday came, apologies were everywhere. No matter how much we talked I knew the wrong I had done.

Monday proved interesting. At work on my lunch break, I made a call as I remembered the words from the Bible *Reap what you sow*, then the words *What goes around comes around.* I had experienced a lot of confusion in past relationships, and I knew I didn't want to suffer the consequence this marriage might bring, so I wanted out. When the lady answered the phone I blurted out, "What does it take to get an annulment?"

I had it all planned out in my head. A simple way to undo a bad mistake. The lady on the other end of the line shattered my senses when she told me, "Annulments in Louisiana are no longer legal, unless..." She ran down a list of scenarios like bigamy, incest, and coercion. And based on the criteria, I didn't qualify for an annulment. For the rest of the work day, I kept thinking, *LORD have mercy. Trouble is on the horizon, and 911 is gone be called.*

Our co-worker Eric had been admitted to the hospital. We didn't get all the info on his condition, but when we got word he had died, a dark cloud descended over our office. And so, by the end of the week, I committed myself to peacefully work my way out of my marriage.

EPISODE III: BLOOD TIES

The Doctor shot rapid-fire questions like, "How have you been feeling? How have you been making it? Haven't you been tired?"

"Well yes," I stammered. ***Weird question***, I thought. Who wouldn't be tired? Who else was going to take care of the boys, and put food on the table? Even though I had a husband, I was the main breadwinner. My husband worked hard in his business, but the money was slow.

Again, at my next appointment, the Doctor started with a series of questions. "How have you been feeling?" he said. "Doctor, I am drained, I feel a tiredness all the way down to my bone marrow" I admitted. "Have you been sleeping?" he asked. I answered, "No", then with no shame, I burst into tears. Floods of emotion burst through as currents of fear, anger, confusion, and guilt filled me. It took a while before my tears subsided.

Reviewing my home life, and past high blood pressure history, the doctor concluded that I was suffering from ***Depression***. I thought ***Yeah Doc but it's more like Desperation!!!*** The doctor concluded that I was suffering from clinical depression, and he prescribed medication. I didn't want to believe what he said, but when he read the definition of clinical depression, I knew I needed help. I had suppressed a deep sadness that I believed if surfaced, I probably wouldn't be able to breathe. Embracing the idea that maybe I could be helped with meds gave me hope. I wanted to be strong and secure in myself, and maybe this was my time when all things would be good.

A subsequent visit to the doctor revealed the source of my energy loss. I was suffering from acute Anemia, and was told that I needed a blood transfusion. I knew disease could be transferred from transfusions, and anything could go wrong. Afraid, I begged for medication instead. The doctor temporarily agreed as he prescribed a dose of 3 huge iron pills and a multivitamin daily. He warned me before I left that if my levels didn't rise in a quick period, then the next option would be a transfusion.

I'd had fears before of dying and leaving my sons without a mother/father. Now, just the thought of having a blood transfusion really scared me. I had to talk to *GOD, Please LORD, let me see my sons grow up before you call me home. Please keep me till they can take care of themselves.* Edward was there when my fears became too much. Leaning heavily on him I diligently followed doctor's orders.

At my next appointment, tests revealed that the meds had not raised my iron to a healthy level. So I agreed to a transfusion and checked into the hospital.

Nervous about my procedure, while drifting in and out of consciousness my thoughts went to a conversation with my mother. She once said, "You better stay around and take care of your children or Ms. Enlow will get them. I can't take care of them!" Puzzled, I asked, "Who is Ms. Enlow?" "She's the welfare lady" Mom replied. Tradition had been passed down the line: this was, after all, what her Mother had told her. Ms. Enlow was the welfare lady who came and took children away when my grandmother was a young mother.

In the hospital, my husband was so attentive to me. Standing in the gap during my absence at home, Edward gained my respect and admiration. I knew I would have to give our marriage a chance; he was trying hard to prove himself to me.

The transfusion was a success, but I couldn't help noting *How fast blood came out of the body, then how very long and slow it took going in.*

When I got home, I had a new respect for my life. I decided to give our marriage my best shot. I told my husband I would trust him to lead our family, and I let him know how much I appreciated him during this past emergency. Not long after, I quit my job and devoted myself to our business venture. My family even stopped going to TKD, and I was surprised when my sons did not seem to care. They were having fun as we traveled to Alabama, Texas, and even Georgia, picking up auction wins of computers and parts. Finally thinking I was on the road to my vision, we registered with the Secretary of State as *Can Do Enterprizes, LLC.*

For a while, I took advantage of sleeping in late. Then I realized that I was a part of the success of *Ed's Computers*. Changing my habits, I got into a routine, working our business like it was a job. I even started a side hustle doing auto title work for a couple of used car dealerships.

EPISODE IV: 5/26/06

This was a "MAD" day for me. Quitting my job seemed like the right thing to do back when, but today would have been a good day to have a job to run to.

Reality hit hard when I admitted the truth to myself: *I could no longer pretend in this marriage*. The emotional feelings of loss and stress that were created by this relationship made me feel horrible. And I started to feel like my life was in danger as I began to mourn myself. Silently I would pray, *LORD, please have mercy. I didn't even consult you in this decision. I really liked him as a person, not as a husband, or a lover. What have I done? Am I truly responsible to make it work because he's a good person? No one deserves this madness*.

Edward changed my life in so many ways, but I didn't have it in me to be his *Good Wife*. Still, a part of me pleaded his case when the voices wouldn't quit, *Stop fighting, you have never had someone care for you like this. You are selfish and arrogant. All you think about is yourself.* Then I asked myself, W*hat is the right way? How could I have followed through with such a wrong decision?* Healing from the pain, peace was needed; but I didn't know what to do.

EPISODE V: 911 EMERGENCY

From the time I said "ido", it was a given that I would have to make this call one day.

Wonderful things were happening in our business, but our relationship was deteriorating. My kids witnessed constant arguing between Edward and I, and our house was a mess. And lately, almost everything rubbed me the wrong way.

"Momma!" Jimmy Jr screamed when he walked out the front door. Alarmed, I asked "What's wrong? He said, "Momma you have a bald spot in the top of your head." From where I was sitting on the step when he walked out the front door he could see the top of my head.

Confused I asked, "What do you mean?" as I reached up to feel a thin spot. Rushing to the bathroom I confirmed what he saw. I had a bald spot in the top of my head. I wondered *How was it that I had missed this empty plug in the top of my head? Maybe this was where all the heated fumes from our incessant arguments had settled.* Upset, I called my friend Ms. Jai the barber. She told me, "Your scalp is stressed. The stresses of your life had undoubtedly settled in that spot, and is making it difficult for your hair to grow there." Pacing the floor like a caged animal, I was ready to end things with my husband that night.

The evening came and by the time Edward got home I was ready to war. As soon as he hit the door, I blasted him. I even banged my head in protest screaming, "Look at this bald spot, I've had enough". When I asked him to leave, he refused, and then we got into a terrible fight. I couldn't stop because I had to get this man out of my house. My children watched in terror as my husband pinned me against the dryer with his hands on my throat. As he choked me, with pure hatred in his voice, he said, "Now, what your Tae Kwon-Do gone do for you now?"

I was filled with rage, but I was also paralyzed because I couldn't believe what was happening. My kids were crying and screaming for him to stop. I don't know if I managed to dial 911 or one of the kids did, but soon there was a knock at the door. It was the police.

"Ma'am do you want to press charges?" the policeman asked. "No. I just want him out of my house." I said. "If you don't press charges we can't make him leave because he lives here," the policeman said. "But sir, we strongly suggest you find somewhere else to stay for the night. If we have to come back here tonight, someone is going to jail" the second policeman said.

When Edward left, I replayed the night over and over again in my mind. I couldn't believe how quickly I had forgotten the self-defense tactics that were taught during each and every class of Tae-Kwon Do. The more I thought about it, the more I knew I was responsible. This man had never exhibited any violent tendencies toward me. I had been the hostile one.

EPISODE VI: STORY OF MY LIFE

July 15, 2006, was Joshua's eighth birthday. I cried because there would be no celebration, but not one tear fell for the man I called Husband. Even though I was still apologizing to my sons for the incident with the police, their hugs and kisses made me feel like they really understood. Again, I swore to always take care of them,

A few days later, Edward showed up. His apologies and

pleadings, along with my guilt, let him back in the house. We held a family meeting with the kids to explain our actions and our plan to make things work. It was very odd this time when we talked to them. Their indifference had me wondering what was on the horizon. I didn't want to make matters worse than they already were, so I did everything I could to make them happy. This was a critical time, and I had to get it together fast. School would be starting soon, and Joshua was starting second grade.

When the kids were in school I isolated myself in deep thought. I kept trying to describe my feelings to myself. Then I saw it clearly in this story:

CRISS-CROSSED

I was once in the desert with no shoes. The sun was beating down on me as I walked. This was a desert of confusion, heartache, lost love for oneself, and misunderstanding; it was a desert of sin. As I traveled, it became apparent that I had to get to the other side or I would die. I was so a blinded by the blazing sun that I couldn't see the end. As my tired, aching, swollen feet became an issue, I was offered a pair of shoes from out of the blue. I accepted them. They looked good, but they were the wrong size. From first sight I got the idea that these shoes needed me, I believed they needed rescuing. I didn't even think about my need for protection from the hot sun and sand.

When I shined them up they looked like beautiful glass against the sand. Even though they were the wrong size, those shoes fit, but oddly. Somehow the right fit on the left, and the left fit on the right. I could only get part of my feet in the shoes at first, but with great struggle, I'd finally get my entire feet into them. And I experienced great pain. I figured there must be a way to correct the fit, but the shoes warned me that I had to learn to walk in them as they were. It was a very tight fit. Throwing them off, and away into the brush, I continued my walk, rebuking myself for such ludacris behavior.

It didn't take long before the shoes showed up again. This time more animated than ever, they shouted, "Please look at me again! I've gotten new soles and laces, look how polished I am! Please try me on again. If you must go through the desert isn't it better with shoes on?"

Considering this I agreed that shoes in the desert was a better way to go. Once again I squeezed my feet into those crisscrossed shoes and continued on my walk through the desert. I was only able to go a little farther until the pain became unbearable. Casting the shoes off again, I continued my journey, bewildered as to why I had put the shoes back on when I knew the consequences.

The terrible desert had gotten hotter, with no end in sight. Just as really crazy thoughts flooded my mind, the shoes show up again, more persistent than ever. I began to think again; maybe I could learn to walk in them. Making rationalizations I accepted the shoes back. Determined, I said "I can do this", and shoved my feet in with full abandon. Oh, my **GOD**, it hurt, the pain was intense. My feet were screaming, but they were out of the hot sand, no matter how painful.

Time went by and I got pretty good at wearing my ill-fitted shoes, parading them through the sand as the best. Going through, my hopes were that these shoes would stretch, and we would eventually see eye-to-eye, and become a perfect fit. There was one big problem though; you can't fit a size ten into a size six and be able to walk correctly. And how can you truly walk with your left shoe on your right and your right on your left?

LORD knows I tried. I thought **He** had presented me with a gift in my time of need. Had I truly respected myself I would have accepted the fact that my feet were too big, and I couldn't walk in the shoes (but the sun was so hot I rationalized). I knew the shoes were not from **GOD**.

I should have stood firm in my decision when I first tossed the shoes off. And I should have encouraged the shoes by telling them, there was someone whose feet would fit beautifully inside of them.

The longer I walked the more I began to despise those shoes. I had forced the fit and walked the walk, knowing I was wrong. I was so intent on correcting the shoes that I failed to even consider I was the one who needed correcting. I couldn't blame the shoes; they were just trying to belong. They wanted to do the right thing and walk me through the desert.

It was time for me to let the shoes go permanently. My greatest regret was that when they were fancy and happy I did not let them go free. I had scarred them up, scratched, and bent them out of shape. Now they would be all alone.

I had been so busy sweating in the sun that I had failed to gauge myself in the desert. I had failed to look back and see how far I had come. Then, I finally realized that through time, grace, and mercy my feet had actually become accustomed to walking in the desert. I was okay, and if I had not accepted those shoes, and held on for just a little while longer I would have found out that I was so near the end of the dry desolate spell I was in.

EPISODE VII: TO THE LEFT

Beyonce was ruling the airway. And I was enjoying a moment of peace on my toilet, listening to her latest song, "Irreplaceable", as it sailed through the door.

GO appeared in my mind like a neon billboard. And I didn't even have to think about what it meant. First thing was that my husband had to *GO*, and secondly, it was time for me to *GO* back to work.

Like a robot, I proceeded to pack my husband's clothes and didn't stop until I packed all of his things. Then I put them by the front door, not even realizing I had placed them "to the left, to the left" like the words to Beyonce's song.

When my husband got home I didn't waste any time, I told him, "You have to leave right now." I wasn't asking and no was not an option as I pointed to the boxes by the door. He was amazed by what was happening. As he reached to touch me, I fiercely blocked his hand (This time I remembered my self-defense moves from Tae-Kwon Do). He let out of screech, screaming "Why you do that?" I merely looked at him calmly, and said, "Don't ever touch me again. I need you to leave now."

As he continued jabbering I opened the door for him. It was only then he realized I was serious. He grabbed the keys to *Taz* and began packing the trunk of our car. As he drove off, I found myself giving him a classic Mrs. America wave, a celebration of my liberation.

EPISODE VIII: F-R-E-E-D-O-M

After I spent some time alone, I realized my life wasn't over; in fact, it was just beginning. Talking with *God* helped me to clear my mind, and I was confident that I would be lead in the divine right way when I penned these words:

CHOOSE LIFE

My time has come to choose, what direction shall I go? Should I stay, or should I go? Can someone please help me find a hiding place? This is too much, hide me now.

*Then one day, out of **His Grace, GOD** touched me. **He** spoke to a place that had been locked away. Steel bolted, barb wired, you know the story. **He** knocked so loudly, but I was afraid to let **Him** in.*

*As it stood, things were bearable, but **GOD** wanted to give me more. With His arms open wide, **He** said **"Come to me! Your trials*** *and tribulations have not gone unnoticed by the Heavenlies. Your faith and perseverant behavior have wrought you a place among the favored".* Now was the time to claim my prize. *To win the race, you must decide to trust in* **GOD**. *Circumstances kept calling me back, telling me to be afraid.* "You can't do what **GOD** has promised. You are not worthy!" *they said.* "But, how can I not be worthy when **JESUS** shed **His** precious blood? *I asked the circumstances.*

JESUS *is only a breath away, and I understand that I must be reborn again from inside out. Radiating love in all fashions, I claim who I am.* **I am GOD'S Woman**, *and I have been given a choice. I know there's only one way.* **With GOD as my guide, I Choose Life!!!**

It had been a week since my husband left. When I saw him drive up in *Taz*, I thought, *Now what?*

He looked rattled when he got out screaming, "Here, take this car!" I flinched when he threw the keys toward me, looking with my mouth open wide. He acted like *Taz* was possessed by the devil, and that he had to get away from the car. Claiming my car as a blessing I thanked **GOD** for the many more blessings to come.

Rising like a phoenix from the ashes, I jammed to Beyonce and had a fabulous night. Boldly I claimed, "I still believe in miracles!" I even had the audacity to dream about what I would feel like with the man of my dreams. Hence this poetic endeavor:

SMILE

When I see your smile, my heart just melts.

Melts into a universe, a place I've never felt.

The day I fell in love, it was such a casual stance.

Sitting there I knew for a lifetime with you I'd want to dance.

I am here, I am yours, and I can't help myself.

For I know time and chance come to everyone.

And the wait for you is worth my very soul.

Let me be yours till we both are one.

Your smile,

let me touch you,

let me love you,

let me into all of you.

And as I wait I know all things are mine.

For your faith in me,

and your smile

takes me to a place of sure fate

*I know **GOD** has chosen.*

EPISODE IX: A STRONG FINISH

My four sons and I surprised our Tae Kwon-Do (TKD) instructor when we walked into the school. Meekly, I explained to Mr. B some of what we had been through and told him I wanted my family to return. As we were welcomed back, I knew I was at home.

In December of 2006 I was refreshed and ready to get back to work. Beating the pavement, I was prepared to knock on every door to find a job. Then I had this amazing thought, ***What if I could go back to my old job? It was a good position, and my friends were there***.

Timidly I made the call, and the manager told me I was eligible to return. Excitedly, I screamed, "Hallelujah!" Turned out I was within the eligibility period to return to work without going through the entire hiring process again. I got my job back, and I was happy, because things were in divine order.

December 16th was my birthday. My boys and I spent the morning working out, then we pigged out at the pizza buffet that afternoon, and that evening while my sons played Xbox, I rested. It was a good day.

Necessity is the mother of invention, so when I didn't have much money for Christmas, I got a great idea for a tree. While the kids were busy, I got strings of light and nail gunned them to the ceiling. Cascading the lights to the floor, I put the gifts we'd received from the Salvation Army's Angel Tree program inside the lights. Then I nailed the lights to the hardwood floor in the shape of a Christmas tree.

The boys thought I had done something special for them as they delighted in our unique tree. We kept our Christmas light tree up for weeks. When the guys returned to school after the holidays, they told all their friends. I enjoyed listening to the stories they shared about how everyone thought their tree was the coolest.

SEASON VI

Growing Panes

EPISODE I: 99 WON'T DO

I was finally able to better understand the lessons taught by my grandmothers, so much so that I even revised the slogan on my t-shirt to: *Mandatory to grow old as long as you live, optional to grow up.*

I was blessed with two awesome grandmothers. Big Momma was no longer with us, but Ms. Charlsie was still here. As the matriarch of the clan, her work ethic rule was **Get it done**. As a frugal spender, she would save for big purchases, and her megawatt smile lit the way for many in dark times.

Ms. Charlsie turned one hundred (100) on February 18, 2007. My mom and her sisters were happy to commemorate the historic moment with a birthday party for their mother. When they wheeled my grandmother into the building, she smiled brightly at all the well-wishers in attendance; she just knew this was her party.

Ms. Charlsie was the first in the family to reach 100. She had raised the bar and given each of us a star to believe on. A few years ago, I asked her for some words of wisdom, and she told me, "As old as I am, I found out that I didn't know everything." After that, there was nothing else I could say.

EPISODE II: MEN-O-WHAT

Since I was seventeen, I always had a heavy menstrual flow.

I thanked **GOD** I didn't have the debilitating cramps some of my friends had though. Practicing Tae Kwon Do did however mean I had to improvise my protection. I learned to double up with my padding, and amazingly I never had an accident.

Even though I was forty-seven-years-old, I really felt like a young woman. My kids gave me a youthful energy. The Big M, or menopause, had never really crossed my mind. But in June 2007, the light spotting I experienced got me to thinking. Knowing for sure I wasn't pregnant, I thought, *Maybe this is the end of my menstrual cycle?* Checking it out on Google, and with the doctor, I found out that I was a premenopausal woman. I didn't want to rush my life cycle; but if the end of my menstrual cycle was near, then I sure wasn't going to be mad.

I had been having hot flashes straight from hell. It literally felt like someone had turned an oven on inside of me. And when the crazy from a hot flash would kick in, everyone would become aware. There were even times in Tae Kwon Do when a hot flash would hit, and our instructor would warn the kids to just leave me alone. Drenched bed sheets from night sweats were also a sign to me that my body was changing. I got happy knowing that the Big M. was not too far ahead.

EPISODE III: GROWN WOMAN CRUSH

The choice to be single and celibate was serving me well as I focused on four young boys that captivated my life. And I didn't want my focus distracted, or forget my resolution to *Let Go, and, Let GOD*. Additionally, I had personal areas in my life that still required my discipline. With three failed marriages, a heck of a lot of insecurities, non-stop worries, and horrifying fears under my belt, the fight for sobriety was intense.

My patience was dwindling as I fought the sad thought *I might never have someone special in my life*. When my patience ran out, I ceased waiting on *GOD* for a mate, and his fullness of time for my life.

I secretly held a fascination in my heart for a good friend. Though tempted before to share my feelings, I'd fought the temptation with a *hands-off* policy. Then, when familiar urges started saturating my senses, my thoughts became obsessed with him. I found opportunities to see him; my car, surplus food I had cooked, whatever. Nothing seemed to matter as I became a force to be reckoned with.

This man never knew of my attraction to him, until the day I pushed up on him. Surprised by my actions, he responded to me. Apparently, the attraction had been mutual, and we both knew how to keep our feelings intact. Once my feelings were exposed, I couldn't help feeling this man when I was in his presence. It had been 27 years since I'd felt such giddiness. We'd had long talks in the past about relationships, and I knew he didn't want to be in a committed relationship. This didn't matter to me though because I was determined to be *The One* that would turn his world around, even if I had four kids.

In time, I became fodder for this man, if he said come, I was there. There were so many lessons about being single that I had missed, but my perspectives changed when I started believing *If a man tells you something, you might want to believe him because it probably is the truth*. When he told me before that he didn't want to be in a committed relationship, I should have believed him, because he meant it.

As much as I wanted him to feel what I was feeling, it just didn't happen as our friendship began to suffer. His honesty about his single life was crushing. He arrogantly told me one day, "I could date your best friend if I wanted to." This was a terrible insult to me. And it hurt me to know that he held me in such low esteem that he would even verbalize those words. I had sunk to an all-time low with myself when I took his words like a grain of salt.

Angry at myself for forfeiting quality time with my children to be with him, I knew I was the only one to blame. There were so many reasons to run as far as I could from this man, but then I would find as many excuses to chase him more. I had fallen deep into a situation that facilitated between, *I love you, I hate you,* and *I don't know what to do.*

Everything started to feel like payback for how I'd behaved with my ex-husband. The five words, *What goes around comes around* seemed to fit because I was now on the butt end of someone else's choice. Poor me, I just couldn't walk away by putting the brakes on: I had to be pushed to the depths of hell with only my tears to put out the fire. When the light finally came on for me, I was able to amicably part ways, no longer having room to keep hope alive as I lost a good friend.

EPISODE IV: BLESS ME *LORD*

August of 2007, this would be a first: everyone's was in school. The twins were in the first grade, Joshua was in the third, and Jimmy was now in middle school, sixth grade. It felt great when my friends and family would tell me what a great mom I was, but I kept my fingers crossed moving forward.

So much time had passed, and I still found myself continually thinking about old things I supposedly had given to the *LORD*. I knew I had to take care of myself, physically, mentally, and financially. The walks in the park, meditation, and mini fasts I had started doing were good for me; if I could only make those lifestyle changes permanent. My *I gotta haves* seemed to be under control as I felt *GOD'S STRENGTH*.

By October of 2007, I still was affirming the life I would love. I had been released from my bankruptcy, my house was now paid in full, and my deed was in the mail. With new monies into the household, I created a workable budget that should've worked out, but somehow I found needs for the surplus monies. The ramifications of my actions were revealed when I started feeling a pinch.

I prayed, *LORD you keep on proving yourself to me. Please bless my faith, and forgive my lack of faith. I truly want to be whole and fulfilled in you and your ways. Let my faith be renewed and strengthened, and as small as a mustard seed is, let me be as big as you are. Thank you for loving me. I pray to be 155 lbs., and that my mind, body, and soul shall come together to make this possible. I am divinely led in my role as Mother/Father. Bless my children with divine perfect health. Thank you for a renewed relationship with each of them. Let me be a lovely lady in all my ways. Thank you for being a Father of your word. Give me a better understanding, and a clearer insight into all the lessons you are teaching me. IN JESUS NAME.*

My sons' father started making regular appearances. The dissension among my troops was unnerving until things started making sense. I realized that since I had started allowing the kids to go over to their father's house, my two older boys had been behaving with an air of superiority and arrogance toward me. I just thought it was just some kind of phase, then I found out that their dad had been sharing his ideas about me with the kids. He didn't like me, and he convinced the kids that he still had a claim to his family and his house. Then he told the kids that I was just being stubborn. Even though I couldn't control what he said to the kids when they were with him, I didn't appreciate it when they would press me with hopes that we all could be family again.

On November 1st, 2007, I called a family meeting, an emergency meeting. I had to get the situation with their father under control. There was a serious problem brewing, and this meeting was my stand to get control. My father's words echoed within me: *You have to get control of your house now, or you will be sorry when the boys are teenagers*.

Everyone was at the meeting but Jimmy Jr. I didn't even know where he was, but I decided to give him some space because this was way out of character for him. After the family meeting, when he got home we sat down and talked. Then, as if I had been blinded, my eyes were opened. For the first time, I realized that I had never given any thought to what Jimmy Jr might have been going through. He had been a solid rock for me, and he never complained about **The Beast** life had put on his back. I felt terrible as I apologized to him for my insensitivity, then I tried to explain the foolishness of my actions to him. Jimmy Jr surprised me that day with understanding words and lots of hugs. His maturity was unbelievable. In tears, I told him how proud I was of him, and how thankful I was for the little man he had become. That day, I honored Jimmy Jr with a new understanding and love that was needed to nurture him into manhood.

EPISODE V: Trials and Tribulations

Going into 2008, I was at a loss.

Joshua was now in a counseling program. The counselors would come to the house, talk with him, and afterward talk to me about his good manners and how well he answered the questions. This didn't seem to be working out because I felt the counselors accepted the act he was putting on: I knew the truth.

Still seeking answers, I took him to see the doctor. He was diagnosed with ADHD and given a prescription for Ritalin. I hesitated as I remembered stories of kids who'd experienced zombie-like states from this medicine. Every morning I diligently gave Joshua the meds and I kept him active in TKD. As time passed, I guess his immune system adjusted to the medicine because by two in the afternoon the school would start calling me.

The doctor wanted to increase the dosage of Ritalin that Joshua was on. Something had to change because I just couldn't see giving Joshua more of this medicine that had mummified so many kids. Unsure what to do, I talked to Mr. B about ways I might be able to help my son. When the invitation for a TKD tournament came, our instructor talked to me about how competing might be a positive way to channel Joshua's pent-up emotions. I agreed, thinking this was an excellent option. My decision became clear when I decided to take

Joshua off the Ritalin.

The devil had big plans in store for me though.

On March 14, 2008 at 10:30 pm I was still shaking. I had just finished starching Joshua and Jimmy Jr's TKD uniforms and cleaning the kitchen. I was anxious to get to bed early because the boys' first tournament was the next day. Just as I reached to cut the lights off, from the corner of my eye I saw a spark and smelled something funny.

Sniffing around, I couldn't tell where the smell came from, or even see where the spark was. I checked the microwave, the refrigerator, and all the small electrical items, nothing. There was a disconnected dishwasher next to the sink that I hadn't moved out of the house. I figured there was no power there, but I pulled it out from its spot anyway. Just as I moved the dishwasher, I saw another spark, then another. There was a break in the electrical wire, (I thought the dishwasher was dead) and the insulation around the wires had been burned. I considered dialing 911 because a fire was about to start, but I felt that by the time they got there, my house would be in flames.

My babies were asleep, and I had to act fast. I tried to unplug the cord, but it was embedded under the cabinet. Knowing that it was a matter of time before the sparks started a fire I grabbed a pair of scissors and tried to cut the wires. The sparks were slowly igniting, and I couldn't waste any more time. Then remembered the knife I had bought from Carl earlier. He told me the knife would cut through anything, even bone. I then grabbed the knife and proceeded to frantically saw on the wires. Carl was right, this knife did cut through anything, and it got the job done.

Proud of myself, I looked at the knife and the blade was burned. Then reality set in as I looked at the burnt blade. Crying uncontrollably, I thought of the foolish thing I had done by using the knife on the exposed wire. It never occurred to me to douse the sparks then call 911. *Oh my GOD, my kids could have woke up in the morning with their Mother dead on the floor* was my only thought as I headed to bed.

That night, I knew for sure that **GOD** was real. After I prayed before bed, I then pondered on my near fatal meeting with death. *You have to do what you have to do. Use what you got. Trust in GOD, because He will send signs when doom is close. He didn't allow me to go to bed with a fire ready to erupt in my kitchen, I smelled the scent first. A car makes noises or starts to smoke before it completely stops. My mind and heart said No before I married my first husband. When we chose not to listen to warning signs, more than likely we will suffer unwanted consequences.*

Still shaking, I drifted off to sleep, professing I would put my book together. I believed this was a part of my life's mission, and it would be manifested through **GOD'S GUIDANCE**. I wouldn't let fear stop me from completing my commission for **Relics Of A Woman**.

Let go and let GOD lead you, Amen was my last thought that night.

EPISODE VI: TINY TITANS

Morning unfolded into a beautiful day.

After the horror of the night before, I was thankful to be alive. It was a big day for the family, our first tournament. The twins weren't competing, but they were excited for their brothers. Letting them sleep in, I took the time to reflect on the goodness of my life. Then, they jumped out of bed, excited and ready for the day to start. As we headed out the door, I whispered a small prayer. I did want my sons to win.

The gymnasium was exploding with people. Our entire TKD class was there to cheer the boys on. Jimmy Jr and Joshua looked great in their starched white uniforms. They didn't even seem nervous as they embodied the principles of Tae-Kwon Do: courtesy, integrity, perseverance, self-control and indomitable spirit. These guys were intense, and ready. The entire day was a phenomenal spectacle.

Everyone was blown away by the guys' performance, and they were having a ball. Jimmy Jr competed in three categories: forms, point, and continuous sparring, and he won 1st (first) place in everything. Joshua competed in two categories: forms, and continuous sparring. He walked away with 2nd (second) place in both events.

Strutting out of the arena like winning peacocks; I knew this would be the first of many competitions, and even gave my sons a stage name: *4JHampton*. The twins wanted to be a part and I vowed to them: *"Next time!"*

EPISODE VII: CELEBRATE DAUGHTERS

Someone asked me, "How could you write a book for daughters when you only had sons?"

This was such a strange question to me. I was a girl, after all, a mother, a daughter, a sister, a niece, and an aunt. Why wouldn't I write a book to encourage girls and women on their journeys? I was a young girl that grew up to be the woman that made many mistakes. So much of me was still the lost little girl who had the biggest heart that put on a mask for the world. My prayer was that *Relics Of A Woman* (ROAW) would bring liberation to me, and many others. I wanted my book to be a *motivating sword*, and also I wanted *ROAW* to be a *listening ear* for all girls young and old within my sphere. Through *ROAW* I intended to present a case for right thinking and living. But more than that, my desire was to let everyone know that they were worthy of *GOD'S LOVE AND BLESSINGS THROUGH JESUS CHRIST.*

EPISODE VIII: OLD SCHOOL WAYS

I pulled my sewing machine out when I got an itch to try my hand at what I called sight design. It seemed like forever since I'd sewn anything. I wanted to make TKD pants for my sons, and I didn't have a pattern. Using the pants from their uniform I was able to design a perfect rendition of their pants. The form and fit were ideal. I even did the same for a uniform I made for Master B.

This got me thinking of all the times I had been asked to replace zippers, hem pants, and sew buttons on. Then I thought *Maybe I could make extra money*. So in July, 2008, I printed out the flyer, had my sons sign and agree to it, and thus, *Low Cut Alterations* was born.

When I got divorce papers for the third time in my life, I was reminded of my visions of grandeur in big business. Maybe I was a serial entrepreneur, one destined not to succeed. I was having trouble with reality, as excuses crept in about why I couldn't win with *Low Cut Alterations*.

EPISODE IX: 08*08*08

It was said that this date would not come around for another thousand years. In a numerology study, the number 8 indicated infinity and new beginnings. And this day was new beginnings time three.

I needed a new beginning.

This day was so important because I was going in for a procedure. Way back when I had spotted, I thought it was an indication that my menstrual cycle was about to stop. That was just a moment in time because since then I had been bleeding even heavier than before. My padding for TKD went from one large pad to a tampon and a large pad. On the verge of anemia again, I started researching what I could do about alleviating these heavy periods, short of having a hysterectomy.

After researching a procedure called "Her Option Cryoablation Therapy" I was immediately interested. I couldn't pronounce cryoablation, but I knew this therapy was for me. The procedure would freeze the lining of my uterus which would then reduce or eliminate tissue shed during my period, thus no more heavy periods. After consulting with the doctor, it was determined I would be a good candidate. So this was the day of my procedure, and I was nervous as I prayed for a positive outcome. Even though I had been informed this procedure was not guaranteed to stop my menstrual cycle, I was desperate and would have settled for a reduction in my monthly output. The procedure was a success, but I would have to wait for the results.

EPISODE X: MY EPIPHANY

By now I had lost 35 pounds, but when I looked down, it seemed like my stomach was looking back at me, and I became discouraged. I had been working out, but had gained some weight back by being complacent. And I hadn't changed my eating habits, which was a total disrespect for all the hard work I had been doing in class. I made an excuse to myself by saying *I'm bloated*, but I looked very, very pregnant.

Could this be the first time I ever really looked at my body? My stomach was a belly, it was huge, and when I sat down, my gut would be in my lap. Asking the kids their opinion was not a good idea, they said, "At least it's not what it used to be." I was horrified as my heart hit the floor. *What in heaven's name did I look like before?* I wondered as I started to feel like a big fat pig. Then the light came on, *You're wasting your time Gwen if you don't change your ways*.

103

EPISODE XI: THANKSGIVING

Nov. 27, 2008. The prayer before dinner was fraught with sorrow.

Our beloved matriarch, Ms. Charlsie had died at one hundred and one years old. I had gained another *Angel Wing*. It had only been four days since she'd left us, but her presence was still strong in the house. My friend, my girl, my grandmother, was gone. Ms. Charlsie was my Shero, a strong woman who had hit many nails, mowed many lawns, repaired, replaced, and painted anything in her path. This woman meant so much to me, to us. And so, though our prayer was sad, our dinner was filled with laughter and smiles as we shared stories about *Mul* or *Ms. Charlsie* as I called her.

On November 28 we didn't have a birthday party for the twins, but I made sure they had a birthday cake. They were eight. Here was that number eight again. New beginnings, infinity times two.

I made sure my boys were okay with going to their great-grandmother's funeral because I wouldn't have forced them to go. They loved Ms. Charlsie and wanted to go. The tears came but the feeling of admiration for such a beautiful life lived was undeniable.

SEASON VII

BOLD AND BEAUTIFUL? SOMETIMES...

EPISODE I: DETACHED FROM REALITY

My 2009 New Year's resolutions disappeared fast when I got a chance to spend time with my *Grown Woman Crush*, the one I had to get away from.

I was still enamored with this man and I found myself jumping through hoops to be with him again. When he called I dropped everything. I knew I was in love with this man, but he didn't feel the same way. I settled on the fact that since I had four kids that maybe this was all I could get in a relationship. I was risking everything to be with him, things I never thought I would do. Leaving my kids alone into the night, drinking and driving, spending money I didn't have: I was just a reckless fool. The thought that our times together were just booty calls was unbearable. I prayed for change because I wanted him to love me. And I tried to pull away, but each time I found myself begging to get back to him. Days turned to weeks, weeks to months.

Sometimes it takes a drastic situation to get your mind right. When he told me, "I am always good to myself." I was left feeling more like a fool than ever. Everything I was doing was not being good to myself. This relationship had me feeling so confused. My gullibility wasn't his fault, and he took no charge for my atrocities. He was honest from the start about where he had been, and where he was headed in his life. No matter what he said, all I heard was, ***Not you, you won't be my lady, but I'm having fun, thanks.***

Though I had been seeking an escape from the pressures of my life, in reality, I was on the road to the looney pen. Finally getting real with myself I took the journey of detoxing myself from this man. The withdrawal pains left me weak. And I silently begged forgiveness from my sons for putting them in danger of losing their mom, swearing ***I will still fight the devil straight to hell for my sons***. Fighting the urges to insinuate myself into this man's life, I prayed he wouldn't call. It hurt when I finally stepped away from the situation.

EPISODE II: PERFECT TO ME

Now was the perfect time, I thought. I would be fifty on my birthday, and I was determined again to be a better woman. I made a bucket list for myself to be accomplished by my birthday.

My list included two things. First on the list was to get a breast reduction and reconstruction. When I was 25, I had gone in for an evaluation for this surgery. The shame I felt after reviewing the before pictures of what I considered my deformed breast kept me away from any cosmetic surgeon's office. That was, until now. The pains from a size F breast could be pretty bad, from the digging in of bra straps into my shoulders, to back pain. Not to mention the disgust I would feel when my breast sat on my lap like a bag of sand.

No matter what they looked like I had never had a complaint from any man, which was a sad testament to what I had been measuring my truths by.

Secondly, I wanted to have the corns on my toes removed. Foot pains from these corns could be worse than a toothache. I really had to get something done before I bled to death after one of my razor trimming episodes. Considering my feet, I asked the question, ***Do I have to live the rest of my life with these painful corns?*** Then I remembered all the times I'd committed ***shoe-icide*** by wearing the wrong type, and size of shoes, all in the name of looking good.

When I got approved for both procedures from my insurance company, I immediately turned in my leave slips for a six-week medical leave. This surprised everyone. They couldn't understand why I wouldn't do one procedure, then the other later. Someone even asked, "Why now?" as if to say I should leave well enough alone. But it didn't matter what anyone thought because I knew this was my perfect time. Underneath everything though, was the haunting thought of Donda West, Kanye's Mom, who had died from complications after cosmetic surgery. I wasn't deterred but I was in constant prayer.

On June 25, 2009 I was so scared about my breast surgery, and I was especially nervous about being under anesthesia for a surgery that could take up to five hours. I cried so much, praying that this would not be the day **GOD** would exact vengeance on me for my foolish ways. When Mom arrived to take me to the hospital, I ran into the boys' room to catch a quick look, fearing the possibility that this could be the last time. Mom and I had agreed she would stay with me till the surgery began, then she would go back and be with the boys.

If I had known the words that were to about to come out of the anesthesiologist's mouth, I would have taped it shut. Reviewing my history, he asked, "So you smoke about one cigarette a day?"

Unable to lie I sheepishly answered "Yes." Mom was sitting there with the most indignant look I had ever seen. Looking like the Queen of the Land she said, "I never knew you smoked cigarettes." She had never smoked or drank so this didn't make sense to her. Then the thought came hard and fast *LORD have mercy, please don't let that anesthetic be a truth serum. I will die if I have to tell momma about the joints I'd smoked.*

Still, I wanted to laugh out loud; she looked so funny. Before the anesthetic kicked in I started defending myself. "Mom, you had six kids, never did you have to raise one alone, Dad was there. You wouldn't understand being single, what it's like after working all day, and then you have to make sure homework is done, and the kids properly fed and everything else all by yourself. They say follow the food pyramid but all you really can do is give them a sandwich. You have to make sure teeth are brushed, hair combed, baths taken. Clothes washed, folded, and put away. The house cleaned and disinfected, dishes washed. Finally, when the kids are in bed, and I have time to myself, sometimes I just want to sit on my porch, whether it's winter or summer and smoke that one cigarette before bedtime. I really don't expect you to understand."

She didn't realize how much I respected her. I would never have smoked in her presence, and I didn't even want her to know I did. I idolized my mother for the triumphs she had endured, and so much more. She didn't even know how much I wanted to quit, and it was not for her, but I wanted the victory for my life. Just as I started to feel bad about how I had spoken to her I heard the anesthesiologist speak "Mom why are you so hard on her? She's a single mother, raising four boys, working hard at a fulltime job, taking care of her household. I would imagine she might need that cigarette a day."

I wanted to kiss that man. Drifting off, I looked over at mom. She was saying something but I couldn't make it out. I prayed for her to understand, but I knew that as a married woman for over 55 years, she probably wouldn't. I did know for a fact that she understood someone trying to quit smoking, my father had been trying to quit since forever.

My surgery was a success. The weight mass removed from my breasts was over eight pounds. I thanked **GOD** for reviving me and giving me another chance. When Mom arrived to pick me up, there was nowhere to run as I sat in the passenger seat on the way home. I knew I had to address the elephant in the midst, *my smoking cigarettes*. Just as I got up the nerves to talk to her, a bulletin came over the radio, "Michael Jackson is dead, also this day we have lost another well-known celebrity, Farrah Fawcett Majors." Stunned I flipped through the other stations to confirm the report.

And here I was, still alive. I believed **GOD** still had use for me and I was so thankful to be reunited with the kids. But as soon as I was alone with them, something snapped and I started screaming at them, "I am *Your Angel*, and I'm still here to take care of *Y'all*! You guys had better start appreciating me!" Apparently, the anesthesia had left a residual effect, and I was heartbroken over the deaths of Michael and Farrah.

Just as I was in the middle of this rant, the phone rang. The man on the other end said, "Hi, how are you doing? Can you say the same things you said to me the last time?" Confused, I replied, "Who is this and what are you talking about the last time?" Then I heard that disgusting, slimy voice say, "You know, those things you said to me last time." I knew for sure the anesthesia was still in effect, because I blasted the man terribly, hanging the phone up so hard, I just knew I burst his eardrum. Profusely, I apologized to the kids for my behavior, and then went to take a nap. I really needed one.

The doctor was pleased with my post-op results. The healing process prevented me from working out, but I didn't mind because I knew I would be a better athlete once healed. Of course, my breasts weren't perfect, but they were perfect to me. I had never been happier with my body; even the bandages made me happy. Asking myself, *Now, how far can you go Gwen on your weight loss journey now?* I was elated that in two days I would be having foot surgery.

Then my period started. My mood turned to dread at the thought of a heavy cycle while my feet and breast were under wraps. It was nice however that my flow was light. Then I wandered *Maybe the procedure I had last year to stop my cycle was finally kicking in, or the big iron tablets I was taking for anemia were now normalizing my blood flow.*

July 10, 2009. I was motivated as I moved forward on my bucket list. I was ready for the foot surgery. Earlier I had mentioned a strange tense pulling on my middle toe to the doctor, and he said he could correct this issue as well at the same time. "Yes, I want to do everything I can to be good to my feet as I get older", I said.

It had been two days since surgery, and my feet hurt badly. At my follow-up appointment, the doctor gave me a pair of hard post-op shoes. At first, I thought the doctor was pranking me when he gave me mismatched shoes, but he wasn't, he just didn't have a matching pair in the closet. I left his office looking like Milton the Monster on crutches. The picture really got funny when one considered the bandages from breast surgery I wore which were reminiscent of The Mummy. Of course, I was the source of many laughs, but I didn't mind. All I kept thinking about was the relief I would have once I was out of those funny shoes, and got to put away my crutches and bandages.

My breasts healed beautifully. I tried to remember if I ever had perky boobs before, and what they felt like. Hard as I tried I couldn't, but I was sure this had to be what perky felt like. Life for me was coming together, and for once I was being true to myself, one hundred percent.

EPISODE III: A THANK YOU

Four years ago, when Mr. B sat down at my desk, I never in a million years could have known the impact this man would have had in my life.

Our class got to witness his promotion to Fifth Degree Master in Tae-Kwon Do (TKD). We all appreciated the many lessons Mr. B had taught each of us, and we wanted to show our honor and respect.

On August 2, 2009, our class celebrated Mr. B's twentieth year in business, and his service to the community with a banquet.

We turned a TKD dojo into a banquet hall. I was proud to be a part of this celebration honoring our sensei for his good works. I gave Mr. B a perfect attendance medal for his service to my family. Since agreeing to pick up my sons for class many years ago, he had only failed to pick them up twice the whole time. Those incidents were due to accidents on the interstate. We had an exceptional ceremony for an exceptional man; my parents even attended.

EPISODE IV: ME, ME, ME

I weighed in at 173 lbs. on August 30, 2009. This was my lightest weight since college. I was flying high at my fifty-pound weight loss, so close to my 155 lb. goal.

With a new pep in my step, my self-esteem was soaring. There was still one problem though: I had not changed my eating habit. Working out was my saving grace, and ritual I continued to honor as I went back to work from medical leave. I promised myself that I would reach all my goals by the end of the year while my momentum was high.

EPISODE V: FORGIVE ME BODY

Even though I had to work, December 16, 2009 was a great day. It was my 50th Birthday. I was so thankful to be alive, and I wanted forgiveness from my body, hence:

FORGIVE ME BODY

Forgive Me Body for not loving you. Forgive me for putting others in front of you. I did not know how precious you would become to me as I got older. Forgive me for the times I ate too much and exercised too little. I abused you with audacious thinking that you owed me. But it was the other way around; I owed you. Forgive me for the war wounds I have inflicted on you, all the scars, scrapes, and burns you wrongfully earned in this life. You are my temple, and it is my desire to be a respectful Queen over her temple. Forgive me for not nourishing you first. I will cleanse you, and work hard to do better. I don't need a husband to complete me, especially one who is more confused than me. My sons deserve a healthy Mother. Forgive me for my past, I appreciate you for standing strong with me. You let me know today again how much you love me and that you have always been on my side. Thank you my body for everything. From this day forward help me to be good to you.

I knew what I wanted to do for my birthday. I printed the flyers and distributed them to the ladies at work. Born on the scene was *Forgive Me Body 90-Day Blitz*. This would be my contribution to health. I would make a commitment to teaching others lifestyle changes through exercise, no matter their fitness level. Mr. B agreed to allow me to hold classes on Tuesdays and Thursdays at the school after work for my co-workers.

I had high hopes for my ladies. In this office alone we had a big assortment of ailments that included obesity, rheumatoid arthritis, back and knee problem, depression, heart conditions, and even more. I wanted to make a positive impact in the lives of my friends, and I was hurt when only six agreed to give me a try. I just assumed everyone would be on board.

Still, I released all negatives thoughts and concentrated on the ladies who came out the first day. Before long, I realized that I had just the right number of participants for me to work with. However, by the end of the 2nd session, two had dropped out. They each had a valid reason, but I knew what a difference this little class could make. It could lead to greater things. At the end of the 90-Day Blitz, I awarded two certificates of completion to Kessa and Shelia.

Upon evaluation of my performance as an instructor, I realized there was more I could have done. I was proud of what I had accomplished, but did not see a repeat of the *Forgive Me Body 90-Day Blitz* anywhere in foreseeable future.

EPISODE VI: PAWS FROM HEAVEN

March 2010 was an interesting month. I'd heard the saying many times, "*GOD* has a sense of humor"; but *LORD* this wasn't funny.

Sitting at my desk I heard *You* clearly say *Go get the dog*.

Looking up, I whispered, "What dog?"

Again *You* said *Go get the dog*.

This time really confused. I asked again, "What dog?"

Looking out into the sea of customers waiting their turn, I imagined them looking at me as though I was a crazy woman talking to herself. I sure was feeling like one. Then I head *You* speak again, louder this time, *GO GET THE DOG!* It was then I understood, you were talking about the cute puppy my sister had.

"Why me *LORD*?" I asked, remembering the stray German shepherd my ex-husband had brought home before. We named him George, but the boys would only call him Troy. When my husband left, Troy was still there. I would be late for work sometimes because he had gotten out through the night, and would be standing at the gate in the morning like Scooby-Do saying: *I'm hungry*.

Feeling overwhelmed, I made plans to find Troy a new home. After all, I had so much on my hands with four boys. My friend Felicia found the perfect home for him. Her father-in-law lived in the country and had agreed to take him in. Everyone was sad the day we had to leave Troy behind. Weeks later, I really felt bad when I found out that Troy had followed us home that night, and that nice old man never saw him again. I never told my kids about what happened.

"Why me LORD?" I asked again miffed by such a demand. And for a second time, *You* didn't answer me.

When I got off that day, I headed to my sister Pat's house. She lived next door to our parents. She and Mom were outside when I drove up. Mom said, "I didn't know you were coming by."

"I wasn't. I came to get the dog," I snidely replied.

"What dog?" they both asked simultaneously.

Tearfully pointing at the cutest puppy I said, *"That dog!"*

My Mom and sister were confused by what I was saying until I explained what had happened earlier at work. I guess my sister wasn't going to argue with **GOD** because she willingly gave me the puppy she had happily named *WooWoo*. Stunned by what had just happened, I couldn't imagine what this two-month old puppy would mean to my home. He was born January 1, 2010.

As I turned the corner I scanned the street for the boys. No one was in sight. When I parked and opened up the tailgate to get the puppy out, I turned and all my sons were surrounding me. I didn't know where they came from, but they couldn't contain their excitement when they saw the puppy. They had loved on *WooWoo* each time they went to visit their Aunt Pat. These guys were smiling like a prayer had been answered, and I wondered, *Did they make this happen*?

We all agreed he needed a new name. I said, Champion, they said Champ, and the dog answered to both. I really liked Champion, but Champ was perfect too. Champion Hampton aka Champ/C-Hamp.

EPISODE VII: NO MATTER WHAT, GOTTA DO IT

When I got my tax refund earlier, I used it to pay up on my bills, take care of the boys, and remodel most of the kitchen, get a new refrigerator, and get some minor repairs done that were needed throughout the house. I was proud that I had spent my money wisely, but I regretted not saving any. This was a refreshing point for me, but I couldn't imagine what was just around the corner.

The van was dying when everything started breaking down in spades; the motor mount, tire rods, tires, fuel pump, power steering, and more all needed repair or replacement. Then my plumbing stopped up, and I need new faucets. Right behind this was electrical problems: I needed to replace a fuse box. I thanked **GOD** for my brother since he financed the electrical work. But everything else left me in a quandary. During the times my van was down, I would drive *Taz*. And that meant I had to update the maintenance, inspection, and tags on the car. I kept *Taz* for times like these, though it wasn't in any shape to be a primary vehicle.

When I walked through the door, I had no idea what I was getting into. I needed help, and the sign outside read, *1st loan interest-free*, and I thought, ***This could work***. I could get this payday loan, take care of my stresses, and pay it right off. Things didn't work out as planned though because before I knew it I was paying off the first loan, then getting a second one. I had gotten in deep when this became a revolving event at different payday loan offices. I even made excuses when I'd tell myself, ***GOD made the way for you to get the loan anyway***, or I'd say, ***At least I took care of some of my van and plumbing repairs***.

Confused, I questioned Carl the mechanic, and Mr. B as to what I should do about the van. Their answers were basically the same; *The van was a cash cow, and I needed to make plans to get reliable transportation*.

My sons and I walked into the dealership looking for Ed. He was an in-law that had been selling cars since I was very young. Ed sold me my first car, and I trusted him and believed he could help. He was out on a test drive, and when he returned we were standing outside waiting for him.

Smiling, he excused himself from his customers long enough to say hi, and asked, "What's going on?". I quickly explained the situation with our van, and what our need was. He looked back at his customers; the elderly couple who had just test drove a brand new car and had decided to trade their SUV in. Ed turned back to me and said, "That's what you need right there."

Intrigued, the boys and I waited till he finished with his customers. Then he took us for a test drive in the 2004 Ford Explorer.

It was immaculate. The couple had been the only owners, the maintenance records were even in the glove compartment, and the mileage was less than 60,000 miles. We all had ample room too. The boys squealed "Yes" and I knew this was our divine vehicle.

A down payment was needed when I was approved for a high-interest loan. I didn't discourage the thought when it first came; in fact, I explored it. And when I was approved for my first internet payday loan, I was able to make the down payment. This loan was totally separate from the other payday loans I already had going.

The day I went in to sign papers for the Explorer, sitting there was my neighbor who lived across the street signing papers for her car. I took this as a positive sign that I had done the right thing. Later when I pulled into my drive and saw both our new vehicles, I couldn't help but feel relief. That day I named my Explorer *Tae* for the Tae in Tae Kwon-Do, which meant to break with foot in Korean.

I applied for additional public assistance when I was overwhelmed with stress. One of the requirements to receive services was to have an active child support case pending through the state on the non-custodial parent. The rule was that parents should first support their children, and I agreed, even though I had never received a dime of support. I just assumed my children's father was not working or had skipped the scene.

When I was asked to produce evidence of an active child support case, I contacted the Department of Social Services in Baton Rouge. I asked for documentation of my previously starting a child support case, and wanted to know where my case stood. When a co-worker dropped a fax on my desk May 07, 2010, I could hardly believe the words on the page. *Child support case closed as of December 20, 2006...receives SSI and has been deemed incapable of working or providing support...*

117

Immediately I called the contact person listed on the form. She explained to me that my ex-husband received SSI, and that the funds he received were for his living expenses only. She said, "The government does not require child support payments to be taken out of his check." I asked, "What is wrong with him? In your letter it said, deemed incapable of working, what does that mean?" What she said to me was something I thought only existed in movies. She told me, "He has been diagnosed with a rare multiple personality disorder."

My mouth was wide open as I thought, ***What the hell! What about my multiple personalities, I need a check my damn self?*** This lady listened as I asked more questions. Before long, she apologized and ended our call. It was one thing struggling to take care of my kids in ignorance of what was going on with my ex, but this new information had the worse effect on me. My problems had been surmounting since April and I tried not to bitterly detest my ex-husband as I called him ***Sperm Donor***. On one hand, I believed he may have had some mental issues, but on the other, I envisioned him putting on a circus act for the doctor in order to receive a check. My finances were in ruins, and my days were spent fretting.

EPISODE VIII: I HAVE TO

The kids were already registered for summer camp in 2010 at the recreation center. But this year there would be a detour. I'd heard about a free Sheriff's Camp for boys, and I immediately registered them. It was imperative that I put my sons in front of real men. Any free positive activity I could involve them in, I always made sure they were there. I was nervous about them going camping though.

When I picked them up that Wednesday after camp, a couple of Sheriffs made it a point to speak to me. They told me how courteous and helpful my sons had been. I really beamed with pride when I was told that my four sons were the only ones out of about 75 boys who had received T-shirt recognition. They were given T-shirts that only the Sheriffs wore.

The Scoutmaster called inquiring if I would be interested in my sons being involved in Boy Scouts and I told him I had to think about it. There didn't seem to be any room on my plate. My boys, however, had a great time at camp and they were all in for Boy Scouts. Now I had two more schedules to keep up with because Jimmy and Joshua were old enough to be Boy Scouts, while Jaleen, and Jeremy had to be enlisted as Cub Scouts. Of course, they met at different times. My sons were growing up, and everything counted now; from church, school, Tae Kwon-Do, and now Boy Scouts. I **had to** do this because they still deserved the best training. I put me aside, thinking *One day this will all be worth it. Then maybe I will rest.*

EPISODE IX: EVERYBODY PLAYS THE FOOL

I had woven a terrible web that I kept close to my heart, only sharing my predicament with a co-worker who was going through the same scenario. Our paydays would find us crying the blues, and once again we would be sick over our poor stewardship of money. The secret was smothering me.

For months I had been tangled in a payday loan nightmare. The first time I got a loan was so easy, then over the course of time, it became crazy. I had heard very little about the dangers of these loans. When I couldn't pay for one at maturity, it was as simple as going to another business and get another loan to help finance the late one. I had about five going at one point. I was so ashamed, and I put my actions way under the covers, especially since I looked like a single mother that was doing pretty good.

When I had to work late, I missed making my loan payments on time. There was no grace period from the payday loan company, so my pre-filled checks, complete with my signature had been deposited into the bank. The next day I went to the bank to check my balance and it was negative. On August 13, 2010, I cried like a baby. It was payday, and I didn't have any money. All of my paycheck had gone to cover the deposited payday loan checks. Crying and desperate, I pleaded with bank personnel about some type of reversal. School was starting the next week, and that paycheck had been designated for school clothes and supplies. When I found out that nothing could be done, I cried some more. It was devastating when I explained to my children that there would be no back to school shopping. I swore, *If it takes me the rest of the year I'm going to get these loans out of my life.*

My sons went to Dallas for the holidays with my brother. I spent Christmas, and New Year's alone with Champion. When the clock struck twelve I prayed and gave all things to **GOD**. Only He could change my life.

SEASON VIII

PERILS

OF A TAE

KWON- DO

(TKD) MOM

EPISODE I: The Journey

JANUARY 2011. Champion turned one on New Year's Day.

All my sons had been behaving so mature, and I'd gained great respect for each of them. I called a family meeting to let them know how I appreciated and loved them. They all had this angelic look on their face, Jaleen even stood there like an *Angel* about to spread his wings. Just as I began to discuss plans for the family going forward, the phone rang.

It was their dad: he had amazing timing. Even more amazing was that he tried to regulate my household with his words. I did my best to be polite in front of the boys, but when I'd had enough, I gave the phone to Jimmy Jr and left the room. Mad, I asked myself, *What's this man's problem? Why won't he stay out of my way or step up to the plate?* I knew at that moment it would be a long time before I would have *any* conversation with this man.

FEBRUARY 2011. The tournament invitation our school received was for Saturday, the 26th, and it came with a special announcement. *The World Tae-Kwon Do Alliance would be hosting the 2011 TAE KWON-DO INTERNATIONAL GOODWILL CHAMPIONSHIP GAMES in Dallas on July 22nd -24th. Tryouts for Team USA would be would be the following Sunday.* The flyer was intriguing, and our class was amazed when we saw our own Mr. B on the flyer with the 1987 Team USA team standing proudly with his teammates and coach. The team had competed in the 1987 World Championship in Athens, Greece. Though we all had heard about him competing in that tournament, this validation of his journey was the best ever. This was a déjà vu moment, the coach for the 2011 Team USA was also Mr. B's coach from so long ago.

On the 26th all my sons competed in the tournament. They all did well, and between them, they each received a first or second place in their divisions and categories. Jaleen and Jeremy were in the same division, which meant they had to fight each other. One received first place while the other received second, or vice versa.

Jimmy Jr and Joshua tried out for Team USA the next day on Sunday. Jimmy Jr was chosen for the team and Joshua had a good showing among the older kids. Trained in the techniques and fundamentals of traditional TKD, what he needed to learn now was team synchronization.

The wheels of my mind turned swiftly as I wondered, *How can I afford this venture?* Remembering something my mother used to say when we traveled, "I want my children to be able to say they've been somewhere." my understanding became clear. I knew I had to find a way to make this a family affair because I wanted my sons to see new places, and met fellow martial artists from all over the world. And they would have great experiences to share with each other one day.

It was the last day of the month and I was up early cleansing my mind, and my house.

Satisfied that I had done a spotless job cleaning the huge hanging mirror on the wall, I turned away, only to be stunned when the mirror fell on my head. Though I didn't bleed, I was however left with a sharp sting at the top of my head. As though a wake-up call, my mind was penetrated by the thought *The mirror didn't break, it was shattered not broken*. I took this to mean seven years good blessings for my sons and me instead of seven years bad luck. I wanted to forever stand on the words *Shattered not broken* as I continued on my journey in life.

I was looking forward to finally paying off those payday loans, getting my bills current, and being able to finance my son's journey with Team USA with the tax refund I was due. I really had to call upon the words *Shattered not broken* when I filed my taxes. The tax preparer informed me that the social security numbers of my kids had already been used by someone else and that my refund had been put on hold. When I called the IRS, I was told, "You will have to prove your right to carry the kids as dependents, and the other person will have to do the same. This could take up to eight weeks, and nothing can be done about your refund until our investigation is over." The IRS would not tell me the name of this person who had done this unless I had an attorney, but I knew who it was. When I called my last ex-husband, he denied any wrongdoing. I was not convinced, because I knew my children's father never had access to their social security numbers after he went to jail. Holding tight to the words **Shattered not broken** I fought the urge to scream my fool head off.

MARCH 2011. We found out that Champion was Shepherd-Chow mutt mix and he was growing fast.

Mr. B stopped by to talk to Jimmy Jr about upcoming events. While he was there, Champion got out. I went to the store while they looked for Champ. My heart froze when I returned, Mr. B and Jimmy Jr were walking away from a police car.

I could see how furious Mr. B was when I got out of the car. Apparently, he had been disrespected and treated rude. As a veteran he had instinctively rattled off his name and presented his credentials, explaining to the officers that they had been out looking for the dog. This did not seem to matter to the police as they began questioning my fourteen- year old son like he was a criminal, every Black Man's nightmare. Mr. B was not only upset at the way the policeman had treated them, but he was upset at my son's indifference about what had just happened.

I defended my son because Jimmy Jr had never experienced prejudice, nor had he ever had to defend himself as a Black Man. He thought everyone loved him.

Before Mr. B left that night, poor Champion got a taste of his anger. Fighting to get Champion back on his leash, Mr. B grabbed him roughly, acknowledging that my dog was the cause of what had just happened. Champion, in turn, bit him on the thigh. I felt my instructor's pain, but I grabbed my dog in horror, knowing a dog could only be a dog. I was infuriated by what had happened.

Later, I tried to explain to my son why Mr. B was upset, and I talked about national news stories of police brutality, and the fight for respect by Black Men everywhere.

The next day at work I called the police station to speak to the Police Chief. I had to leave a message. Later he called me back. As I explained what happened, and the implications of what could have happened he assured me he would look into it. It is strange how things happen, because the next day his daughter was involved in a serious police matter. I didn't think I would hear from him again, but I made sure my son and Mr. B knew I had lodged a complaint.

I had a lot to think about. I knew the devil was on my tail, and he hated me as much as I hated him.

My son's participation with Team USA would cost me money I didn't have.

When I received the team information packet I immediately put in my leave requests at work through June. I really appreciated my supervisor for her compassion, and understanding of how important this was to my family. She signed off for my requested time. Now that I had the approval, plans had to be made to raise money. I wasn't afraid to beg and was determined that no matter what, my son would experience this exciting opportunity.

APRIL 2011. On April 1st, we traveled to Texarkana, TX. for Jimmy Jr's first training session. *I hope this ain't a sign* I said to myself as I thought about April Fools' Day.

We got lost two times on the way to the location. This was when I realized how unprepared I was for the trip. I couldn't get GPS because my cell phone was government issue, and I did not print out directions from MapQuest. After a few circles around the town, I finally found the school. Jimmy Jr was phenomenal, the other kids on the team started calling him "Freak." I was glad I hadn't forgotten my camera because I captured some amazing photos and video footage. On the way home, he and his brothers had a great time reviewing his performance.

Motivated by my son's performance in Texarkana, I put fear aside. I got on the phone and began knocking on doors to raise monies for the rest of the training camp series. The word got around. Mr. Livingston, a writer with the local Black paper, *The Shreveport Sun* called to say he wanted to do an article on my son. He felt this exposure would also help to generate more money for the cause. When the paper came out on April 14, I made sure to buy ten copies. Before reading the article, I smiled in appreciation at our picture at the head, it was our family portrait from when I had turned fifty. The article was titled: ***4JHampton: Region's First Family of Karate***. Mr. Livingston had done a beautiful job sharing our family's journey in the martial arts. I was proud and ever so thankful. Mentioning that we would be traveling the next weekend to the Ozarks for training, he ended the article with a plea of support for our upcoming trips.

There had been heavy storming in Arkansas during the week. A trip to the Ozarks in the rain was not ideal traveling conditions for me. Expressing concern that I might not take the trip, I contacted the Assistant Coach of the team who lived in Hot Springs near the lodge in Deer, Arkansas. He assured me that the roads were clear and even offered to meet us in Hot Springs so we could follow him up the mountain to the lodge. Considering the coach's offer, I then decided to make the trip with just Jimmy Jr. I knew my way to Hot Springs but had never heard of Deer, Arkansas. The coach gave me different directions to Hot Springs and I assumed that since he had made the reverse trip to Shreveport for the try-outs that he surely knew what he was talking about. It was a beautiful morning for a road trip, and I started out early because I had decided to take the unknown route.

Headed down Highway 71 north of town we were stopped by a traffic jam. My vision was limited but from my vantage point, I could see an 18-wheeler flipped on its' side. ***This is crazy***, I thought as I sat in traffic waiting. Fear struck my heart as I contemplated us making the six-hour trip alone. I talked to my son, and he still wanted to go. That was all I needed to hear, and I was back in the game again. It didn't seem like the traffic situation would be cleared up anytime soon, the police weren't even on the scene yet. Checking my watch, I then calculated how long it would take to get to Hot Springs if I u-turned and went the way I knew. I believed we had enough time to make the scheduled meeting with the coach.

As I crossed the bridge to Bossier City I caught Highway 3 to Arkansas. I had not gone this way since the honeymoon with my first husband. We were making good time, but I started getting worried when my calls to the coach went unanswered. I wanted to let him know we were on the way, and for him not to leave us. I asked myself ***Where is this man?*** Then we were slowed down just as we got into Hot Springs, the city was having a Corvette Rally. There were fine cars everywhere, my son was enjoying the cars, but I was a nervous wreck. It was getting late in the afternoon, and I still had not gotten through to the coach. Pulling over I filled the tank then grabbed the info packet and found the number to the lodge. I called the host explaining what was going on. He then told me the coach was there. "What?" I asked with acid in my voice. The coach had gone ahead to work on roofs that had been damaged in the storm and complete work needed before the teammates arrived. I got mad because he had forgotten us, and I couldn't turn around.

The host of the event gave me sketchy directions to their location. *Go up to the top of the mountain then go down the mountain to the bottom, make a left, and go down the gravel road to the creek.* Then he warned me that the electricity had been out, and the road crossing the little creek leading to the lodge was out. I was told to call them when I got there so they could send someone out to pick us up, explaining that I would have to leave my truck on the other side of the creek till morning.

Scared to death, and unsure of everything, I started up the mountain. I had to keep it together because we still had a long way to go, MapQuest said two hours and fifty-one minutes exactly. Driving up the mountain was so hard. I was petrified on the two-lane highway, as the 18 wheeler trucks zoomed by or passed me. When it started to rain I drove real slow. The 1000 foot drop with no railings to our right was terrible and made me drive even slower. This had become the longest day of my life.

In a moment of panic, I looked over at my son, and he was peaceful with the world. Wanting him to feel some of what I was feeling, I screamed: "Don't you understand what I'm going through?" He simply said "No." I never wanted to hurt my son before, but for an instant, I wanted to open his door and kick him down that 1000-foot drop. It took me a minute, but I found a laugh. I remembered that Jimmy Jr was a cool kid. Part of his mystique as a champion was his poker face. His casual, nonchalant persona could be disarming. Many times I found myself screaming at him like a mad woman trying to make a point, he, in turn, would look at me like he couldn't figure out what my problem was. He would make me feel silly. There were times when I would have to stand my ground, with my hands on my hips I would quietly yell at him: *"I AM THE MOMMA!!!"*

Up, up, up the mountain we went. There was very little life on that road. As we neared the top I started looking for someone to ask for directions. It was past dusk by now. At the very top of the mountain, there was a group of people outside of a building. I pulled over, jumping out of the car I immediately felt like a fish out of water. Standing there was a group of middle-aged white men from the mountains: I think they were at a dance at the local school. And here I was this strange black woman up on their mountain with a little black boy in the front seat. Bravely I walked over, "Hi, my son is a member of Team USA for Tae Kwon Do, and we are headed to a martial arts training camp in Deer. Do you know where it's at?" The man standing near me looked at me strangely, then he looked over his shoulder and called out to another man. "She's looking for that martial arts place down the road." The other man started laughing when the man started giving me the directions to where I needed to go. "Go down the mountain for about ten minutes, when you see the church start looking for a sign that says Limestone. There you will make a left. The place is down that road."

Feeling confident I could find my way from there we started down the mountain. When the rain started again I was undeterred because I was so close to my destination. I truly needed to get to that lodge soon, I already didn't drive well in the dark and with rain in the mix, I was in a difficult situation. Almost missing the little Limestone sign, I made the left. Then, we were on a muddy gravel road with no lights. I pulled over and called the lodge. They told me to keep going till I got to the creek, and they would send someone to meet us. When I got to the creek, Jimmy Jr and I got some of our things together for the night. The truck pulled up, and for the first time in my life, I crossed a creek. I was a bundle of messed up nerves, and I still was a little angry, it was a good thing the Coach had left for home already. After exploring the lodge, and checking in with home, I finally drifted off to sleep thinking this trip was a play out of the Gilligan's Island playbook. Gilligan and The Skipper started out on a short boat ride then ended up lost in a storm stranded on an island.

I could not believe the view. Morning in the Ozarks Mountains, was magnanimously magnificent. Darkness held nothing to this morning light. The marvel of nature was breathtaking. This was an ideal place for the kids to clear their minds, and get ready for their training. The mountains around in the front of the lodge rose like a green wall, and in the front yard there was a deer grazing, like he was at home. Then there was the huge mountain not far from the back door. After breakfast the team was assigned a hike up that mountain. They were ready.

Still wound up from the night before, I decided to join the kids on the trek up the mountain. I was doing well till we started down. My son stayed behind to walk me back down. This was a good thing because within a few minutes I stepped on a rock, and twisted my ankle. Then the young lady walking with us tripped, bruising her ankle. Jimmy Jr looked like a **Rescue Angel** as he assisted both of us back to the lodge. Knowing I had to drive home, I elevated my feet for a long time: I didn't want to stay in those mountains any longer than I had to. Later I did manage to take a slow walk down by the creek with the team, got a chance to forgive the absent coach, and then I swore to never depend on anyone else for directions.

The weekend was well planned. The kids worked out hard and I got some really good pictures and video. After we said goodbye to everyone, I decided to follow one of the teammates who lived in our area down the mountain. Headed back down the gravel dirt road was revealed what was missed in the dark the night we arrived. You could see a deep drop off beside the road among the trees. If I had seen that the night we got there I probably would have cracked up. Following the truck ahead we were lead to the interstate. **What, the interstate!** I couldn't believe I had been given a treacherous route to this place, and the interstate was so close.

GOD smiled on us with good weather all the way home. When we arrived home, I looked at the clock and realized TKD class was still in session. Making a detour, we went in and gave a mostly good report to our class, with my bandaged ankle and all my anxieties.

MAY 2011. Mr. Livingston's article had garnered some great interest. Friends and family I hadn't seen in a while called, offering help. Pastor Green even invited us to his church and made a plea to his congregation. Everyone was so kind. We had a rummage sale with donated items received of linens, household items, and odds, and ends. We raised enough to finance our next training camp which was scheduled in Tampa, Florida.

I wanted the entire family to go, but I had a severe case of doubts the closer the time came to leave. Regardless of any feelings I was having, school excuses were cleared for all the kids and the plan was set. My neighbor had agreed to feed and water Champion while we were away. Knowing he was okay didn't stop the pain I felt when we pulled out of the driveway before sunrise.

The miles kept the odometer rolling. Mile after mile, they just kept rolling, Mississippi, Alabama, then Florida. By the time we reached Pensacola I was too rattled to go any farther, I couldn't wait to find a motel. I needed time to assimilate what I had just done by driving this far as the only driver, with four lively boys. As amazing as this was, we still had six more hours to Tampa. It had been about twenty years since I had made this trip and I had forgotten how long the trip was. Tomorrow came too quickly, that morning after repacking everyone up, and grabbing a to-go breakfast we were on our way again. I had promised myself to take my time and enjoy the day and that's exactly what I did as we rolled down the windows, ate up the miles, and sang to the radio.

By the time we made it to Tampa I had lost track of all the pit-stops taken. Then, I couldn't believe the mistake I had made. Just cruising since morning, it never occurred to me that we would run into five 0'clock traffic in Tampa, Florida, which is exactly what happened. I had also forgotten that it was a holiday weekend: Mother's Day was on Sunday. The traffic was very heavy when I missed my turn. I felt a lapse of consciousness when I realized how lost we were; my heart skipped a beat, and my breath became short. When the interstate split I was taken way off the route. Panicking I pulled over, and asked for help. Going over my directions with a **Good Samaritan**, I was back on track, and back in traffic. Finally,

131

we arrived at the hotel; it didn't look clean. Hurriedly I rushed the kids back to car. Driving a short distance, I spotted a beautiful hotel with a nice nightly rate to match. After we checked in, I quickly got the boys settled down in front of the TV with snacks from earlier. I would get them dinner later, but I needed time to think.

The first training session was starting in 45 mins, and I still had no idea where we had to go. Slipping off to the front desk, I nervously asked the desk clerk for help with my directions, so sure he was going to tell me I needed to be on the other side of the world. I wanted to fall on my knees and kiss the floor when he said, "The place you need to go is about a mile down the street this way" he pointed. Feeling like I could finally breathe again, a great big smile crossed my face. Jimmy Jr was confident and cool when he walked into the training session without a care in the world. I walked in praising **GOD** for his goodness and mercy, **IN *JESUS* NAME**.

While Jimmy Jr was in training the next day, I thought the other guys might enjoy a day at the beach. A unanimous "No" was sounded. These guys wanted to stay at the hotel and spend their day poolside. I truly believed they wanted to be close to their brother. They must have been psychic though because we had the pool to ourselves all day and Jimmy Jr even got in on the fun later.

When the training sessions were over, we got in a little sightseeing. Sunday, May 8th, was Mother's Day and it was time to go home. Just outside the city limits, I started to feel heaviness in my chest. Fear was creeping in as I contemplated the long trip ahead. I knew there would be no sleeping over in Pensacola, because we had to get home. It was Mother's Day, and my child, our dog Champion was at home alone. As we made our way toward Pensacola I found myself in deep thought. While the boys slept I shed a few tears while praying. I asked **GOD** for direction, and help to be the best Mother I could be. I was questioning **GOD** about my decisions concerning my sons when a truck pulled up beside me. I looked over and written on the side panel was ***All My Sons***. Excited, I knew **GOD** have given me a good answer to my question, and I screamed with joy. I quickly shook the boys awake, made Jimmy Jr grab the camera and get the picture. Just in time, he captured the back of the truck where the words *All My Sons* was happily written. Mother's Day was turning out to be great. From that point on, my fear was relieved, and my driving confidence was restored. I knew I was doing right for *All My Sons*.

Again the miles turned into hours, as we changed time zones. Crossing into Mississippi found me in good spirits. Searching the radio to find something familiar on the radio had become our game. Then one of the boys shouted "Momma this is dedicated to you." I had never heard this song by Kanye West, but hearing the words "Momma I'm so proud of you" made me listen intently. I had never been so proud to be a Mother than when my sons started singing the words, "Momma I'm so proud of you..." I was very happy, even though I was now driving in the dark.

We had made many pit stops, but when we got into Ruston, La. I asked: "We are almost home; does anyone need to use the restroom?" They all said "No," and each agreed that they could wait till we got home in about hour. I believed them, and my thoughts were then focused on getting down the road, home to Champion. Not far along I looked over at Jaleen who was sitting in the passenger front seat. He had a cover over his lap and appeared to be squirming in his seat like he was hiding something, so I asked, "Jaleen what are you doing?" He said "Momma, when you asked if we had to go to the bathroom I said no because I didn't have to then. Then I had to, so I peed in a bottle, and some of it spilled!" Quickly thinking, I said, "Throw it out the window!" That was just what he did. When he threw it out the window he bent down to pick something up. Our windows were down and I and my other three sons got a backsplash of urine in our faces, I guess the top wasn't on tight. For a minute we were all shocked, then we all cracked up laughing. It was a well-timed comic relief. Sitting up Jaleen realized what had happened, but he couldn't figure out why we were laughing. He thought we were making fun of him. He didn't speak to us the rest of the way home.

It was midnight when we pulled into the driveway. Champion barked loudly as he welcomed us home. By the time I got to bed I was totally exhausted. Thank *GOD* I had the next day off from work to rest.

The next training camp was scheduled for Tulsa, Oklahoma. Even though I had put my leave in for this time, making the trip was becoming a dim possibility. Donations had waned, and I was unable to finance this trip. Finally, my income tax refund was cleared, and I got a check. Paying my bills forward, and outfitting the boys with needed clothes I made plans for a six-hour trip to Tulsa, Oklahoma.

The weather reports said to expect additional rain in Oklahoma and they were 100% accurate. While traveling on the Indian Nation Turnpike we were fascinated at how low the dark clouds were. Then it was as if the sky literally opened up and poured buckets of water on us, the rain came hard and fast. My limited visibility had me very tense, and nervous; I practically screamed at the boys to be quiet. We had to get to Tulsa so I continued to creep down the tollway. I was never one to pray, *Rain, rain, go away* because I believed *GOD* had his way and *He* had every right to do what *He* wanted to do. But, just as I was prepared to say this prayer, the rain subsided, then it stopped. I let out the loudest sigh of relief, and lead us in a group prayer of thanks. I was speechless when I looked over to the right, and there neatly imprinted on a grass mound was the word *JESUS*. There had to have been *Road Angel*s who did this, to encourage drivers like me, during times like this. This was just what I needed as my confidence was restored. And we made it to Tulsa unharmed.

The first day of training was fun as we sat in on the session. Jimmy Jr and his brothers even got to train a little together. Again, everyone was friendly and helpful. When it was time to go, I was feeling very good. Then, I thanked *GOD* for an uneventful trip back home.

I was headed to Bossier City to pick the boys up from Boy Scouts on May 28, 2011, at 4:15 pm. They had a lock-in the night before, and now I was picking them up after a carwash fundraiser. To cross over to Bossier, I had to merge with I-20 traffic while yielding to the traffic incoming from downtown. Having a clear entrance to the lane I continued to enter the highway. Looking back at the traffic behind me, I saw something fly from what I assumed was my car. Confused, I slowed down as the traffic whizzed by me from the interstate. Then I stopped when I realized the traffic behind me had stopped. I couldn't figure out what was going on. *Had someone hit me* I pondered. The next thing I knew; I was backing down the interstate on this busy afternoon. I didn't have any fear, which was a surprise but everything made sense when I got out of the truck.

There was an 85-year-old lady behind the wheel of the car that was now holding up traffic. She had been sideswiped by an 18 wheeler. What I saw flying earlier was her side view mirror. She was hysterical when I reached her, she just kept crying "He never stopped, he never stopped!" By the time the police got there, I had managed to calm her down, and get her story. Mrs. Robinson had been in town visiting her son. While he was out, she had gone exploring. Had I not been where I was, the truck would have probably taken the entire front end of her car off. I felt like an *Angel In The Right Place At The Right Time*. This could have been a horrible situation for her son. When the policeman got there he was astounded at the damage done and that she was unhurt. With Mrs. Robinson in the backseat of the patrol car, we all got off the interstate at the first exit. I gave my story, checked on this young lady, bid my prayers and farewell. Very late by now picking the boys up, I couldn't fully explain what had just happened. All I knew was that *GOD* had kept Mrs. Robinson and me that day.

JUNE 2011. We were scheduled to travel to Scotch Plains, New

Jersey on June 9th for training camp. My mind was set to go. Then I started considering **ALL THOSE MILES**. I couldn't purchase airline tickets, so I would have had to drive because riding the bus would have been too much. Going into my manager's office I rescinded my leave. My decision not to go was alright with my sons. By now the thrill was gone, and they were no longer motivated to travel by truck. I didn't blame them. Thank **GOD**, time was nearing for the championship. A trek to Minden, then a final trip to Texarkana would finalize the training camps. I was looking forward to the end.

Sometimes **GOD** drops nice surprises in our life. *Tae*, my Explorer had taken a beating with all the travels. On June 20, 2011, I took *Tae* in for maintenance, and a few repairs; something was up my front end. My bill was $222.00. When I paid, the customer service rep told he would to check to see if my warranty might still be in effect. I was ecstatic when he called to say it was and that I would receive a $122.00 refund from my claim. "Ain't **GOD** Good, **IN JESUS NAME**" I told the man.

On June 25, 2011, we took a thirty-minute trip to the Baptist Church campground. This was a nice change, and I even invited Monica to go with us. She was a student in our Tae Kwon Do class, and she and Jimmy Jr were the same age. I knew she would enjoy hanging out with the boys because they were close. The campground was nice, but I was surprised at how deep in the woods it was. Most of the teammates came out for this training camp. After lunch, I realized that I had lost an earring from a pair my mom had given me.

When the session was finished, I loaded up the kids because we weren't staying overnight. The short drive would allow us to get back early the next morning. On the way home, I mentioned to the kids that I had lost the earring. Then Jaleen said, "You mean this one?" as he pulled an earring from the console. He had found my earring in the midst of fifty people, grass, cars and everything else. I laughed at satan because nothing he had done to ruin the weekend worked. Rebuking him, I enjoyed the nice weather and the short drive home. Things were good.

EPISODE II: GOOD NEWS/BAD NEWS

Five months ago Team USA infiltrated my life, and I was off on a fascinating journey with my sons.

Right before we were scheduled to leave for the championship, Mr. B dapped the family with a five-hundred-dollar donation in front of our class.

On July, 22nd we left for Dallas, Texas. This was the weekend for the *2011 TAE-KWON DO INTERNATIONAL GOODWILL CHAMPIONSHIP GAMES.* Jimmy Jr was still unfazed by everything and he was ready to rumble. Some of our classmates from Tae Kwon-Do made the trip to Dallas. Mr. B stayed in Shreveport because there was a class the following morning. My brother Jerry and my nephew Karvin lived in the area and came out to support Jimmy Jr. The event became a family affair. During the weekend my kids and I got to meet people from all over the world. The best ever was when I got a picture of my sons with a competitor from Ethiopia.

Jimmy Jr won **FOUR GOLD MEDALS** that weekend, two in individual competition and two as a member of Team USA. He didn't shout, but I saw the look in his eyes when I took his picture with all four of the medals on. I was one proud Momma, and if my son got a chance to go to the Olympics, then I would do whatever I had to do to get him there. Team USA had become a big part my life, and I hardly had time for myself.

I was scheduled for a bone marrow biopsy on July 29, 2011. Three weeks before my white blood count was 400, this day it was up to 1100. The doctor had no explanation for the difference, except that I had been under a significant amount of stress. But for more details, I would have to wait on results from other tests taken. My sons were very worried, even mentioning the day I was in the hospital when Michael Jacksons died. I was so thankful for their love, but inside I was unraveling. The prospect of having **Cancer** was frightening.

On August the 10th I got a clean bill of health, but I was instructed to take my blood pressure pills, and continue losing weight. I didn't mention I had gained ten lbs. since the beginning of the year. Agreeing to do better, I put together a plan to get on track. Again I prayed that **GOD** would bless me to get past my gluttonous habits.

When the phone rang on September the 3rd I tried not be irritated; it was very early for a call. At first, I didn't get the voice, then it dawned on me that it was Jimmy. I felt skin hairs rise as the words ***Sperm Donor*** kept repeating in my mind. Not once had he ever attended a class or a tournament with his kids. And when he missed Jimmy Jr's win at the Championship, I didn't want to talk to him anymore.

He wanted me to bring the boys over to his house later. Explaining that his car was down, he told me he would pay me what a cab would charge to bring them over. ***Really man!*** I thought as I shook my head. What he suggested was not an option and I told him, "I am not a part of that arrangement. I have to go, and have a nice day".

EPISODE III: WISE WORDS/KEEP BELIEVING

Dreams do come true, but you have to believe.

Challenges on every hand work hard on keeping you blue.

No matter what it looks like,

No matter what it tastes like,

You gotta tell your fears to take a hike,

Because your journey may require you walk, run, or take a bike.

I can't do everything right. I can't say all the right things. I can't be everything to just anybody. But I can be everything to me.

SEASON IX

LOVES OF MY LIFE

LIFE

EPISODE I: PLUM DAYS OF FALL 2011

Some days are just so good they remind me of taking a bite out of a big, sweet, juicy plum. The taste is delectable, and you just can't stop smiling because the plum is *so* good.

Jimmy Jr bet me he would outdo me in class. He had just won $5 off Jeremy with the same bet. I accepted. After he royally outdid me, I asked him what he wanted. He said, "Nothing Mom, I just wanted to see you do good."

My sons and I were invited to a fencing class. Suiting up in our fencing gear with our helmets and swords was amazing. This was our first time, and we enjoyed everything.

Jimmy Jr and I sparred for five minutes in class. I took a beating as he kicked me upside the head, and pounded my tummy. The mothers on the sidelines were screaming, "JIMMY JR! No!!! That's your Momma." I understood them, but they couldn't understand my joy: I was able to do this at 51 years old.

Later on, I was madly laughing when my sons impersonated me. It was like looking in a mirror. They had me down good, and they were so funny. They had all of me, sad, happy, angry, afraid, screaming, and crying. ***Can I really be this bad?*** I wondered. Immediately, I recommitted myself to doing better.

Everyone was very healthy after wellness checkups.

My pride soared when I received my Red Belt in Tae Kwon-Do. I was so proud to have progressed from white, yellow, green and blue belts. Next up, was my black belt, and I wanted to be in the elite group of certified Black Belts in Tae Kwon- Do, I liked to call, ***4JHampton***.

What's more, my friend and co-worker Sand had gotten her book published. I was among the first to buy. Speed reading to the end, I was amazed at her testimony. You just never know what someone's going through unless they tell you. I was thankful to Sand for sharing with me her publishing journey. She gave me some valuable information and resources. And as she encouraged me to complete *Relics Of A Woman*, I was filled with a bold powerfulness.

EPISODE II: OPPORTUNITY KNOCKS

When the job was posted, I couldn't believe how many in my office applied. Our manager was being promoted, and everyone was encouraged to apply for her position. The office staff was short-handed, and I was pretty sure I didn't want the managerial responsibilities so I didn't apply. After a long conversation with a co-worker, I reconsidered. It had been a long time since I was an office manager.

The interviews were scheduled for November 15th in Lafayette, La. 200 plus miles away. All the job applicants from our office piled into state cars as we headed south. Making a stop in Alexandria we were all surprised when our former regional manager walked into the door. This was the same Manager that had demoted me years earlier. She had since retired. I didn't have anything to say but, "Hi", then I asked myself, **Is this a bad sign?**

When we arrived in Lafayette, the interviews began. At 6:10 pm., we pulled into our office parking lot. June 10th (6/10) was my son's birthday, and I didn't ask any questions as to the significance of these numbers: I didn't want to know. Anxious to get home, I wanted to be with my boys, especially since they were leaving in just a few days for winter camp with Boy Scouts.

On December 6th, I found out that I didn't get the job. When I congratulated my friend, I wished the best. Heaven knew she would need it.

EPISODE III: HOME ALONE AGAIN

The boys got to spend Christmas break in Dallas again. So again I was home alone with Champion for the holidays. And I hated that he was just a dog, and couldn't talk to me.

On December 28th I was looking forward to picking the boys up in Dallas on that weekend. Mr. B called and wanted to know if I would hem some pants for him. I told him I would. He then suggested I stop by to pick the pants up and bring Champion. This was an unusual offer, but a ride would be good for me, and I knew Champion would really enjoy it.

When we arrived at Mr. B's he invited us in. Champ who is a runner was watching everything. He found his moment at one point when Mr. B opened his door, then he bolted across the yard and out of sight. We were unable to find him, as he disappeared into the night. I was terrified. Champion had never been in that area before, and there were woods close-by where there had been sightings of bobcats and coyotes. Also, traffic in the area could get be heavy at times. We looked for Champion until finally, I had to go home.

When I pulled into my drive and there was no Champ, I burst into tears. I could hardly sleep because I keep thinking about the next three days when I would have to explain to four boys that their dog was lost. Then, I was really torn up with guilt when the words *My dog is lost in the wilderness* persisted in my consciousness. After praying I began to relax, thinking *Maybe, I don't need a dog. Maybe, he'll find a good home.* Finally, I was able to sleep, and I woke in a rush to get to work on time.

It was just after five when I bolted out the door at work, and headed to the dog pound. I called, thinking he might have gotten picked up, but didn't get an answer. The pound closed at 5:30 pm., so I had just enough time to get there.

When I got there, the office had closed early for the holidays. I stopped by Mr. B's to see if there was any word on Champion. He asked me, "Do you want to put up lost and found posters? The earlier you get the word out, the better the chance of finding him. When I said "No, maybe I don't need a dog", he looked at me very strange. I understood what he was thinking: *This dog is a part of your family.* I was so ashamed.

We had the day off on Friday, December 30th. I went to work-out in the early TKD class. Mr. B was not there; this was unusual because he was normally there early. Since I couldn't get in, I decided to go and pay a bill. When I returned it near class time and Mr. B still wasn't there. My heart wasn't into working out anyway, so I took this as an excuse to leave. And so I drove off a second time, this time headed home.

Dreading the next day, when I would pick my sons up, and have to explain what happened to Champ, I decided halfway home to turn around. I knew a workout and good sweat would be ideal. When I got back to the school Mr. B was there. When I bowed in to class he asked me, "Is there any word on Champ?"

"No", I said.

"Go outside, and walk around the building", he said.

It was an odd request; I guess he thought I needed some fresh air. As I turned the corner, sitting there tied to a stake was Champion. Choked up, I profusely thanked my instructor. He went on to explain why he was late: On his way to class, he noticed a sign on the pole at his corner. *Is your Dog Lost?* the sign read. Pulling over, he immediately dialed the number, recognizing the voice as his neighbor's across the street. The neighbor and his wife had found Champion; they had even commented on what a beautiful dog he was. Turning around, and pulling into their drive, Mr. B retrieved my dog. I was very thankful that he took the time, and that Champion was safe. I stayed for class, and worked out real hard.

When we got home, I saw a fear in Champion. His eyes were flickering, like lights in the night. After putting him in the back, I continued to check on him throughout the day, touching him to make sure he really was home. I reminded myself of **GOD'S GOODNESS AND HIS GRACE AND FAVOR TOWARD ME.**

On December 31st Champion and I loaded up for the road. We were off to get the boys, *my buddy and me.* The weather was beautiful and Champion enjoyed hanging his head out the window catching the fast breeze. After spending time with Jerry's family, my family hit the road headed home.

EPISODE IV: SEASONS

Today was historical, but normal in this neck of the woods. On January 17, 2012, the weather cycled from rain, heat, sunshine, cold, breezy, then freezing.

Pulling up in my driveway that day I saw Champion in the neighbors' yard. I quickly jumped out to get him, then I looked at our back gate. My dog was there. I looked back and realized it was a smaller stray version of Champion. This made me think about an old saying, *You can't believe everything you see.*

Things at work were becoming tense. The rumor was that our jobs would probably be outsourced to a private agency. It was hard living with the threat of job loss every day. The thought *I might not be able to care for my children financially or physically* distressed me. I tried to blot out the rising prices of food, especially gas; I just wanted to cry on the way to work every time I'd pass the Exxon station. When they changed the price on the sign one day to $3.65 a gallon, my heart started palpitating. I knew I had to get my mind right; the busy tax season was upon us at work, and we had been working overtime.

At work, my mind would start drifting to a long-ago place, ***Can Do Enterprizes***. While daydreaming I would wonder ***Maybe this is the time I can fulfill my mission in life. I want to live my purpose; if the trees, the sun, moon, and stars know and do what they're supposed to do, why not me?*** I knew so many hurting people, and this just intensified my desire to inspire the world.

So I prayed, ***LORD I believe in you. Increase my faith. I trust in you. Strengthen my trust. I love you. Let me love you more. I am sorry for my sins***. One thing I knew for sure: Perfection wouldn't come on this side of heaven. No matter how hard I tried, I would still make mistakes, but it was my blessing to have ***GOD*** on my side.

EPISODE V: LOVEDAYS

I truly appreciated what my sons did for me on Valentine's Day in 2012. When I got in from work, they were all dressed up, with chocolates, and a beautiful card. When they played Kanye West's ***Momma I'm so proud of you***, it took my breath away. Crying like a baby, I hugged them tightly. My princes put on the Ritz for me, and I felt like a Queen on her throne.

Again, a flyer was sent to our Tae Kwon-Do school with a tournament notification: The flyer advertised The International Pioneer Cup that was scheduled for July, 20-22nd in Memphis, Tennessee. I was a very proud Momma when the brochure for the training camps had my son on the front executing an awesome sidekick on one of his teammates. The first listed camp was being held in the Ozarks in Deer, Arkansas. My first thought was ***There ain't no amount of love that would get me back up in those mountains again with my son***.

On February 25, all my sons did well in the tournament. Jimmy Jr was again selected to be on Team USA. I was sure Team USA would become a tradition in the future for my sons, one that might have even lead to the Olympics.

EPISODE VI: DOUBLE TROUBLE

Monday March 5, 2012 was a very stressful day. I felt a frightening crack on the inside of me. I had never felt this way before. My sons recognized the gloom, and even commented on how bad I looked.

There was a war raging within me. I called it The Dr. Jekyll and Mrs. Hyde of me. This was a situation where my two dueling personalities could never come together for my good. These personalities entered into a fight, and the rumble was: *The Fat Girl vs. The Fit Girl*. And both wanted to rule. The Fat Girl was the depressed one, who over lived life, and caused havoc. She didn't take care of money or her health, and she lived in clutter and uncleanliness and stayed mad most of the times. The Fit Girl made sound common sense decisions about her health, money and her spiritual self. Every intent in my life was for good, but more times than not I didn't follow the right road.

I had to live with the complexities of my life, but it was not required that I live them with my kid's father. I couldn't even use senior in his name because I didn't respect him as such. But I did honor my son as Jr, because it was his legal name. I knew these unforgiving feelings had to pass, but I didn't know when.

When Jimmy picked the boys up on March 17th, at 8:00 pm, I didn't even come out. The negative feeling I had toward this man felt like a heavy winter coat in the middle of summer. I didn't want to alienate my sons from their father, but I prayed, *LORD keep me here, this man will not take care of my boys, and they need me*.

Then on March 18th, at 9:46 am. the phone rang. When Jimmy said good morning it felt like someone had poured slime on me. *Why is this man calling me? The boys are with him* I asked myself. There was no emergency, but he wanted to have a conversation. I couldn't believe he was casually asking me personal questions. Being civil was no longer an option when he asked me "What have you been up to?" My first thought was, **Raising four boys, duh**. Damn, he did it, he pushed the wrong button, and there was so much I wanted to say. He didn't know the other day I saw the woman who had accused him of rape, so I wasn't feeling good toward him anyway. After a quick prayer, **LORD let me tell this fool so he'll understand without popping a blood vessel over here by myself. If I died, he'd have my sons. GOD forbid.**

I then let loose "U want to talk? You've had 16, 14. 12 years to talk. You listen to me; I am going to make this fast. Then I'm getting off this phone. You have many skills, you're a carpenter, a cement finisher, you even know about cars. You haven't taught your sons anything. You haven't put a dime in this household for your sons. Not to mention: Do you remember taking the siding off the house saying the house would look better? Great, I know you sold it. Well look at the house now it needs painting badly. You could have taught you sons how to paint it. I'm getting off the phone now, I will see you after seven when you bring the boys home." I was so angry, and this made me think about the prognosis from the doctors as to his disposition, **Rare Multiple Personality Disorder**. *Maybe I was so angry because I really DID understand after all* I thought. I understood because right then *The Fat Girl* was winning this round over *The Fit Girl*.

EPISODE VII: ALL IN THE NAME OF MOM

I had enrolled the family in computer classes. Spring was always a good time to learn something new. Even though I worked on computers, there was basic information I still wanted to understand. Plus, I wanted my sons to be more computer literate. When the manager Mrs. Beard told me, "There is enough with just your family to have a class of your own," I agreed. Sitting in the class weekly learning with my sons made me so proud.

Shuffling the boys from tennis to soccer to TKD to Boy Scouts, time would fly and my days would go by in a blur. I didn't mind because they deserved the experiences. One day I prayed they would do the same for their children.

Leaving TKD one day, while backing up I stopped. Looking over at the boys, I started laughing. My mind reverted back to high school. The book, *Gulliver's Travels*, was a favorite of mine. A story about little men called Lilliputians and giants. I was laughing because my car seemed like a Lilliputian and my sons were the giants. They have grown immensely, and I felt like the incredible shrinking woman. The fears I had before children were real. No one could have told me the magnitude of responsibility and obsession that would overtake my life in so many ways when I had kids.

SEASON X

I'M DIZZY AS THE WORLD KEEPS TURNING

EPISODE I: HELP!!

It was not a crack this time, because today I felt a tear in my soul.

Looking in the mirror I confessed: **YES**

I

AM

THE EPITOME
OF
AN
ANGRY MAD CRAZY BLACK WOMAN!!!
(THIS IS JUST ME, BUT I KNOW: I COULD BE ANY WOMAN)

Things at work were tense now. Part of our office operations had been outsourced to a third party. My mind started wandering at work, especially when I was moved to another desk. Looking out at the sunshine streaming through the doors had me longing to be outdoors gathering support for *Can Do Enterprizes*. I felt a burden as I started to internalize the situations and circumstances of the people I met. Then I started to rush *GOD* to make a move in my life.

Involving myself in more community events I was sure I'd find my way to where I was supposed to be. The Founder's Day celebration for a women's program allowed me to make contact with city dignitaries. When I got a chance to speak with the Director of the program, I gushed, "Your program is wonderful, and its right in line with a vision *GOD* gave me many years ago. I want to do something like this one day."

As though on defense she told me, "That wouldn't make me happy. You'd be competition."

I was taken aback. Her organization helped so many women, but it felt like I was talking to satan. *** This woman couldn't mean this***, I thought, but I knew she was serious. Leaving quickly, I turned and looked back saying to myself, ***There's more than enough people needing help, but there aren't enough helpers***.

It was only a few days later when I saw that woman again, sitting there in the audience at my job. She even peeked around at me. A weird sensation overcame me as she approached my desk to get her picture taken. The look in her eye said she recognized me, but I didn't say a word.

Strange things have happened to me at that picture station. I met a man once who invited me out to see Al Green. I laughed to myself because his last name Champion was my dog's first name. Before the date, we had a long talk about all kinds of things. And we had agreed to meet at the concert. Three days later, he found his way to the desk where I was standing. Smiling, I thought maybe he had come to ask me to lunch, but he shocked me. He whispered vehemently, "It's over, no dinner, no concert, it's over!

...You seem to have trust issues."

All of this in one breathe. I just looked at him, not even wanting an explanation. And I was glad I hadn't introduced him to my kids, and had not agreed to ride with him to the venue. When he left, I knew I had dodged an ugly bullet. The truth was, Champion was a dog, and that made sense to me.

EPISODE II: FORGIVE ME BODY 2012

June 30th. It was an honor when my friend asked me to be a part of her ministries women's conference. My segment was, ***Forgive Me Body***. I was blessed to share my testimony of self loathe and body shame. Leading the ladies in relaxation and stretching exercises, I started believing I might have a true calling as a health coach.

EPISODE III: WOUNDED WARRIOR

My sons performed well again this year on the tournament circuit. Team USA was scheduled to compete at the World Pioneer's Cup Tae Kwon-Do Championship in Memphis, Tenn. The family supported Jimmy Jr's decision to be on the team, even though it wasn't the road to the Olympics. There were no endorsements or sponsorships for his winning four gold medals at the International Goodwill Games last year, but I wanted to believe my son's alliance with Team USA would lead to greater things, that he would excel, and have a great experience.

The training camps this year were close to home. Absolutely refusing to go back to the Ozarks that year, we attended the additional training sessions, two in Bossier, and one in Texarkana.

Mr. Livingston even did another story for Mother's Day on our family for the local paper. Praising Jimmy Jr for his four gold medal wins last year, and seeking a sponsorship for us. The phone barely rang, but the way was made for our trip to Memphis.

July 20th. Our drive to Memphis was pleasant, no pitfalls or strange happenings. I was glad when we crossed into the city limits on a clear sunny day. We were there early enough to enjoy a sightseeing adventure before competitions began. It was lots of fun, and my son was ready.

There were individual competitions my son was to participate in, in addition to the team ones. He was doing very well in his first fight. Everyone knew he had won, but the judges gave the win to the other fighter. I had it all on video, and I knew what had happened.

While waiting for his next fight one of the judges asked me, "How old is he?" The way he asked the question was like he was implying Jimmy Jr was in the wrong division. I didn't have a good feeling about this event. My son was a very tough competitor at 16, and he was a good kid. In his second fight, the judges disqualified him. They said he was using excessive force. This was unbelievable, because we had witnessed some fights during the day that were brutal. I started feeling like we were alone in the room, and there was no one there to defend us. By the time Team USA competed, Jimmy Jr had lost heart and nothing was ever the same.

This wasn't the first time I had to explain to my sons how judges could be biased. This time, however, was a tough conversation. Never would I have imagined that I would have to explain such blatant prejudice to my sons at this type of caliber event. But again, my son's cool composure shined, by the time we got out of Memphis he was over it. I was very proud of him. His biggest issue was having to go back to class and face his sensei, mentor, and instructor, Mr. B. So it was back to the training mat for Jimmy Jr.

EPISODE IV: 9-11-2012

"Happy birthday Daddy," I said when I called. Today I was frantic. **LORD** help me, for the first time ever on my father's birthday I heard, *911, what is your emergency? I AM THE EMERGENCY.*

Am I dying today? I asked **GOD**.

Never had I been in such a dark place. I didn't know how to get out of it, but I need some help. And I had to make it through the workday. When the door closed after the last customer, I was unsure if I could ever walk through those doors again. The best I could do when I got home was hide behind my closed doors and pray the dread would pass. The crack inside of me was getting wider and deeper.

EPISODE V: PENNIES FROM HEAVEN

Yesterday, they buried my Auntie Vennie. She had lived a very vibrant life as a wife, mother, sister, retiree, and international traveler.

My admiration for her was huge.

On October 7, 2012, Jaleen, Jimmy Jr and I were headed to the grocery store to pick up a few items. But I changed directions, and we ended up at a store we didn't normally shop at. As we walked alongside the meat counter, I saw this woman in front of us. She was walking to the meat counter with her buggy head first.

This looked strange to me, and then I realized she was moving backwards. No she was falling. Her hands came up and she hit the floor. She was bleeding from her head, and foaming from her mouth.

We were very frightened. Then, Veronica, an old friend appeared around the corner of the aisle where the woman had fallen. She had also seen the lady fall. Thank **GOD** she was a nurse. As Veronica attended the woman, I ran to the front, found management, and had someone call 911. Racing back, I grabbed the ladies purse from the buggy and found her cellphone. It was a smartphone, and I didn't know how to use it. Passing it to Jimmy Jr, I instructed him to call the last person she talked to, while I searched for her license. Her name was Penny J.

Jimmy Jr gave me the phone. It was Penny's friend who lived in Benton, which was about 35 minutes from where we were. The guy said she didn't have any family, but she did have seizures.

Just then the emergency crew came down the aisle. As they loaded her up I asked what hospital they were taking her to. I told her friend where they were taking her, then put her phone back in her purse and gave it to the EMT.

On the way home Jimmy Jr told me that I should get some kind of citizenship award. I guess from his standpoint I had done something heroic. I thanked **GOD** I was in the right place at the right time. On the way home we all agreed that whenever we saw a penny,

155

from then on we would pick it up in honor of Ms. Penny, and life. I thought about Ms. Penny for a long time. The image of her blood on the floor of the grocery store was unforgettable.

One day, I had a few extra coins in my pocket, and I decided to go to the casino. I stopped by the restroom on the way inside. When I walked in it appeared that I was alone. While in the stall I heard a woman's voice. I was surprised when she spoke the words, "When someone finds a penny, it means someone has lost a penny," I was spooked. Unmoving, I looked up at the ceiling asking, **GOD, what is this, an Angel?**

Then *She* spoke again: "When someone finds a penny, it means someone has lost a penny."

I walked out of the stall and was washing my hands when a woman walked out of one of the other stalls. I had to maintain my composure because the woman was a cute midget dressed in a plaid shirt with jeans tucked into cowboy boots. And she had long fire red hair. All I could do was say "Hi." Still spooked, I made the way to my car after that.

EPISODE VI: FAMILY FALLS

I believe when a family member dies we gain **Angel Wings** which strengthens us on our journey. I didn't keep up with how many wings I had gained, but I knew every time I got a pair that it was from **GOD**. When my brother Terry died, he left behind his daughters Kerrie and Sherrie, and my sister-in-law Annie. Sometimes I think **GOD** does one thing to prevent heartache somewhere else. I didn't believe Terry could have handled the news that his daughter Sherrie had committed **SUICIDE**. Annie and Kerrie were devastated. I keep asking myself, *What could have had her so hopeless that she would leave behind her teenage daughter to fight alone in this world*?

By now, losing loved ones had become a normal part of life for me. I never liked it, but I never questioned **GOD'S WORK**. That year alone, I had lost four loved ones. My Auntie Vennie, Sherrie my niece, my cousin Michael aka Trick, and a dear friend named Gloria. It was only with faith and love that my heart would be comforted at these times and again my strength renewed.

Gwendolyn Hampton

SEASON XI

GUIDING

LIGHTS

EPISODE I: AT THE CROSS

I still had a job, though I haven't found my heart's love. The kids were doing well; keeping them active, I was confident that they would be good productive men. My mother was very strong these days, and her patience was amazing. Dad was showing early signs of Alzheimer's and Dementia. He didn't seem to have a care in the world, spending his days doing whatever he wanted to. I saw so many persons going through, and I had no answers, not even for myself. My personal challenges still haunted me, but I still sought contentment. I did however recognize that my life could have been so much worse, and I was not as bad as I used to be.

Taking long drives alone had always been a great fix for my depression. So that's what I did.

The One Hundred Foot (100 foot) **Church Cross,** east of the interstate seemed to call my name. I pulled into the church parking lot singing, "At the cross, at the cross where I first saw the light, and the burdens of my heart rolled away…"

My heart was so full. I didn't get out, but I knew I'd be back soon. Headed home, I realized the hotel where I had my first public appearance for *Forgive Me Body* was directly in line with the cross. This made me want to understand more about my journey. I prayed hard as I headed home.

The intrigue of the *The Cross* held me captive all day at work. I knew I had to return, and I knew that night was it. Once I got my kids settled in at home, I then started my trip to *The Cross*. It had gotten dark, but I had tunnel vision. Still, I had to touch *The Cross*. I needed to be close to *GOD*.

When I pulled into the drive there was a Security Guard directing me *to the left;* His left, my right. My mind flashed quickly to my

159

previous marriage, and to Beyonce singing "To the left, to the left". The thought gave a me a funny snicker at the ironic parody of it all. Just thinking about all the issues I had bought into my life from that relationship with Edward, and how I still hadn't learned from hard lessons had me scratching my head. Just as I turned, a smiling face greeted me by giving me a Christmas CD, and directions. I then drove through a *Live Nativity Scene*, realistic of life during *JESUS'S TIME*. This was the most humbling experience ever.

At the end of the scene I pulled over and stopped. Kneeling at *The Cross*, I breathlessly prayed, "Thank you *LORD* for loving me, for believing in me still, even through my failures. Please *GOD* help me be the Gwen that I was created me to be. Thank you that from the beginning you knew what my purpose would be through the annals of time. Thank you for believing in me up to this very moment of 53 years. You chose me to have the strength to keep pushing, and pushing harder. I feel like I am in labor, and I have to get my body, and spirit together right now. When I get to the end of this saga, I'll have a good understanding but for now I am pushing. I am using my shoulders, my stomach, and my thighs because my babies are near. *Relics of a Woman*, and *Can Do Enterprizes*. Thank you that all things are in divine order. **IN *JESUS* NAME**." The beginning of the true essence of my faith in *Christ* was sealed that night.

The next day my sons listened as I went on and on about the live nativity scene at *The Cross* the night before. We made plans to all come the next week. They were looking forward.

On Saturday December 9th *Momma and 4JHampton* headed to *The Cross.* When I gave Jimmy Jr the keys to *Tae* that night, I had a nervous ache in my stomach. I was still getting used to having a teenage driver in the house. And even though he was a great driver, I still had timid moments if we had to take a different route. That night, Jimmy Jr was driving us across the bridge to ***The One Hundred (100 foot)*** **Church Cross, *The Cross.***

Everything looked new to me that night. As Jimmy Jr's passenger I got a chance to read every billboard along the way.

When he pulled onto the highway headed to *The Cross* I got a close look at the hotel where *Forgive Me Body* was born. Then, I could only gape with my mouth wide open at the little shack sitting on the right just past the hotel. It was the shack Jimmy; my sons' father had used for *Jimmy's Car Detailing* our business at the time.

What a revelation, *The Cross, Forgive Me Body, and Jimmy's Car Detailing* were all in line with each other. I could only deduce from the evidence was that *GOD had been watching over me for a very long time*. This realization added another dimension to our sojourn to *The Cross*.

We rode in silence through the nativity scene, then we stopped. Encircling the huge base at The Cross we kneeled; each sending up a prayer, we each agreed to new life, and new liberty. Pulling out of the church parking lot, we loudly sang, **"At the cross, at the cross..."**

EPISODE II: END OF TIME 2012

December 16th was my birthday.

After church we headed to the mall to celebrate. As a gift to myself, I was getting my ears pierced. I thought *Why not? Why not now? They did send me an AARP card in the mail! And I'm a Baby Boomer.... Tomorrow ain't promised to me.*

It had been forty years since my cousin did a homemade ear piercing job on me. It didn't take long after that before I developed large keloids on both earlobes.

My mother took me to a doctor who agreed to cut them off before they got larger. The doctor instructed me to never get my ears pierced again; he said the keloids would come back, and maybe even larger. This was enough to scare me off from ever doing it again, and I never forgot the sound made when he cut them off. It sounded like paper being cut by scissors, which made my flesh crawl.

"It's My Birthday! It's My Birthday!" I sang as I pranced into the mall. It was my birthday and I was going in. When I strolled out of the mall with shining studs in my ear, I started dancing again.

My sons were off to Dallas for the Christmas holidays, and I was glad because I was wearing thin. My personal loneliness was setting in; I just didn't want to be alone. Then, I connected with my grown woman crush. We had a good time, and I even rested on his chest listening to "Silent Night." On the way home, I cried, knowing I had fooled myself again. After a long talk within myself, I decided to file this night under *Just for Fun.* Then, I went back to my seventh grade anthem, singing myself to sleep, "*GOD* gave me a song that the Angels cannot sing…"

I picked my sons up in time for us to celebrate the New Year at home. I was refreshed and ready to step out of 2012. As always I was prepared to be unprepared for everything. Heading into a new year always called for reflection of the last twelve months. As always, *GOD* showed up in my life during the last year, and unexpectedly rescued me from myself. It was then I thankfully acknowledged the many fun times I'd had in 2012. *GOD* had been good to me. And I wanted to always keep my eye on the positives forever. 2013 had to be *The One*.

EPISODE III: KEEP HOPE ALIVE 2013

It was truly amazing that I had not given in to the madness of my life. Feeling manic, and insane most times, I would feel like a locomotive on a very long track headed for disaster.

When I was invited to do a self-defense segment with my sons for the youth attendees at the church leadership conference, I immediately accepted. I had determined that whenever, wherever I would always help children learn ways to defend themselves. It was encouraging to know that the kids already had some idea as to what they would do if they ever had to defend themselves. Motivating them to truly understand real dangers in life helped me to recalibrate my mind on what I had been doing to myself. I needed a class on defense from self-sabotage. My sons were very shy about helping me, but in the end, their popularity soared as *4JHampton, The Black Belt Brothers.*

The conference inspired thoughts of *Can Do Enterprizes (CDE)*. As my mind locked in on *CDE* I became hopeful of the manifestation of *CDE*. Then, I spoke to *GOD Our families do deserve a program like this. But LORD, how can I make this happen?* I asked.

Gwendolyn Hampton

SEASON XII

WAR OF THE WORLDS

EPISODE I: satan, YOU ARE A LIAR!!!

I realized the job of the evil one was always to rob, destroy, and kill. It was one thing when present danger was before your eyes, but when the unforeseen happened, you could never be prepared. It's good to know that **GOD** has *Angels* everywhere.

Jimmy Jr had become an excellent driver and I was comfortable riding with him. Even to the point of reading the newspaper while riding as a passenger.

We were all nervous when the roaring sound started. There was nothing apparent that we could be seen, until then tire exploded. Panicking, I finally remembered that I had roadside assistance. Before I could complete my call to State Farm, one of their assistance trucks pulled up behind us. It was a miracle. The nicest man got out, calmed our fears and got us back on the road. Thank **GOD** my spare was in good shape. And *Road Angels* were still on their job.

EPISODE II: MARCH MATTERS

My mission was accomplished when my four sons got their Black Belts.

It was a given that the day would come when each would exert their will to either continue on in the martial arts or not. I was totally unprepared on March 2, 2013 when Joshua quit class. Joshua was having a fit in class that day, and nothing seemed to matter to him. When the instructor asked him if he wanted to even be in class anymore, Joshua calmly, and sincerely said "No."

My stomach dropped. And as much as I wanted to deny his request, I had to agree with his desire. After all, he had put in eight years, when he started at seven-years-old. You could almost see the

165

wheels turning in the minds of Josh's brothers when he quit. They looked like jackals plotting their escape. After class Joshua walked out cocky, like he had just defeated Goliath.

Jimmy Jr had started to regularly drive my car *Taz*. It was hard to let him drive off to school alone for the first time. I was nervous all day at work. Over the years I kept up the maintenance on *Taz*; my intent had always been to see my sons drive *Taz*. As I traveled, I would continually anoint *Taz* as a **Road Angel** and **Bless** the roads **IN JESUS NAME.**

The day Jimmy Jr drove his brothers to Tae Kwon-Do alone, I forced myself into solitary confinement. I was frightened to death: what if something terrible happened to **All My Sons**. Mr. B had been officially relieved of his promise to pick my sons up. I desperately wanted to go to the school after work and follow them home. But, we were working late that night and class was over before I could get there.

Instead, I went home, sat on the porch praying as I looked up and down the street awaiting their arrival. When *Taz* turned that corner I jumped and ran to the edge of the drive: I was finally able to breathe. This was a milestone in my life as a parent. What a sight, my four sons pulling into the drive with their brother driving: they were all grinning.

Jimmy Jr aka *Jimmy Jam* asked me if he could drive to a school dance, I agreed. My concern wasn't whether he was a smart driver or not: it was hard for me to let go. I was surprised by the shock I felt just knowing my cool cat Jimmy *Jam* even wanted to go to a dance. I shouldn't have been surprised by anything he did because he was still the kid with a cool demeanor, and a poker face. That same face he used on me when he asked the question. On the outside I showed him absolute trust, but inside fear was eating me up.

The night of the dance *Jimmy Jam* left home with a new cool. The dance was downtown on a Saturday night, which meant there were people hanging out partying and drinking. My stomach was queasy at the thought, so I followed him.   As Jeremy and I pulled into the parking lot, I was shocked to see that in his haste to get to the party Jimmy Jr had straddled two parking spaces.   Knowing this could be an incident waiting to happen, I decided to move the car; almost sure my son wouldn't be aware of the change.   This would have been a great getaway if for two things; I had changed purses and my spare key was in the other purse, not with me.   I couldn't just leave the car like it was, so I sent Jeremy in to get his brother.   He was glad to go, ashy knees and all.   When Jimmy Jr came out, he shook his head, moved the car, and smiled as he sashayed across the street saying, "Bye Mom".   I knew this was it: all my kids would be driving soon.

On March 30, 2013, I received my Black Belt Certificate. Getting to that point had been a very challenging journey.   All the jumps, turns, and kicks I did, were nothing compared to the forms I had to learn with all the moves in each.   Feeling like Superwoman, I was proud to have accomplished something as phenomenal as that at fifty-three.   It wasn't the belt that made the issue, but the determination, stamina, intensity, strength, and everything else that went into the Black Belt program in Tae Kwon-Do.   My memories were innumerable.   There was one time I got off work early; I had enough time to stop for gas, and be on time for class.   After filling my tank, not paying attention, the nozzle fell and was pointing up with an overflow of gas that ended up all over me.   Closer to class than home, I sucked it up and strutted into class smelling like a gas tank.   Stinky me finished the class.   Now, I was the proud Mother of a five Black Belt household.

EPISODE III: FATHER KNOWS???

I heard it said again, "A woman can't raise a man!" Still fighting the urge to be angry at my son's father, I knew I would never defend that statement again. And if I heard it again I would scream.

I knew as a woman there were things I couldn't teach my sons like; how to urinate standing up, or show him how to shave without getting razor bumps, or teach him anything that was a man's alone. But, what I could do as a woman to raise a man was to bring real men into the lives of my sons who were willing to share their stories and teach my sons all things **man**. Then, as a woman to raise a man I could exhaust all avenues of research to give my sons answers to their questions. Then as a woman to raise a man I could make sure the physical, mental, and emotional needs of *All My Sons* were met.

As a mother, I could raise curiosity in my children by exposing them to the word of *GOD*. And as a mother what I could do was not give up on the sons in my care; one day they would be men and have to teach the good seeds sown in their lives when they were young. Most importantly I could teach them to love and fear *GOD* and learn the ways of *JESUS CHRIST*.

As a woman, I could teach my children that *JESUS* was the way, the truth, and the light in my life, and their lives. If this wasn't raising a man, then I didn't know what was. I knew these things were true because I was raising men, and all my sons were baptized believers in *Christ*. I had to believe for six, me, my four sons, and our boy dog Champion until they could believe for themselves.

On March 13th my ex Jimmy knocked on my door. It was immediately apparent that he was not there to see his kids, as he began his friendly, friendly toward me. Not once did he ask to see his sons. Standing on the porch maintaining civility, I listened to him. Fighting an uprising emotion to scratch his eyes out, I continued to listen. I knew I had to get past the hostility I had toward him.

While standing there, we saw a group of kids walking down the street. Looking at the kids he said "Lots of kids around here." I said, "Yes". Then this man made a comment that changed everything "I bet most of them don't have a Father." Feeling like he was mocking me, I said: "Excuse me!" That was it, I was boiling on the inside, and I didn't want to know where our conversation was leading. Quickly I said, "I think it's time for you to leave." Then he clapped back at me, "That's why men can't ever see their kids because of the woman!" I saw red, and I couldn't believe he was insinuating that he didn't see his kids because of me. *Hell No!* I said to myself, that was it. I told him to get off my property before I called the police then I slammed the door on my way inside.

EPISODE IV: ALPHABET SUE/GWENDOLYN SUE

On my way to work, just pass my driveway I saw a large piece of colorful cardboard.

Curious, I got out and picked up what looked like a sundial with alphabets on it. My mind went straight to the negatives of my life. *A-anger, B-bankruptcy, D-depression, F-fear, N-NSF's, O-obesity, P-payday loans, S-single mother*, I knew I could fill in all the blanks. Before I could get back to my car, I looked over and saw the second piece of the sundial with additional letters. Determined to have a good day at work I replaced the negatives with positives. *A-adventurous, B-beautiful, C-compassionate D-diligent, H-hard worker, M-martial artist, S-seamstress, V-valiant, Z-zealous*, I knew I could fill in the blanks.

Having a good attitude was so important because I was becoming a disgruntled employee. Struggling I'd pray, *LORD please open the doors, and show me now. Lead me to my place. I know experience counts, but I wouldn't wish many of my experiences on anyone. Don't let my life be in vain.*

EPISODE V: I HATE YOU

July 13, 2013, I had to ask, *Am I going crazy?* I had started writing backwards; like counter clockwise. This was really funny to me because it was legible. I thought this should register higher than being ambidextrous.

Working hard at maintaining my positive, I was out enjoying a drive a few days later. I couldn't help but smile when the four bikes passed me. They looked like Power Rangers zooming down the parkway. Watching them as they pulled into the park, I followed. As I parked, I was so tickled as they embarked off their bikes. I had a fun visual of myself, and my four sons out enjoying a ride on our own bikes. Then *Bam!* Off came the yellow helmet, dismount off the yellow bike. *Bam!* Off came the black helmet, dismount off the black bike. *Bam!* Off came the red helmet, dismount off the red bike. Then *Bam!* Off came the blue helmet, dismount off the blue bike. I was so excited; I'd never seen anything like this.

I got out, introduced myself to these young men. Making sure they understood I wasn't a pervert, I explained my interest in them was as a Mother of four sons. I was gushing; they were such a beautiful sight. It was amazing; these young men were new airmen from around the country stationed at Barksdale Air Force Base, out for a ride. I gave a short scenario of my vision, *Can Do Enterprizes* with a request that they might become a part of a mentoring session one day. Each agreed; giving me their phone numbers. When I got home I put a smile on my boys' face with the story of my adventure with the Power Rangers.

Things can change very fast. A smile can be turned upside down in a blink. On July 19th, the word came that my nephew's beautiful mother Betty had died. Her birthday was two days after mine, and she was a year older than me. This meant she had made it to 54, and I hadn't. Her death made me truly admire the life she lived. I wanted to do better in my life, and live to see my sons as adults, as she was blessed to do. I promised myself to live strong, and courageous.

It was a very somber week. Friday night as I rushed off to the family hour for Betty, my neighbor stopped me. She said. "Why didn't you tell me about K?" "What do you mean?" I said. "You didn't know? K was molested the other night!" she said. I was flabbergasted: K was only seven. Since I was running late, I told my neighbor that I would go to K's house, and talk to her Mom the next day.

Walking down the street I didn't know what I was going to say to make things better for this family. When K answered the door her hair was down; she looked like Cali's doll Wild Woman. Cali is the daughter of a friend, and Wild Woman was the name I gave her ragged doll when she was young.

I asked K. to go get her Mother. When her mom walked in I started, "I heard what happened to K. I really hate this happened. I would have been down sooner, but I didn't know." She loudly proclaimed, "You didn't know? What do you mean you didn't know! It happened in your backyard." Speechless, I stared at her, as the question crossed my mind, *Was it one of my sons?* Then finally able to speak I said, "What do you mean in my backyard?"

She went on to explain: K, her brother and my son Jaleen had been playing hide-and-go-seek outside around dusk. Jaleen had been hiding so K. decided to go in the backyard and look for him. She was not afraid of Champion so she boldly strutted back there. Her brother who was afraid of our dog finally decided to follow her when she didn't come to the front right away. He thought she had found Jaleen. When he got back there he saw his little sister being forced to perform oral sex on an unknown white male. Frightened he ran down the street to get help. By the time he got home K was coming down the street.

I was so upset, because I remembered that night. We (my other sons and I) were in the back room next to the backyard watching T.V. It was a sickening thought that this baby was being molested while

171

we were watching a movie; laughing and enjoying ourselves. Then to make matters worse, Jaleen knew nothing about what had happened that night. I'm sure he would have fought for her. This affirmed my belief that kids should be taught self-defense for such an occasion as this, K might have been able to do something. I thanked **GOD** that K was alright , and that neither of my sons were implicated in this matter.

After hearing the story, I knew that K would forever hold a special place in my heart. K's hair was down that day because Ms. Christine was braiding it that day. As a show of solidarity with this little girl, I asked Ms. Christine if she would braid my hair as well.

This was major for me: I had gotten my hair braided about four years ago when I turned fifty. It hurt so bad and took so long that I swore never to do it again. This was different though: I was ready to fight with a new hair-do.

K sat on the stool while Christine braided my hair. In a hush tone Christine shared another shocker with me. Her granddaughter's virginity had been taken by a man who had broken into their house. Not only had he forced her with oral sex, but also anal sex. I was sick to my stomach. **LORD** have mercy on our babies and families. I wanted to get away; go for a drive to clear my head. If I could have flown away I would have. Then I remembered one day: Sitting at the red light I saw a man walking, ready to cross the street at the light. Suddenly, he took off running, flapping his arms as if he was flying. I started clapping as he continued running up the block, then he stopped. The light changed but I sat there, blowing my horn I cheered the man while holding up traffic. This time, however, I wanted to fly away and disappear.

Later, I called a family meeting with my sons to discuss this matter. My priorities included again; 1) stranger danger; there were many transient people in our neighborhood, 2) awareness of one's surrounding; we did live in a highly populated area for sex offenders, and 3) taking self-defense skills taught seriously; you never knew when you might have to use them.

EPISODE VI: AUGUST HEAT

The weather was stifling, and I didn't want to do it anymore.

My job required that I master working with all kinds of people while maintaining my composure. I had to resolve their issues while not getting into any undue conversation. I had already been warned and written up for talking too much. It was hard for me to be indifferent to the storms raging in the lives of my customers, some who were my friends. I was never surprised at how many people sought solace at the DMV. They just wanted someone to listen to them about their job loss, the death of a loved one, even their broken relationships. My own personal, silent tsunamis roared inside of me: I understood. I was always compassionate for the people on the other side of my desk, never knowing what might have happened to them at the breakfast table, or the red light, or even in the parking lot. How could we know; someone might have been at the breaking point, and a smile or kind word could have been the hope they had prayed for. My superior told me I talked too much, but what she didn't know was that I was praying a lot of times with my customers. And this could happen within three minutes of their sitting down at my desk.

Road tests were very different though, I'd be in a car with people for fifteen plus minutes. During this time I was not supposed to get into extra conversation with the testers. Needless to say, this didn't always happen. A perfect storm of emotions sometimes left me in the parking lot after the test wiping tears away. One day, the heat, and the array of misery I confronted was more than I could handle. I didn't want to do it anymore.

One day I declared war, there wasn't a notion of not following thru with my vision *Can Do Enterprizes*. Looking at K smile at the dining table sitting there between her two brothers was a joy to my soul. No perception of the horrendous crime done to her earlier was evident, even though her Mother told me she was having nightmares. That day when I looked over at K I felt a new blood flowing in my vein, like Wonder Woman, I believed I could do anything. I was taken aback when K called me Momma while sitting at the table. Gently I explained to her that she had a Mother who loved her very much and that her mom was hurt over what happened to her. I told her I was a Lady that also loved her, and was going to help her and her family.

She was eight-years-old now, and I was so proud of her; beautiful, sassy, and smart. It was very odd when she read the T-shirts I had displayed on the chairs in the dining room: no kid had ever taken time to read all five of them. While I fixed lunch she read each one of them, taking her time, meticulously pronouncing each word:

"If I agreed with you we both would be wrong."

"Love is the key."

"Congratulations Mr. President."

"It's time to choose *JESUS*."

"Growing old is mandatory: growing up is optional."

There was still a glimmer of hope that Joshua would return to Tae Kwon-Do class. But this was squashed when Joshua denied the opportunity to get back in. Then, I inadvertently hastened the moment when the 4JHampton domino stack would begin to fall. One day, while talking to Mr. B, he asked me about the disposition of the other boys toward continuing class. I mentioned that Jimmy Jr was having doubts. This was one of those times when I should have stayed in a woman's place and stayed out of this men business because Mr. B immediately approached Jimmy Jr, asking him if he wanted to quit. And of course, Jimmy Jr's "Yes" was as nonchalant as it could have been. There was nothing I could say because he was being honest, but his unintentional candor was unsettling coming from a seventeen-year-old.

Now I was two Black Belts in, and two Black Belts out of Tae Kwon-Do class, not including myself. The twins were still holding on. On August 2nd Jeremy was very distracted, and his actions made Mr. B zero in on him. When asked if he wanted to quit, Jeremy said "Yes". I didn't work out on that day, which was a good thing because sitting there on the sidelines I could hardly see as my eyes filled with tears. And, I probably would have gotten put out of class that day anyway because I was so sad. Then there was one left from the 4JHampton group. Poor Jaleen, he held on for me, jumping, kicking, and rolling in class so that I wouldn't be alone.

Pain often precedes joy. My feelings of gloom were soon replaced with happiness. School started and Jimmy Jr was now a senior in high school, Joshua was a sophomore, and the twins were in their last year of middle school. As the Mother of these four young men, I was overjoyed. The prospect that my oldest would graduate, made me ever so thankful. As a family, we had been on quite a journey. I was surprised when Jimmy Jr told me he wanted to join the military and asked me to set an appointment with a recruiter. My son was becoming a man. Also, he was in his final stages of completion to finish his Boy Scouts requirements to be an Eagle Scout. Things were looking good.

EPISODE VII: 9-11-2013

The decision had to be made because my life was at stake. I had made an appointment to see the doctor. My nerves were shot, and I was preparing to put my request in for a family medical leave. My emotions were off the chart and I was trying to keep from killing anyone.

My doctor's appointment was scheduled for Tuesday, September the 10th and I had my Family Medical Leave papers ready for him to sign off on them. I needed some time off because I was having a mental breakdown. ***Surely I can hold out till I see the doctor*** I kept thinking. Then, four days before the appointment, my Friday morning was ruined. The Doctor's nurse called me at work to inform me that my appointment would have to be canceled. She said, "The Doctor has an emergency and won't be back in the office for the next three months."

Though the doctor had an urgent family situation in India he needed to take care of, I didn't think I could hold out for the three months he would be away. ***How crazy am I LORD? How crazy am I about to get?*** I kept asking myself when I thought about a customer from last week. She was there to get an identification card. When she asked, "Can ***schizophrenic*** be put on my ID?" I thought she was joking. She said, "I'm serious." Intrigued I asked what she meant. She was asking for her sister who had inherited schizophrenia from their Dad, who inherited it from his Dad. She suspected her sister's two children had it because she was used to how schizophrenics acted, like her Dad, and sister. She then said she was not affected. As I listened I thought it might be a good idea to put a grade 1-5 as degrees of schizophrenia on everyone's ID, like a medical code. But here I was at a 10 on this scale of 5. ***What would I be considered?*** I asked myself.

On September 11th I called my father before work, "Happy Birthday Daddy! I love you, and pray you will have a wonderful day". As well I prayed to have a wonderful day myself. I had decided to turn in my resignation at work that morning. Everything at work had become too much, and I had had enough. Sure that this would be the most emotional thing I would deal with this day, I acknowledged my pain as I thought about the friends I would leave behind. I had no plans or arrangements other than in two weeks I would not be at the job. I didn't want the ambulance to be called for me as it happened to a co-worker, or have the coroner come because I was dead like that old man who died in our audience one day.

There was no preparation for the news I got later that morning from a co-worker when she asked me "Are you going to the funeral?" Alarmed I asked, "Whose funeral?" "You know Mr. Livingston, they are burying him today," she replied. I was floored.

Mr. Livingston was the news reporter that had introduced my family to the area. He had touted my sons' accomplishments, went to bat for us to raise funds when we traveled with Team USA, and he had become a family friend. I was forever grateful to him.

The last time I saw him was at an event he hosted. He had invited my sons to do an exhibition for the event. And they were happy to oblige.

Mr. Livingston was a good man who always spoke highly of his wife. He was also a social activist, who fought for the rights and equalities of the underdog. As an inspiring writer, he touched many with the deep social issues he explored. And he also encouraged me as a writer to complete *Relics Of A Woman*. I really admired this man and was sad I couldn't attend his funeral. I didn't even ask if I could get off work to go: we were shorthanded that day.

The news of Mr. Livingston death made me determined. I was going to live my dreams. He had been a great example of someone who lived their dreams. Having a sense of fear and relief at the same time I was satisfied with my decision to turn in my resignation earlier. That was until I laid down for the night. That's when **GOD** spoke to me, *Not Now* was what he said. I couldn't even fake that I didn't understand. Obedient to **GOD'S COMMAND**, the next morning I went back to work and rescinded my resignation. I was very ashamed. Funny thing was though that as the days passed, joy started coming. And I thought *I must be going crazy now for sure.* Smiles and laughter even graced my face as I started feeling better. And I promised to continue to work on the vision of my unborn 13-

177

year-old baby, **Can do Enterprizes**. I thought *Here we go*. *Win or lose or draw I will put things together*.

EPISODE VIII: DONE DEALS, FALL 2013

Jaleen held out as long as he could as the last of my sons still practicing Tae Kwon-Do. You could see the hurt in his eyes. Jaleen was the master at doing splits in the family, but now his pain was evident; even in his splits. One day, Mr. B gave him an easy out and told him he didn't have to do class anymore: Jaleen took it. I wasn't mad, but I was missing him already. Not wanting to add insult to injury, I tried not to talk about my sons anymore in class. I knew Mr. B had hopes that my sons one day would be around to help keep his school's legacy going.

After 8 years **4JHampton** had fulfilled their destiny at our school of Tae Kwon-Do. These young people had other things on their minds, like having fun, and freedom as teenagers. I let them go, but I also made it clear that quitting Boy Scouts was not an option. We would finish the program to become Eagle Scouts like they had become Black Belts in the martial arts.

When my kids quit class, I was left with a big hole in my heart. By now our class had dwindled to Monica, and I. She was a seventeen-year-old who had gotten her Black Belt shortly after I got mine. Like Jimmy Jr, she was a senior in high school. And if you looked closely you could see that same faraway look in her eyes that said *I want to be somewhere else*. It wasn't long before a way was made, and she was out of class.

Then there was me: The last woman standing in the class alone with **Sukahorro**r. This was the name I silently called Mr. B when his intensity was a 50 out of 10. It was a sight to behold. I truly admired Mr. B, and though he was five years older than me, for the first time I was truly afraid I wouldn't be able to keep up, but I vowed to give it my best. I had to step everything up several notches because there was no place for me to hide. It took a while for me to release the negative feelings I was having from my sons' departure.

When I looked at Mr. B I just wanted to apologize for my son's seemingly ungrateful exits from his class. This man had been a positive force in each of their lives, and not one of them said thank you to him for being the good man in their life. I promised myself that I would make up for their callous ways by doing good in class: I would show Mr. B how much I truly appreciated everything he had done for me and my sons.

EPISODE IX: CHANGE-THE POEM

If *everything must change, then why am I still the same?*

Is it me? Or is it you????

How dare I ask the question, when I already know the answer.

IT'S ME!!! IT'S ME!!! Standing in the need.

Planted was the seed, since the beginning of time

I must make reason for the rhyme

To earn my wings, I must loudly sing

Learning along the way many new things

Worlds unknown, mysteries unveiled

Time to set my sails

*It's my time to fly with the **Heavenlies** high*

***LORD** if you will, please keep me still*

As you set my course, open the doors

*With **JESUS** AS MY **SAVIOR**, Let salt be my flavor*

Don't change if I choose, don't bend and I lose

To lose is to break

I don't choose to lose

When I can choose to win

Can't be afraid, for it's just a new beginning, not the END

And whatever it looks like

It is what it is

And I am who I am

October 25, 2013

Gwendolyn Hampton

EPISODE X: NOVEMBER REVELATIONS

I was glad the workday was over. The sun was still shining as I headed home.

Just as I merged onto the expressway, I saw a man dressed in an overcoat with a hat on walking toward traffic carrying a loaded trash bag. Blinking several times, my mind clicked after I had gone a short distance. ***That man looked just like my Daddy. What! No, that couldn't be*** I thought. My mind was in a tizzy as I pulled over to quickly call my parent's home. My aunt who was there visiting from Los Angeles answered the phone. Frantically I asked her, "Is Daddy there?" She looked around and didn't see him anywhere, and then she asked my Mother where he was. Mom didn't know, and said she hadn't seen him since the morning. Now I was panicking, as I told my aunt about the man on the interstate. Quickly I got off the phone, headed down the freeway to the next exit where I made a U-turn, returning back to where this had all begun. I saw the man again, he hadn't advanced very far, so there he was.

I couldn't believe my eyes. I stopped the car, ran over to my Dad screaming at him with a barrage of questions, "Daddy what are you doing out here on this freeway? Where have you been?"

When he shot that irresistible smile at me, I fought back the tears. He was oblivious to the dangerous situation he was in. I opened the trunk, and we put his bag in the back. He had been out collecting cans for recycling all day. I called my Mom, told her about what had just happened, and that we were on our way home.

My Dad had been headed down this busy highway, miles away from his home, in the wrong direction. The reality of my Mother's life with my Dad was becoming clearer as deep signs of Alzheimer's became evident. My siblings and I had no idea how far our Dad's health had declined.

Stories I heard about some of Dad's actions were very horrifying thoughts. It all made sense how diligent Mom had been in keeping up with her husband. There was the story of my Father driving his riding lawn mower down Line Ave., a very busy main street. Mom had previously given his driver's license to me and I told him he couldn't drive anymore: *Doctor's orders*. This was necessary, because he had many dings and run-ins with curbs in the past. I took this opportunity to make Mom a promise. I told her, "I won't fight with you when your driving become a hazard to you and others on the road. Momma I will take your license without asking." She promised to willingly give them up: I wanted to believe.

Fishing on the lake was my Father's beloved pastime. He even had a bumper sticker that read *Work is for people who can't fish*. He **LOVED** to fish; every day, any day, in the rain, in the cold, anytime. It didn't matter if he went near or far, in a Pero boat on a small canal, or a huge boat on the Gulf of Mexico. It was no surprise when I

181

heard this story shared by Mr. Robert, his fishing buddy: They had met at the lake, each in his own boat. When it got late, Mr. Robert left before Dad. The two men had decided to meet up again the next morning, at the same spot. Arriving as planned, Mr. Robert got a surprise when he looked out and Dad was already there. He soon got a great scare when he found out that my Father had been out there all night alone. When he talked to my Mom later, he promised to keep an eye out for him. From that time on, Mr. Robert would pick him up so they could go together. He did this for my mother: he didn't want her worrying about her husband.

These story horrified Mom and she began keeping a short leash on her venturesome man. My mother did everything for my Dad as she was faced with the challenge of keeping tabs on him almost every minute. She made sure he ate, picked out his clothes, and drove him everywhere. They were inseparable. I admired their love and could only imagine what it would feel like to have such passionate concern for someone as close as my right hand. They had survived many joys and pains.

By now, everyone was on vigilant watch. It was hard watching my hero go through this unknown territory. I even approached my Mom with the idea of us (my family and her and dad) moving in together when I said, "What if we both moved into a bigger house? I could help out with Dad, and you can help with the boys." She sternly told me "No." Explaining she wanted to keep her independence as long as possible. Respecting her decision, I still wanted to help more: I witnessed the long hours she put in taking care of her Mother, Ms. Charlsie.

Tremendous amounts of our family time was spent practicing Tae Kwon-Do. Many times over the years I would invite family to come work-out with me and the boys. It was a blessing when Dad finally bowed into class at eighty-years-old, my pride soared like an Eagle. He focused very hard in class, and you could see the Army veteran show up. It was so impressive seeing him do push-ups and sit-ups. I was enjoying this so much until the light went out, and he was now ready to go home: He wanted Momma. My regret was that I had not pushed harder for him to work out with me and my sons earlier. *What difference would this have made on the fast encroachment of Alzheimer's and Dementia?* I asked myself. Maybe one-day Mom would bow into class with me.

EPISODE XI: WHAT TIME IS IT???

It was in December of 2013, when I was determined to take time for myself. I decided to no longer work out on Sundays, now that my sons were off doing their own things.

The hurt I felt when they quit Tae Kwon-Do never left me. I just dealt with the reality as best I could. Mr. B would use the scenario that I should cut the umbilical cord. This was so true: I had to admit that I accomplished what I set out to do in the martial arts program. My life's mission was accomplished in part when I got to see all my sons get their black belts. I knew there was so much more ahead, and I was thankful to be raising independent, self-sufficient kids.

When I had a chance to get Jimmy Jr his first job I didn't hesitate. He was hired as a janitor. Impressed with my son for his humility in working, I allowed him to drive to work. This was hard for me: sometimes he didn't get off till after one in the morning then had to be in school for eight. I knew that this day would come, but that didn't stop the angst I had in the pit of my stomach: not to mention the little sleep I got while praying when he was out late.

My sons declined the invitation to be self-defense presenters at the church conference in January of 2014. This was okay because I'd invited two special guests to attend. It was K, the girl who had been molested in my backyard, and her mother: I thought it would be fitting to share with the kids the reality of what could happen on any unsuspecting day. I had a long talk with K's mother to assure her I description cut.

wouldn't exploit K in any way. When I introduced K to the kids, she was excited and happy: We had a great time.

It was a great day when I got my tax refund back with no problems on February 9, 2014, I paid off *Tae* my truck and paid my bills in advance. I was proud to have gotten bankruptcy, and multiple payday loans behind me. I finally believed I would live wisely and my hopes were high.

I heard loud music and a man singing in the Wal-Mart shopping center. Curious, looking around I drove around the parking lot. Then, I saw the man with his recording equipment sitting on the tailgate of a truck singing into a microphone, "There will be peace in the Valley." As though a personal message from *GOD*, I loudly said, "THANK YOU *GOD* FOR *JESUS*!" confirming what I truly understood; *Life is a maybe, Death is for sure, Sin is the cause, Christ is the cure.*

SEASON XIII

SEARCH FOR
TOMMORROWS

EPISODE I: NEW BEGINNINGS 2014

My body ached, my head hurt.

I was crazed about everything in my life, but I didn't want to give up. Weighing in at 184 lbs. all I wanted was a season of joy and happiness... financial freedom. I had to hold on.

Champion and I took a walk one day. Though it was cold outside, that day the trees seemed higher, and the sky appeared bluer. Trudging through the park, I took a new route. On the sidewalk was a big hammer, and I laughed because I wanted to be a carpenter. Part of the **Can Do Enterprizes** vision was called **Menagerie Trades** which included a plan for home repairs for participating families. **Is this a sign?** I asked myself as I picked the hammer up. Before I could get an answer, just two more steps down, I found a flathead screwdriver. Excited, I was sure this was another a sign. I'd always wanted to work with my hands and learn furniture redesign, and restoration. I also wanted to hit some nails, and pour some cement. I was sure these were inherited desires from my grandmother, Ms. Charlsie. One Christmas we pulled names at work. We were told to make a list of three things we wanted. My first two were toolsets. The young lady who pulled my name thought I had made a mistake. When I told her my requests was correct, she looked at me with the weirdest expression.

EPISODE II: MARCH MADNESS

Until I had children I never knew how many ways my heart could, or would melt.

Jimmy Jr would be graduating soon in May 2014. We had a long talk about his job, graduation activities, the prom, and completion of his Eagle Scout requirements. I told him he could quit his job. Then our talk went to a new level when he told me he wanted to be a Marine. Earlier, he had considered the Air Force, but this day he adamantly stated that he definitely wanted to be a Marine. When I asked "Why a Marine" he told me, "I have researched, and the Marines are the best. That's what I want to be, the best". Sick to my stomach at all the possible situations being a Marine meant, I agreed to make an appointment with a recruiter. I was proud of my 17-year-old son standing before me espousing what he believed.

After meeting with the Marine recruiter, we finally agreed that my son would enroll in a Delayed Entry Program: He would work out on weekends with Enlisted Marines as a Poole. He enjoyed the physical challenges and the comradery he had with the troops.

Jimmy Jr also agreed to finish his Eagle Scout certification because it would mean advanced placement in the military. I pushed him really hard: He only had a 90-day window of completion before his 18th birthday.

Several opportunities came around during the spring for my sons to make money as a group. A friend of mine hired them as waiters for her church banquet. Then, Kel, my nephew hired them out to help burn CDs, and organize accessories for his business. I was always on board for them making honest money.

I should have kept my eye on Joshua though, not that I didn't trust him, but I should have been observing him. This became evident when I returned home one day after class. I found out he'd taken the keys to *Taz*, then he and a friend went joyriding down the streets, in broad daylight. When I sat him down later to discuss his actions, Joshua then confessed to me that this had not been his first time. Mouth wide open, I listened as he relayed his trip down Youree Drive in the middle of the night. This was so like this young man: He believed he could do anything. Apparently, he also thought he could get away with everything. Now I would have to hide my keys. What next? I talked to a friend who was a Sheriff: He told me to set a time for my sons to come down and visit the jail.

It was unfortunate that I hadn't made the appointment earlier at the jail; maybe it would have prevented what happened a few weeks later. Kel, my nephew stormed down the street one day. There was a watch missing from his inventory. He accused Joshua of stealing the watch but he didn't indict my other sons. Vehemently Joshua denied any knowledge of the missing watch. But, after much prodding, he finally admitted he had taken the watch. Then, my furious nephew punched Joshua in the chest. I felt that first blow as though I'd been hit. My breath was taken away. Then, I stepped back because I knew Kel was right.

My nephew explained to Joshua that he didn't have to take from him because he could have asked for what he wanted. Kel used a whole lot of words that I won't even mention. Joshua ran all around for cover. As I watched my son brutally pummeled by my nephew, I knew I couldn't call the Sheriff for help now. I would be arrested for child abuse. When Joshua escaped down the street, I, my nephew and Jimmy Jr jumped in the car in pursuit. He slipped by when he went through the brush at the dead end of our street. I was left alone when the guys jumped out and took off in different directions.

I drove back to the house, and sat on my porch with bated breath, not knowing what might happen next. As hard as this had been to watch, I knew Joshua needed a reality check. I had fought through so much for his life, and I would be damned if he would start this stealing scene.

When I saw my nephew (still taking his anger out on my son) come around the corner breathing heavy with Joshua in a headlock, I wanted to run to my son. He was crying, screaming, and apologizing that he would never do it again. My nephew dumped Josh on the step where I was, and I excused myself to the bathroom. Poor Josh thought it was over when I went in. Listening, behind me I heard the last of the episode. Kel had made his point. The other three Hampton boys were in shock, even the men in the neighborhood stood by in amazement.

Everyone knew of Joshua's antics through the years, and they cheered my courage for allowing this discipline; it wasn't courage, but a necessity. After this incident, I called a family meeting, taking advantage of the momentum that this fury had presented. I threatened each of them, telling them "Order was **Mandatory** in this house". I even went so far as to tell them I had spies in the neighborhood watching their every move: I think they go the message.

I ran into a friend I hadn't seen in a long time. She was recovering from a mild stroke: She had no tell-tale signs like I envisioned someone with a stroke. From what I knew about the effects of a stroke, Belinda was a very blessed lady. I made a mental note to make a doctor's appointment. *Gotta check myself on what's real* I thought.

The weather was beautiful the day I had a fantasy about a Spring Fling. I relished in the thought that a picnic in the park after a long walk with a fine man would be the bomb. Anyway! I had to stop myself when the loneliness crept in. I sat on my hands when the desire to call my *Grown Woman Crush* rose up. If I had the chance, I knew I would drop to my knees, and beg him to make me his own. This man and I had maintained an undefined relationship over the years, and it seemed as if I was unable to just walk away from him. Was this Love or Lub? I asked myself. For me, Lub was that bereaved, unrequited, never fulfilled love I had. Again, I got over the fantasy and didn't make the call.

Many times in the early mornings when I would meditate, my heart would flow to *Can Do Enterprizes*. I was more on edge than ever as I beseeched *GOD*: *Please don't take Your vision away from me. Thirteen years have passed since You showed me this vision, please lead me to the manifestation of this amazing dream. So many people would benefit.* Cleaning one day, I ran across part of an essay Jeremy had done in elementary school. He posed the question *How do you help a neighbor build a fence? First you ask if he needs help, if he says yes, then you help him*. I wanted to be in a position to ask that question, and be a help.

EPISODE III: TO LOSE IS TO LOVE

It was going to be April showers, but they would be more like torrential storms for me.

When I read the Saturday paper on Monday the 14th, I was almost too late. I wasn't expecting to find anything special in the news that day, but on Wednesday the 16th, there was a kickoff party planned for *The Startup Prize*. *The Startup Prize* was a contest starting soon for new start-up businesses to compete for a chance to win cash, and mentoring help to build their winning idea. This was right up my alley, and could be just what I would need to go forward, especially since I no longer had a job. I knew **GOD** had put many opportunities to succeed in my path before, and I also knew that I'd been blinded by fear for years to do what was required of me to win. When I thought about The Startup Prize competition, I said to myself *I won't miss this chance, this has to be a sign. LORD remove the scales from my eyes. Awesome, Awesome, Awesome*.

I barely slept that night; tossing and turning I'd had a fitful night's rest. After a disturbing dream I was worried. In the dream, I was in a lot of pain. There was a finger pressed into my neck, and it wouldn't move. I couldn't see anything else but this finger pressed just below my jaw bone. The intensity of the pressure from the finger was so severe that I began throwing up what looked like bile. There wasn't anything else about this dream except the direct contact from that one finger, and how painful it was. This dream woke me up with a loud prayer on my lips "**LORD** help me to understand and go forward in my mission in life. satan, you've had your finger on me too long. I bind you **IN THE NAME OF JESUS**. No more!"

The dream I had earlier started to make sense when I was forced to make a decision later at work. Early in the week, the blatant mistake I made was revealed: I was now on the firing line. Again, my life was at stake as words swirled around in my head, and I could hardly think. Panic-stricken, I found myself begging mercy for my job. Knowing I could make things right, I silently prayed ***LORD, I have done my best to raise my sons. I have worked really hard. Will you still take care of me after this bad move? You have never left me, please don't leave me now, I need you.*** Later, I was told; either continue to fight for the job or quit. And of course, the words *Right To Work State* was mentioned. Beaten, I couldn't fight anymore: I decided to resign. And I no longer had to daydream about being in the sunshine anymore, because now I would be given full access to its rays.

There were dignitaries present at the party that Wednesday for *The Startup Prize*, and I had opportunities to give snapshot info of **Can Do Enterprizes** to quite a few people. That night I collected names and numbers that came with the offer of help when I was ready. I was encouraged, and I believed those numbers would be used soon.

Since the episode at work last year: when I quit, then rescinded my decision, I had been waiting for **GOD** to move in my work situation, then an incident at work forced me into making a decision; quit or fight and I took this incident as my answer. On Thursday, April 17, 2014 I went to the office to turn my resignation in. This was harder than I anticipated; I truly thought I would prance into the office, say my goodbyes, and be off to make ready for my son's graduation, which was a month away. This was not the case: I became a blubbering mess when I found out that a very good friend Kimberley, who called me "Momma" had turned in her resignation that day as well.

When I left, my phone continuously rang with congrats and condolences. One friend told me "You have been delivered." I said "I know, and I'm praying for yours." Another called,

"Congratulations on your Resurrection Day." "Thank you, I really like the sound of that, cause this sure feel like a resurrection," I said. I even got a job offer, to which I commented to myself, *No, not now, gotta deliver these babies*. My babies were *Can Do Enterprizes* and *Relics of a Woman.*

On the last night of *The Startup Prize reception* someone gave me a T-shirt from Cohab, the hosting organization. I wore my T-shirt the next day to a city town hall meeting at our recreation center. The councilman for our area recognized the *Cohab* logo, and approached me, inquiring if I had entered the contest. I said, "Yes". Again I had an opportunity to give a snapshot of my vision. Reaching in his pocket he gave me his card, with an offer to help. He even introduced me to his wife, and child.

Just then, our Mayor Glover walked in. Recognizing the *Cohab* logo he asked, "Are you entering *The Startup Prize* contest?" I said, "Yes, and Mr. Mayor I would like to talk to you about my proposal. Can I call you?" "Yes," he replied. "What is your number, sir?" I asked. He then rattled it off as he hurried to his seat. A week before I had a job and no idea about *The Startup Prize* contest. That night I had no job, but I had already attended a launch party for The Startup Prize, and got to meet the Mayor and Councilman for our area. I was inspired as things seemed to lead all roads to *Can Do Enterprizes*. I found out that night at the rec center how big this contest was, and the impact it carried in our city. I was hopeful. Wearing my *Cohab* T-shirt was a great idea.

Just as I was sitting down, my friend Belinda sat in the chair next to me. It was good to see her, and she was looking great. Belinda explained that the stroke she had earlier left her slightly incapacitated in some areas; especially her memory. I was amazed at her strength: She had overcome so much. She then started telling me about the closing of Providence House. Providence House was a transitional facility for women and children in need. This was a worry to me, because I knew the vital impact this great institution had made in the lives of so many families. When my life was at a pivotal point, I made Providence House my #1 charity, because one of those families could have been mine. This was a sign to me that **Can Do Enterprizes** was on the radar.

The meeting was held at the rec center where my kids were regular campers. My sons helped to keep the area clean that night. Jimmy Jr had been pushing a broom earlier; cleaning the floor. We were standing next to each other when the Fire Chief came over, shook his hand and commended his actions. Jimmy Jr didn't have much to say after a quick thank you, but like any proud Momma, I jumped in giving the chief a spill about my son, sharing the fact he would be finishing his Eagle Scout requirements soon, and that he had enlisted as a Marine. Impressed, the chief shook Jimmy Jr's hand again. That was a good night, and I fell asleep with words playing over, and over again in my mind *Believe, freedom, love, dream, faith, peace.*

I couldn't believe it had been just a few days since I left my job. Truth be told: I had mentally left my job long before.

My first priority was to organize my home, so I started with my closet. By the time I finished cleansing and pruning my closet I had collected many bags of used clothing for Providence House. There was a table in my closet, and I was astounded when I moved it. Under the table on the floor was what seemed like another closet full of clothes. I started again, even though I wanted to take a nap by now. Plowing through the clothes I was determined to finish because I had a busy day ahead. When I got in too big of a hurry I stumbled. Reaching out with my left hand I tried to break my fall.

My hand landed on the wall in the precise spot where there was a nail sticking out. It was a bullseye hit, and the nail was imbedded in my hand. When I regained my balance I inspected my hand, there was no blood, but there was enough pain to let me know the nail had been there. When I looked at the nail I was surprised at how far it protruded out, and that I had never seen it before. I wondered *Is this is a coincident GOD, today is Good Friday?* The date was April 18th. Then I started to talk to the **LORD**, "This day we celebrate the nails that were pounded into your hands. This day you were crucified for our sins. Is this a sign? This nail in my hand sure feels like a confirmation". I was very happy, as I carefully cradled my hand. I felt **GOD** was with me, and had given me a personal point of contact with him.

On a roll now I was swiftly moving through the rooms in the house cleaning. My bathroom was the last stop. I didn't move fast enough before the vase broke. The biggest piece fell in the toilet, while glass shards were left on the floor. For the first time, I saw just how dim the light was in my bathroom as I cleaned the glass from the floor. Apparently, some of the glass was still on the floor because I got a bad cut. I couldn't believe I had missed cleaning up such a large piece of glass until I noticed the 40-watt bulb in the light. *How did I ever get my mascara on right in this light?* I mused. My bathroom in the morning was used for major face repairs, morning breath, and hair horrors. Before I finished cleaning I changed the bulbs throughout the house to 100-watts. Raising the wattage, now meant clearer vision, and clarity and probably a higher electric bill.

After cleansing the house, I called the senior center for men. My Dad was fading in so many ways. I was seeking a day facility where he could interact with other elderly men. The center didn't have a spot, but they put his name on the waiting list, saying he would get veterans preference. I had already ruled out the free senior programs at the city recreation centers. These programs were mostly attended by women. Dad was a handsome, charming man, with a nice smile, and I could just see my Mom getting jealous as these women fawned over her husband of sixty-one-years.

I had an appointment that afternoon with a fine young man. Jimmy Jr and I headed to the tuxedo shop where he was getting fitted for his prom attire. When we parked I had a flashback. This was the same tuxedo shop I worked in for a short time when I was in high school. I was very proud as he tried on the different combination of tuxedos; he was handsome, and the perfect build. I couldn't believe he chose white shoes, but they worked with his chosen ensemble.

Tae Kwon-Do class had been canceled for the weekend, so I enjoyed piddling through the night with my kids. I went to bed one satisfied woman, but sleep would not come easy. I lay awake for the longest time trying to objectively view my life from a clinical standpoint. Questions started rolling through my brain like ticker tape; *How did I get here? How did I go through so much madness, and still was able to maintain my family, and hope for a better day? Why hadn't I ever been in a straitjacket after so many game changes?* Then talking back to myself I said: "One step back, one step forward. Go back, ten more steps back. Forward two, five steps back, ten steps forward, one step back, back, back, and back. This day on Good Friday I believed my steps are ordered. Just because I am not where I expected to be in my life, didn't mean I wasn't where I was supposed to be. I have to believe, no matter the circuitous routes I've taken."

EPISODE IV: RESPONSIBILITY

One day my kids surprised me with a clean house. In doing this, they reminded me once again what my fight for them was about. And why I had taken the heat, so they wouldn't get burned; even though they could be disloyal, disrespectful, and disgusting. I knew my job was to teach them to live with fire, but not be consumed. They would have to learn so much more as they matured.

So it was with the kids walking down the street. They all ran over "Hey Ms. Gwen!" and gave me the best hugs. These times with my neighborhood kids were always special. Sometimes, my borders as a parent were so inclusive that my responsibility flowed out into the street. My house was the Kool-Aid House; a place to get, and give hugs, get an orange, apple or a peanut butter sandwich. When I would invite the kids in, normally my sons would roll their eyes, or go outside, because they knew we were about to have some conversation. We talked about school, what was going on at home, even the martial arts. I told them all one day I would like them all to be in my class.

Thank **GOD**, I was not the only parent extending their wisdom to kids not their own. Mr. and Mrs. Green were just those parents, taking great interest in my sons' welfare, by treating him as family. Jeremy was a friend to their son Jonathan, and they would have sleepovers. Once, when Mrs. Green dropped Jeremy off, she invited us to church. She was a beautiful, energetic, hard-working young wife, and mother, and I was compelled to go.

It was truly amazing how my spirit was quickened on that Easter Sunday before church. I prayed: *Today I am going to lay it all down to you LORD, this holy day. I feel privileged to be starting a new life on this celebrated day of your resurrection JESUS, you gave your life for mankind, when you commended your spirit unto GOD and gave up the ghost. Today GOD, I commend my spirit to you, as I give up the ghost of my past. Today, I step into a new way of doing things right, especially since I no longer have a job. I need a new brain, an organ donation, a brain transplant, even a lobotomy (SMILE), however you see fit LORD. Please just don't take me yet, my boys still need me. Ms. Charlsie stayed with us till 101, I would like to see 102. Make me over again I pray IN JESUS NAME.*

My family was blessed to share the day with such good people. Celebrating the Resurrection of Christ at church, I earnestly expected a miracle from **GOD** that day. I had asked the **LORD** for a do-over. Before leaving the church that day, one of the mothers of the church stopped me to say, "**GOD** has something for you. It's in your belly." "Yes Ma'am, I know" I said.

Determined to live my gift, I enjoyed the day. Refreshed and renewed I was ready to start my new life as a feeder and not a needer. Later before bed, I had a vision that went like this: *There was a zippered veil before me. Partially zipping it down, I stepped into my new life, but my hands were left behind. Knowing I had to get all of me in I unzipped the veil all the way. That time all of me was in my new life.* I knew **GOD** was waiting for me, and he wanted a closer relationship with me. And I wanted **GOD** to reign over my circumstances, as I stepped into my new life. At first, I couldn't figure out the significance of my hands being left behind, then I remembered that most sins I had committed were done with my hands. I had signed contracts that lead to financial devastation, and I had picked up forks and spoons that lead to my obesity. Leaving my hands behind would have meant I would probably make so many more of the same mistakes.

EPISODE V: A DAY AT THE BEAUTY SHOP

My hair was a mess the day I met Mr. Lee.

The day I met Mr. Lee, I was lost in thought, and feeling down because I had been thinking about my niece's suicide. My thoughts were rambling as I headed into the store. Then this man said, "Hi, you sure are a beautiful lady. You should come to my shop and let me do your hair." Then he gave me his card as we entered the door. I thought *Boy, this man is hitting on me hard. I ain't feeling beautiful, but my hair is a mess: I'm going.*

When I went to get my hair done a few weeks later, I got to meet Mr. Lee's wife, Ms. Mary. It was refreshing when I realized Mr. Lee was sincere and had no malice thoughts when he invited me to his shop earlier. Eventually, he and his family became *Guardian Angels* to me and was always in prayer for me and my boys. At one point I asked Mr. Lee "Why do you bless me so?" He said, "I decided to help one person this year, and I chose you as that person." Some of us are going to get lucky, but most of us are going to have to rely on blessings, grace, mercy, and favor from our ***Higher Being***.

The freshness of a new hairdo could be a major catalyst for any woman's change. I was looking forward to a special appointment one day; there was some things I wanted to talk to Mr. Lee about. He was a farmer, and I wanted to share with him my idea of a food co-op. Also, I wanted to share info I had received from a Cattle Rancher who basically told me if you got land, and water you could raise cattle. Plus, we had lots of other things to talk about; he was my friend.

A young lady I had never met prepped my hair for a perm. I asked her name, and she laughed as I pronounced it incorrectly. Then she really laughed when I told her "I don't know if I will ever call your name right because I really like calling you ***Amiracle*** because I am expecting ***A Miracle***".

When she corrected me again I said, "Oh, crazy me!"

Banish that word crazy I thought to myself when I remembered a past customer from work. While waiting on a young man one day I used the word *crazy* in our conversation. This young man sat up straight and said, "Ma'am I don't use that word. I work with the mentally ill, and there really are some people who are crazy. There really is a 10th floor." I knew what he meant and decided then I wouldn't use the word *crazy* again.

"Ouch!!!" I squealed. While combing out my hair ***Amiracle*** hit a knot, apologizing, she thought she hurt me. "It's okay, I know it's rough" I said as I laughed.

You get so much information at the beauty shop. One woman talked about how her husband didn't like her afro, and had told her to get a perm. She said, "I like my natural hair, but I want him to like me too. I needed to do something nice for him." She then us told us about the wig she bought for her husband in the color she wanted her hair in. "I gotta stay married y'all" she said. Then another woman clapped back, "My husband don't like my natural hair either. What's wrong with Black men?" I laughed, thinking to myself, *Ladies, I respect what you are saying, but I'm siding with the husbands. I'm getting my perm today*.

Mr. Lee was a great hair stylist; I think he touched every strand of my hair when he permed it. Mr. Lee and I had had many talks about me converting to natural hair, and my strutting a new color. And I would always reply, "Mr. Lee, when I get tired of combing my hair, I will go natural."

I had never seen anyone roller set my hair as fast as Mr. Lee. There must have been a million rollers in my head as he ushered me to the dryer. Counting down, I knew for sure I still had at least an hour left at the beauty shop. My phone rang and it was my Mother. "Can't talk, under the dryer" I told her. Truth was I didn't want to talk to her because I wasn't ready to talk to her: I had yet to tell her about quitting my job. I couldn't bear just yet what I thought would be scathing questions about my decision. I didn't think I could fully explain what I felt, but I would be able to say *I am so glad this is behind me*. It was so hot under the dryer, my hair was drying, but I was sweating, having a hot flash. I needed a fan.

When Mrs. Joyce walked in I had to remind her who I was. She hadn't seen me in a long time. Her sister Michelle was the friend I was with when I met my first love at nineteen. It was good to see her.

Only at the beauty shop.

I was glad when Mr. Lee took out the last roller. My hair was beautiful, and I was proud of my salt and pepper streak that lined up like a skunk streak. This was my legacy from my Mother. When a young lady told me once "You should get your hair dyed" I replied,

"You should keep saying good morning, just keep getting older." I had no shame in the colors **GOD** had chosen for my hair from his palette of many colors.

EPISODE VI: EARTH DAY

The emphasis for April 22nd, 2014 was recycling. It was Earth Day.

On the way to my parents, I stopped by to say hi to my friend Larry. It was always nice when Larry and I crossed paths. He was a great inspiration, and he always had a good word for everyone. When we were younger he was shot, paralyzed, and unable to ever walk again. This did not stop him; maneuvering his wheelchair like a race car, he also drove a Cadillac. I was proud of Larry; he had taken what was left from a tragedy, and made a good life for himself, and others.

When I got to my parents, Mom, Dad, and my nephew were having dinner, so I stayed awhile. After dinner, I followed Dad when he headed outside. When Dad would get lost in himself he would piddle around in their yard. He had unknowingly created a fascinating moat around the front yard. And that evening I finally figured out how the moat must have come about.

Standing next to Dad, I watched as he pulled grass from the edges of the yard. Then, as if in one motion, he would fling any grass he pulled into the middle of the yard where he was working. Then he would repeat the process till he tired. Almost daily, Dad worked in his front yard. Over time the dugout area around the perimeter of the yard never grew back, but the grassy areas of the yard grew very high and evenly. And my parent's yard looked like a planned landscape portrait.

The grass had grown about five inches higher than the concrete. One day I ran across a picture where all the grass had been flush with the concrete drive. This day though I wondered, *What would it take to make their yard like it once was? I'm sure a bulldozer*. It was a fact that there would be no recycling there at the Bradford household in their front yard.

Back in the house, Mom told me about their doctor's visit. She was shown x-rays of the spots on Dads' brain. The doctor explained his fading memory in terms of Dementia, and early Alzheimer's. There would be no turning back time, no meds to reverse what had started some time ago. I was very sad there was nothing I could do except forever love both of them, and I wondered, *Were we blind and just didn't want to recognize what was going on? Was there something we could have done sooner that would have made a difference?*

My heart was breaking for my parents, but for different reasons: My Mom was losing her best friend, and my Dad was forgetting she was his best friend. I loved them so much. They were two wonderful examples of growing old gracefully at eighty, and seventy-seven-years old and they shared sixty-one-years of marriage. I did get Mom to laugh when I told her, "I'd have to live to be one-hundred and one for a man to love me like that."

EPISODE VII: THIS IS MY LIFE

My morning school day ritual sounded like a broken record each morning. "Jimmy, Josh, Jaleen, Jeremy, it's time to get up". This day, however, things were different. Once my kids were gone to school, the silence of my house sent a lonely echo of things past. The eerie quiet was unnerving when I realized I had no job to go to, and no man to run to. I was left alone with *Me, Myself, and I.*

Jimmy Jr's graduation was great, and I cried as I lightly patted myself on the back. I was proud of my son but still was unable to be truly happy about his decision to be a Marine. I was consoled somewhat with the fact that as an Eagle Scout he would have an upgrade in his rank upon entry. As the weeks passed I became very unhappy, even angry at the fact Jimmy Jr had lead me on about his intent to complete his Eagle Scout requirements. His eighteenth birthday came in June, and it was over, he had reached the deadline for completing his Eagle Scout rank. He would forever be a Life Scout, and I was upset that the years, time, and money spent on the goal of reaching Eagle Scout seemed to have gone down the drain.

When the Startup Prize weekend came, I was not prepared for the intensity of the competition. It didn't take long before I realized that I had gotten in on the rear end of the competition. I found out quickly that the contestants were there to win with their A-games in place. I, in turn, didn't even have a formal business plan for Can Do Enterprizes, nor did I have any real organization of my thoughts. However, I took great notes and networked my butt off. I believed that all the information I had received would one day prove invaluable. When the closing session ended I felt really lost. Even so, I thanked **GOD** that I still had dreams.

I was disappointed in Jimmy Jr for not finishing as an Eagle Scout. It didn't take long to get over what I thought was supposed to be because I refused to let my son go to the Marines knowing I was disappointed in him. As hard as I could, I kept my feelings under wraps by showering him with love and letting him know I would always support him. Jimmy Jr had been assigned to leave in August for boot camp, which meant he would spend most of the summer at home. He enrolled in a business camp, where he won second place for his business plan. I was able to share with him some of the tools I had learned at the Startup Competition. Joshua was hired as an Aide at the Recreation Center, where the twins were enrolled for summer camp.

Tae Kwon-Do had become a lifeline for me since losing my job. I was now working out in the morning and evening class, Monday, Wednesday, and Fridays, and morning class on Saturdays. Struggling through my classes, I promised myself I wouldn't quit. The truth was that the choice might not have been mines to make when Mr. B started expressing his thoughts of closing the school.

Just thinking about our school closed made me sad. I could, however, understand how after 25 years a business owner might want to pursue other avenues. Plus, for the time being I was still the only student in class, so I could see Mr. B's side. I was proud of my instructor when he finally accepted his induction into the *Martial Arts Hall of Fame*.

Since I wasn't working, one day I decided to get something started. I found myself downtown applying for a business license for a new business venture called **Miss Gwen's**, a cleaning service. There was not much I could do financially at that point, but a cleaning service would allow me a chance to make money immediately doing what I was good at. My first job was fulfilling, as I spent the day cleaning nooks, and crannies. When I finished, my clients were happy, asking that I come back a second time to complete the job. After that I never sought any other jobs, it was as though having the license was enough.

I even worked part-time with a friend to develop a position for me in his hair care company. I bowed out when I realized I didn't have the commitment needed to benefit his company.

When my friend invited me again to speak at her conference, I accepted. The topic, *Wear Your Own Shoes* intimately resonated with me. Immediately, I was reminded of my poem *CrissCrossed* about shoes that fit on the wrong feet. I spent weeks plowing through so much paper as I looked for the poem, knowing the words were very fitting for the topic chosen. It was 4:00 pm. on the day of the conference and I had almost given up on finding the poem, when I decided to look one more time. There it was, thank **GOD** because I had not prepared anything else for my segment. Walking shoes were my specific ones to talk about, with the subtitles, *Wary, weary, and worldly*. **How did she know where my life was** I wondered? Reading my poem to the audience had me really choked up, when I looked up, they were intensely listening, some with misty eyes.

Cleaning one day I found a padlock, different from any lock I had ever seen. Quickly I became obsessed with the lock. I went so far as to call a locksmith, describing the lock I had hoped I could get some information on the artifact I had found. There were no numbers on it, and the knob didn't turn, but moved from side to side, and up and down. North, south, east, or west. The locksmith must have thought I was crazy, but he tried to understand what I was saying; in the end he was no help.

When the kids came home from school, I couldn't wait to press them for information about this lock. Jaleen was the one with information. He had been walking home one day with his friend Tristan kicking dirt when he saw the lock. Excitedly, I asked him, "Do you know how to open it? He replied, "Yes, but I forgot how, but Tristan knows how". I was glad we didn't have to go find Tristan since he had come home with Jaleen. Passing the lock over to him, I watched as he opened it up. Two clicks east, one north, three south: I lost track but was fascinated when he opened it. Curious, I asked them how they knew how to open it. They said they just played around with it and got it right. Now that the mystery was solved, and I was excited to share this story with my neighbor Blue when he stopped by. I laughed so hard when I showed him the lock, and he said, "I bought one like that last week." *Where was my life going when I was so immersed on the trail of a lock?* I had to ask myself.

EPISODE VIII: THE CHASM

When I received the statement of funds from my retirement plan from my job, I was surprised.

In this retirement account after many years there wasn't even a full year's salary there. Logically I was supposed to roll these monies into an IRA for future growth, but when I looked at the peeling paint on my house, and the painted shut old windows I knew what I would do. I had been in my house for 18 years, and during this time, I had only replaced four of the nineteen windows.

My first order of business was getting current on my bills. I did not qualify for unemployment, and I had no incoming funds coming in. I could only wonder *LORD, will there ever come a time when I won't have to struggle, and my finances won't be wack?*

Once I took care of my immediate personal finances, I assembled a crew of handyman homies that I knew would take care of business. I just wanted to be able to raise my windows, open my front door, and breathe fresh air. When I pulled into my driveway I wanted to feel joy and warmth coming home, so I even had Rickey expand my driveway.

I enjoyed going from Home Depot to Lowes price checking windows, wood, and materials. In the back of my mind, I was a carpenter at heart because I always had a thing for hitting nails. When work started in my sons' room, I knew there was no going back. The front of my house was exposed for days as they replaced the windows.

Choosing my paint color turned into a great revelation. At Home Depot that day I was having trouble making a decision: There were so many beautiful combinations. Anthony, the carpenter had been very patient. I had taken a long time when he suggested, "What about this?" It was a beautiful green combination. Immediately I said, "Yes" and was astounded when the name of the darkest shade was called, *Hampton Green*. My mouth fell open, then I excitedly went through the scenario with Anthony of how this was a good sign, *Hampton Green-Gwen Hampton*. When the work on the windows was completed, and my house was painted my joy flew straight to heaven because this color was perfectly me.

While work was going on at the house, I stared connecting with elder friends at the Recreation center for their senior program. As the

205

baby of the bunch, I would enjoy great fellowship, and I even got in on piano lessons that were taught by a good friend.

I had missed Mrs. F who was a regular at the center. Her husband, Deacon F had recently passed and she had been on my mind lately. The day I stopped by her house, I had a feeling of relief when she answered the door. It was nice visiting with her as we reminisced about "Deac." I was intrigued when she told me her family had his office building up for sale.

Always the entrepreneur at heart, immediately I tallied in my head how *Can Do Enterprizes* could use this space as a home office. I told Mrs. F that I was going to see the location right then, and that I would call her later. When I got there I crept my way into the dilapidated building: It was an ugly sight. It reminded me of the first time I saw my house; the cobwebs and dirt was enough to make anybody run. I saw past it all though and saw the beauty it could be. Even eighteen years later, I still never regretted choosing the house that became my home. I could almost see Deac moving around in the building taking care of business. He ran a successful business at that spot for many years. The ceiling was caving in now, and the building was structurally damaged. I made a call to Anthony who was at my house working on the renovations. We made plans to come out the next day.

Anthony was always honest with me, and today was no exception. Standing outside, we both agreed that the building was in a good starter location; sitting there on the corner. When we went inside, not wanting to hurt my feelings, Anthony started talking about what the building could be. Then with his upfront honesty, which he knew I appreciated, he hurt my feelings as he broke down the possible cost of the major repairs needed as we went room to room. He even commented that I would do better tearing this building down, and building a new one. Discouraged somewhat, especially since I didn't have any money to buy the location, much less do repairs, I walked outside prepared to leave.

As though for the first time I saw the surrounding area. Across the way was an empty lot on a corner, I thought administrative offices and business lab for **Can Do Enterprizes**. Down the street was a huge empty building with a parking lot, I thought once renovated this would be an ideal spot for a gymnasium and an event venue. These were unexpected moments, so much so that I forgot what Anthony said. My hopes were renewed, as I saw great possibilities in the whole area.

My room was the last in the house to get windows replaced. While inspecting the window frame after the first window was put in, I could hardly contain myself when I saw the name on the wood. It read **Premium Hampton**. I was blown away at this positive sign, and I could hardly wait to show Anthony my name on the wood.

I had chosen stark white paint for the carpenters to finish off the windows.

One day when I was really tired I plunked down on my bed. Some kind of way my right hand hit the wall and connected with a nail that was protruding out from it. Now there was no reason a nail should have even been there, but of course this seemed like a good sign to me as I remembered the nail that imbedded in my left hand while in my closet on Good Friday. I wanted to believe my life was in divine order, even though I still had no plans.

Then, when they finished painting my room, I was alarmed by a panic that sweep over me. Like a crazed woman, I proceeded to tell the workers to please complete everything they had started that day because they would not be coming back. Looking at me like I was an insane woman, they tried to get me to explain what was going on. I couldn't because I didn't have an answer. On the verge of a scream, I was relieved when they left. Even though there was still some work to be done, it didn't matter, because they had to go.

I was literally depleted when the men left. I didn't even have the strength to put the pictures back on the walls of my bedroom. After that I felt like all that was missing from my life was a straitjacket because my white room became my antiseptic room. I cried so hard because I knew I had snapped. I had fallen into a pit without a way out. There was a great divide inside of me. Tore up from the floor up, I screamed at **GOD**, asking him over and over, "Why did you give me this vision?" I was so unprepared for the answer to that question because "Why did you give me this vision?" was answered with, *The vision was a premonition*.

Out of my mind, I couldn't believe what I heard: I just keep repeating *The vision was premonition*. I rationalized with myself; my job is supposed to help the masses in areas of family, fitness, and finances. But the reality was; if I had just personally followed the rules of engagement for Can Do Enterprizes then my life would have been in order. If I had just learned what I wanted to teach to others then my family, my fitness, and my finances would not have been negatively compromised on so many occasions.

Then came the answer to the question, "Why did you have me keep up with all this stuff?" *GOD has a sense of humor* was true once again when *He* gave me a funny answer, *I had to give you something to do, or you would have lost your damn mind*. I was shocked to hear the word damn, then I prayed *LORD, I think what 's happening right now is I'm losing my mind. Please help me, I can't stop crying, I'm very distressed, and totally depressed.*

My days were spent in a scary place inside my head for days. Then on July 20th at 6:00 a.m., I woke to clearer thinking. I was aware of the fact that my antiseptic room would also have to be my healing place, and fast. Within the next 30 days, not only would Jimmy Jr be leaving for boot camp, but school would be starting for everyone else. These two occasions would bring about added grief, along with more depression if I didn't act fast.

When I raised my beautiful windows later that morning, I

examined the fresh white trim of the windows, then I took in a panoramic view of my white picture less walls. I thanked **GOD** that I had not been committed to the mental ward. Champion moved quick sniffing the fresh air flowing through the open window. Meditating on the madness of my insane life, I concurred once again with myself that I had several nervous breakdowns before, but was unable to take them.

I knew I couldn't be mad at **GOD** for his guidance for my life given in the form of a premonition called, *Can Do Enterprizes.* Thirteen years of strife, hard work, tears, perseverance, obesity, begging, borrowing, even being close to stealing, was a lot. I started thinking *What if I had understood the lessons GOD had wanted me to understand? Would I have met my goals, would I have been healthy, wealthy, and wise?* Then I pondered, *How much was I supposed to go through, and how much did I put myself through.* I then surmised, *80% was my doing, 20% was GOD'S WAY. Today I want to stand as a testimony. Whatever time I am blessed with surely I can change things. I recognize that change comes fast for some, but in my case as a hard-head, many times I had a hard way to go. Today, I am a witness as I pick my face off the floor. I can't stop pushing through my pipeline to get to my breakthrough. I stand tall, and pat myself on the back. I have done some good, in spite of everything*.

It was 9:30 a.m. and I was almost dressed when I looked out my open window to see my son's father drive up. I stepped outside as he walked up the driveway. He wanted to hang out with the kids; again he had ignored my request to call ahead, so plans could be made. Deciding not to entertain him, politely I went inside to tell the boys what he wanted. The older two declined his invite, but the twins said "YES"; they were ecstatic. When I told him what they said, he said, "Well it's all of them or no one!" Shocked at what he said, I tried talking to him as though he was a rational person. I said, "You have two kids that want to be with you!" Turning away, hurt for my sons, I refused to allow him to ruin my morning, especially since I had just spent $200 on groceries. This man had no skin in this game. Before I could get inside, he asked me, "What's wrong with your hair?" I didn't even dignify him with an answer, instead, I said, "Goodbye, have a nice day." He had interrupted my dressing earlier and as an *Ode to Exes*, I intentionally hadn't comb my hair, and I didn't wear a bra when I slipped a T-shirt on.

My recovery was moving in the right direction. Getting out of my madness, I started assessing where I was, what I needed to do, and where I needed to go. Then I remembered Deacon F. Jumping in my car, I speedily made my way to his office. This really was not a place I should have been alone, but I was born fearless in so many ways; having done things that could/should have been the death of me.

Satisfied with my thoughts for the inside of the building, I then did a detailed tour of the grounds. When I got to the corner of the building, headed to my car, on the ground, there was a pair of crutches and a pair of shoes. *No More Excuses* the crutches said to me, and then the shoes spoke, *Time To Move*. I got these clear messages as I loaded the crutches, and the shoes in my car.

SEASON XIV

DIVINE

Appointments

EPISODE I: NEW PAINS/ NEW GAINS, MORE TEARS/MORE FEARS

Jimmy Jr's leave date was fast approaching.

The weekend before Jimmy Jr was scheduled to leave I was blessed with a room at the hotel. The five of us had a great time as we swam, worked out in the weight room, ate take-out, and watched TV.

The following Sunday would be my last church service with all four of my sons. Jimmy Jr had been invited to his friend's church, and in turn, he invited us. The small congregation was spirit filled. There was a mighty anointing that sweep through the place, when the Pastor made the altar call. Looking over at my four sons, unable to sit, I found my way to the front, where I gave it all to **GOD**; worshiping, praising, and thanking **Him** for all **He** had done, was doing, and would do for me. This was the first time I heard the song, *Break Every Chain*. As the songstress sang, my tears were out of control: The song expressed the depths of my desires that **GOD** would break every chain in my life. Standing there, meditating in The Spirit, I looked over, and there standing next to me was my son, Jimmy Jr. This was a monumental moment in my life. Hugging, and kissing him my heart was lightened. I gave my fears for his life to **GOD,** as I realized I had done right by this young man, and he was armed to stand as **GOD'S MAN** in this treacherous world of the enemy.

August 4th came too soon. The day had finally come, and Jimmy Jr was preparing to leave. My parents, my sons, and I rode together for his swearing-in ceremony. I was vigilant over everything that happened that day; I even got a picture of him signing his pact with the Marines through partially open blinds in a closed room. My heart was breaking. Jimmy Jr was leaving for boot camp and I was hurting all over. When he was sworn in, it became really hard to see through my tear flooded eyes. I put on the best face I could, and my emotional outburst was no surprise to Jimmy Jr. All of my boys were used to me crying, in good, and bad times. I had always tried to make sure neither of them was immersed in my inner toil, and I would fake it as best I could, believing I would someday make it.

Joshua, Jaleen and Jeremy seemed to be alright with their brother leaving. They were proud of him. My Mom was beautifully cool. Then I looked over at my Dad, and realized he was leaving us also. This made me cry more.

I didn't want to see Jimmy Jr go, but I had no choice when the new Marines loaded up in a van, and headed to the airport for their trip to South Carolina. My family had to convince me to let him go, as I was so close to following the van to the airport. No one seemed to understand. As the van disappeared from my view, I knew this would be the last time I would ever call my son Jimmy Jr. Because I had raised a man that I would forever refer to as Jimmy.

Later, I talked to my Mom about my pain. I asked her how she felt when we left home. She told me "I was alright with it. I had done my job." This was strange to me. She even explained how she couldn't understand why I had traveled all over the place for my son when he was competing. I wasn't upset by what she said, but I was shocked that I was alone with my feelings. She didn't understand, and I had no one else to talk to. I ate my feelings that day.

As much as I missed Jimmy, his brothers still required my best. But for now the tables had been turned; My sons were now consoling me with hugs and kisses, telling me it was going to be alright.

I had to get focused when school started. Things were different now. My morning routine had changed to "Joshua, Jeremy, Jaleen get up. It's time for school". This sounded so strange to me. When they left in the mornings for school I still had moments of meltdown, but I was getting stronger.

However, when the dreams started, I wasn't quite sure what to do. In the first one, I was standing outside my bedroom, about 10 feet away from the corner of my house looking up at the roof. The skies were blue, and hovering just over the edge of my bedroom was a peaceful cloud. All of a sudden out of nowhere a solid cloud that looked like a block of ice settled abruptly just atop of the calm one. I watched as the solid one lifted from the back, trajected itself toward me and like an arrow, fired at me. Moving to the left just in time, the cloud crashed to the ground into smithereens. *What did this mean?* I asked searching for an answer. Then I believed that the dream was a revelation for me to understand that *GOD* was always with me; leading and guiding me. No matter what weapons were formed against me by satan, and his agents I would be okay.

A revealing second dream helped me understand more. The morning of August 21st I had a dream. In it the skies opened as two horsemen descended toward the park. One was dressed in dark clothes on a dark horse, the other was on a white horse dressed in white. I had been walking with another woman when I saw the horses. I stopped, but she kept walking. When I went to go get her, the spirit said *No!* Then the spirit went on to say, *You are the one who need help*. When I awoke, my understanding was that satan was always along for the ride. Then, I began to understand the truth; I was always trying to help someone else, and yet I had not helped myself.

I even had a dream where I saw *THE FACE OF JESUS* when the sky cracked open. People were running everywhere confused. Earthquakes were taking place as streets opened wide, and there was flooding in some areas. I knew this must be a view of *The Rapture*. And there were weeping and gnashing of teeth. This was a terrifying dream.

When September 11th came, it wasn't until late afternoon when I called Dad to say "Happy Birthday Daddy!"

On September 17th, I had missed the call, but the message left me terror-stricken. It was Jimmy, "Mom, this is Jimmy. I am in the hospital, but I am okay." *In the hospital* was all I heard as I started to pray. Listening to the message a second time I got the information needed to call and check on my son. Jimmy's Gunnery Sergeant called assuring me my son was okay, as he used the medical term *Rhabdomyolysis.* The sergeant tried to explain to me in plain terms what this meant, but the words **Muscle injury, dehydration, and nauseousness** frightened me as he continued to talk. I was on the phone so long asking questions that the Sergeant practically had to hang up on me. As soon as Jimmy was stable, he kept in constant contact with me. He had to because he assumed I might storm the gates of the military base demanding to see the commander. I was panicked the entire time Jimmy was in the hospital. I knew what had happened; he was like a kid in a candy shop. And boot camp was his chance to showcase his bionic skills to the extremes.

Because of his length of stay in the hospital, Jimmy's platoon had advanced too far; he had to be assigned a new one, and a new graduation date was given. Everything was good at that point because Jimmy was strong, healthy and back at work. Again I told him, "You don't have to prove anything to anyone but yourself, and you should do your best.

Having sent out an **SOS** for help finding a job, I had started getting some hits. The boys helped out when they earned money working for one of the candidates during the election. Even though I knew I had to get back to work, and I was making motions in that direction, I just couldn't commit to the follow-ups. Two reasons held me back. My Dad's condition was getting worse, and my son's graduation from boot camp was approaching. Mother was there every minute for Dad; to give her some relief I would take charge of him, especially any Sunday she wanted to go to church. These times with Dad helped me to understand the saying, "Once an adult, and twice a child." My Daddy was a good man and I wanted to be available for him. When I considered Dad and Jimmy's graduation, I then put my job search on hold.

A friend can ask for anything from me, **GOD** knows I will do anything possible to help.

When Ms. Jai, my friend forever, asked if I would make a dress for her seventieth birthday party, instinctively I said "Yes". Later, after I thought about it, I wanted to renege on my word. I even made plans several times to meet with Ms. Jai to back out. But each time we got together, she would smile at me with gratitude and excitement about her finished dress, and I would recommit again to making her dress. During our twenty-year friendship, she'd never seen anything I had sewn, except the free-styled Tae Kwon-Do pants I had made for my sons and a uniform I made for Mr. B I was surprised she had such faith in my sewing skills. This proposition really had me paranoid because those pants and that uniform were the last things I had made, and that was years ago.

Though I still wanted to say no, I finally put my foot down and took her to the fabric store to get her fabric, pattern, and notions. I almost fainted when she chose lime green satin. I hadn't sewn with slippery sliding satin since high school. Paralyzed with procrastination, the weeks passed as the fabric lay sprawled on the rocker in my room, like a menacing beast about to pounce.

Then the time came when I couldn't put my task off any longer. I had one week to create a magical dress for Ms. Jai's seventieth birthday ensemble. Reprimanding myself at the first cut, I fiercely worked to make a masterpiece for my friend. On November 7th, just three hours before the party, I pressed my last seam. It was amazing, the dress fit Jai like a glove, and no one would believe she was seventy. She had a beautiful celebration with her son, six daughters, and many grands. She was very proud as the compliments rolled in. And I was proud of me for accepting, and completing the challenge.

EPISODE II: MISSION POSSIBLE

Jimmy's graduation was scheduled for the day before Thanksgiving. This was great timing because he would be home for the holidays, and his brother's birthday. I knew there was nothing that would keep me from attending his graduation. It was hard to contain my excitement as plans were made. My brother Jerry was making the trip possible, and he even intended to caravan with me on the trip. I was thankful to him for his thoughtfulness.

I had my vehicle checked out and it was cleared for travel, even though my engine light had come on. The technician told me it would be okay, but be sure to have a thorough inspection once I returned. Everyone was excited as we started our journey. The miles and the states passed, and we keep going. When we got to Atlanta GA. it was about 5:30 pm. It was getting dark, and the traffic was thick. When we missed our turn, we pulled off the interstate to check our directions. We wanted to be sure we were in sync, especially since the darkness was approaching, and we still had a long way to go. Our goal was to be sleeping in our hotel room that night.

Just as we got ready to pull out on our last stretch, my car wouldn't start. No matter what I did, I couldn't get it to start. Not one to panic, my brother helped to keep me in check. We were in a serious situation, it was the holidays, and there was no auto shop near where we were. After much discussion, my brother and I thought about a mobile mechanic. Thank *GOD*, because we were able to contact one who wasn't very far away. The diagnosis was that my alternator had gone out, but the good news was that he could fix it if we got the parts. *GOD* was on our side because across the street was AutoZone. We got the parts, and the man fixed my truck. Back on the road, somewhat frazzled, I prayed hard. My night vision was still not the best, but I mastered the journey. Over into the morning, we arrived at our destination just outside of Parris Island, South Carolina.

This trip was unlike any I had ever been on. Here I was in South Carolina preparing for my firstborn's graduation from boot camp for the Marines. It was amazing to me that Jimmy was now on his own as a grown man. And that we as a family was there to celebrate with him on his journey into adulthood.

We arrived the day before graduation so we could spend time with Jimmy on Family Day. Leaving my brother in the hotel, my sons and I traveled the short distance to Parris Island, South Carolina. It had been a long time since I had been on a military installation. My heart pounded heavily, and my breath was short as we waited for my son to be released for a short leave. I didn't know what to expect, he had been gone for over three months. Then he appeared, and I was able to calm down. He looked great; strong and happy. I was impressed at how much he had matured, but also how he was pretty much the same. Jimmy took us on a tour of the base. He then took us to the basketball court where he and his brothers got reacquainted, as brothers do. The brotherhood between my sons was beautiful. It was chilly so I sat in the truck. Watching my boys, I began to understand the magnitude of what was going on. It wouldn't be long before all my sons would be off doing their own things as men.

Hanging out in the truck, I took the time to read the newspapers I'd brought from home. Catching up on the news, I read the tragic story of a Texas family of eight headed to Disney World in Florida for a holiday of fun. Both parents, sibling's age four, seven, and fifteen did not make it out of Louisiana. They were killed in a terrible automobile accident. The news report stated that on the night of the accident, the sixteen-year-old son fell asleep at the wheel. Snapping awake, he overcorrected which caused the vehicle to roll over. It was so sad that none of the deceased had a seatbelt on, but the driver did. My prayers for this family were unending. ***Only an act of GOD would allow this kid to have a normal life***, I thought. I could only cry when I looked out at my sons laughing and joking with each other on the court. Then, I was embraced in a moment of fear when I thought about our fourteen-hour trip ahead with four teenagers, my brother and me.

It was raining extremely hard on Graduation Day, but we are on schedule to be on time for graduation. Finally finding a parking spot, we began our wait outside with the other anxious families. By the time we got inside, everyone was wet, but no one seemed to mine because like me, they were there to support their Marine, and take them away. When the platoons filed in, the only way we had to recognize Jimmy was to identify his platoon. All these young people looked alike. We had chosen great seats because Jimmy's platoon was stationed right in front of us. It was an awesome, sobering ceremony. So much of what was going on I didn't understand. I was just a proud Momma waiting for it all to be over so I could salute my son, and once again tell him how proud I was of him. He was continuing a family tradition. My father was an Army veteran, and my brother Terry had been a Marine vet.

When Jimmy was in the hospital he must have taken a super motivational drug because he was identified among a very few. He was chosen the Ironman of his platoon. And he became a Squad Leader, and was meritoriously promoted to Private First Class. Then he was even inducted into the elite 300 Club as an all-around recruit with 595 out of 600 points earned. His Drill Sergeant said to me, "Your son was my best recruit", then he told my son "You will do good. Keep up the good work". Jimmy had done what he intended to do; become a Beast at boot camp. I knew he would excel going forward, even as a Life Scout, because Boy Scouts and Tae Kwon-Do had served him well. A part of me felt like he was saying; See Mom, I got this.

During boot camp, my son had not driven, but during the trip back I let him help me drive. Being chauffeured once again by

Jimmy was nice. I was looking forward to the ten days he would have at home with the family.

Thanksgiving Day was on November 27th and I had so much to be thankful for. The family gangs all showed up at my parents' house, and we all attended church service that morning. Then Mom hosted dinner, while Dad smiled and he enjoyed his family. We also enjoyed a birthday cake; Jeremy and Jaleen's birthday was the next day.

I enjoyed the ten days with Jimmy, but they went so fast. I was tasked with the responsibility of getting him where he needed to be on his next leg of his journey. On December 8th, at 5:00 a.m. I took my son to the bus station and I stayed until the bus pulled out of the terminal. Jimmy had a thirty-hour bus ride to Raleigh, North Carolina where he would complete his training before being dispatched to his duty station in Twenty-nine Palms, California. On the way home I cried and cried some more. I would miss this guy; not knowing when I would see him again. The Marines were looking for a few good men, and I had sent them a good man. My day was spent texting back and forth with Jimmy until he arrived at the base. I thanked **GOD** for ***His Road Angels*** blessing the road, and the bus driver.

EPISODE III: GIFTS!!! FOR ME?

I was dreaming about what my home could look like as I rifled through the Christmas ads from a furniture store. There was an array of beautiful chairs. One particularly awesome one called the *Gwendolyn Glider* caught my attention. I wanted that chair, but I didn't have the funds to purchase it.

One morning just enjoying the scenery on my way home, I spotted a beautiful hardwood chair on the side of the road amongst some other thrown away items. This was a low, wide chair that evoked my memory of the *Gwendolyn Glider*. I made a block in the truck before going home to see if the chair was still there. It was, so I lifted my hatch and put *The Gwendolyn Throne* in my trunk. When I got home I cleaned and disinfected it, exclaiming "Ain't **GOD** amazing, ain't **GOD** good" as I found the perfect spot for the chair.

Two weeks later a friend asked me to drop him off at work. Across from where he was working was two chairs by the side of the road. I got excited as I remembered *The Gwendolyn Throne*. There was a man outside the house where the chairs were. I stopped and asked if I could have one of the chairs. He said, "Yes, my Mom was hoping someone who cared would get it". I told him how much I loved the chair, and asked him to please tell his Mother that someone who cared had gotten her beautiful chair. This low wide chair I called *The Queen's Throne*. When I got home, I cleaned and disinfected it, exclaiming again "Ain't **GOD** amazing, ain't **GOD** good" as I found the right spot for the chair. Now I had two vintage chairs that were even more beautiful than the *Gwendolyn Glider*. I claimed them as my birthday gifts from **The King**. I even tried to figure out how to prototype the chairs into new age rocking chairs for grown folks.

December 16, 2014, was my birthday and I was fifty-five-years-old. Five was the number of balance and **GOD'S GRACE, GOODNESS AND FAVOR**. Also, to **GOD**, five was important to man, his creation, when he gave us digits on our hands, five senses, and five toes.

Ready to get back to work, I accepted a part-time position at the Legacy Senior Day Center. The clients there were mostly elderly adults needing care while their family members worked; they did, however, care for babies as a multi-generational agency. It was a humbling experience to work with elderly persons with limited mobility and Alzheimer's degeneration. It was a blessing to watch their eyes light up when their families picked them up in the evening. I was sure working there would give me additional insight into how to best help my Father during his transition. By now he was getting physically weak and in need of a more vigilant watch.

It was a beautiful day when I picked my sons up from the park. They had just completed a fifteen-mile bike ride as a requirement for the fulfillment of their biking merit badge for Boy Scouts. Headed home, I decided to stop at the nearby grocery store for a quick in and out for dinner. At the register I asked the cashier where the raisins were, as she directed me I headed to the back. On my way back, near the counter I tripped on a raised grease cap on the floor. My quick trip to the store then became a quick trip to the Manager's office to file an incident report. I didn't need 911 emergency; but I was hurt.

Starting treatments at the Chiropractor, I found myself torn about continuing in TKD. Though I was not ready to give up yet, I realized that I had actually quit in my mind. I felt terrible because I was making a dishonorable split from a life that was good for me, and I was not being honest with the man who had made a monumental difference in the life of my family. Also, it was getting hard to face Mr. B; I knew I was a changed woman toward Tae Kwon-Do, and I should have been mature enough to discuss the matter with my instructor.

Class was fraught with frustration for me one day, when I walked out the door, I never imagined it would be my last. Realizing I had left my engraved Black Belt in the locker that day, I was too embarrassed to go back and get it. I didn't think Mr. B would ever understand what I was going through, and I was sure he considered me a quitter and a coward, and by my actions, that was what I felt like. My actions were not honorable, and I knew I was disrespecting the Black Belt that I have worked so hard to earn. Totally losing my zeal, I never returned.

Therapy at the Chiropractor was no replacement for working out, but I was having some mental relief. Dr. Mike insisted I lose weight, get active, drink more water, and get some fresh air by walking. During one visit he even told me he felt a blood clot forming. It didn't occur to me that this might be what was happening when I started experiencing unusual leg sensations that at times were painful. I attributed what was going on with my legs to the fact I had stopped working out, and my body was rejecting that fact. Also, I believed I was carrying too much weight. I decided to heed Dr. Mike's suggestion by drinking more water and walking Champion.

Gwendolyn Hampton

SEASON XV

GAME CHANGERS

EPISODE I: FRESH START 2015

I can think of many fun, and exciting ways to celebrate the New Year, parties, fireworks, and streamers.

It's never a good thing when the New Year start off with car problems. My explorer aka *Tae* was sick. She needed a transmission, which would cost $2000. Since Jimmy left I had parked *Taz*, but a call to the mechanic meant I had to get tires fixed, oil changed, and battery charged to get her roadworthy. I thanked *GOD* for two cars because I didn't have to be a nuisance to anyone.

On January 4th at 12:00 a.m. I started the best day of my life. My head was clear, and my aim was direct when I got the impetus to put the pictures back up on my bedroom walls. It had been six months since I had taken them down. I had been living in my antiseptic room, but the day had come and I was giving up that way of life. Push pins worked as I hung my pictures back up on the wall. I was very thankful to be out of my dark place again... I even told satan loudly, "You have no place at 146!"

I was again invited to be a presenter for the women's conference on January 24th. Engaging the kids with self-defense tactics was a great enjoyment for me. The kids must have enjoyed me as well because I was back for the third year. My kids declined again this year, which was okay because I had established a good rapport with the young people. Earlier, I had attended a sheriff sponsored self-defense class where I received some very good literature that I used as handouts.

On January 27th, *Taz* was running like a super machine as I headed to work my first day. I had gotten a job as an After School Instructor for the City of Shreveport. Even though I needed full-time work, I accepted a part-time position. I had been advised that everyone started part-time, but to hold on, and chance would present itself for a full-time position. Ready for a change, I imagined how much fun the kids would be. Even thinking I might be in a position to institute the principles of **Can Do Enterprizes** into the program curriculum. Things were looking up when I ended my first day on the job.

The news was horrible on January 31st when I read about a seven-year-old girl who had been hit by a drunken driver while waiting to cross a busy street on her bicycle. The child was critically injured. Her address was listed as one that was a block from my house. I couldn't help but think; ***This little girl would have passed by my house on her journey.*** Pictures of her pretty face were all over the news. And as hard as I tried, I couldn't remember her: I thought I knew all the neighborhood kids.

On February 1st, the little girl died. I was sad as I prayed for her family. There was a memorial set up at the spot where she was hit. Tears filled my eyes each time I passed there. When the news came out as to the identity of the driver, I recognized him, this time praying for his family. I didn't personally know this man, but I had waited on him several times at the DMV. He seemed to be a jovial guy, and we had shared some laughs together. I couldn't imagine him sobering up in jail to the reality of what he had done, and the turn his life was about to take.

Days passed, and I still couldn't recognize this baby. One-day standing outside, watching the middle schoolers embark off the bus, I saw two brothers I hadn't seen in a while. I called them over to speak, and ask them how was things. I was floored when they went on to tell me about the death of their little sister, the same seven-year-old that was killed. My heart sank. Knowing it was just so much I could ask these brothers, as not to intrude on their grief, I went inside to get my favorite ladybug wind chime. I told them to give it to their Mother as a remembrance of their sister from me. Hugging them tightly, I told them how much I loved them. I wanted to follow them home to offer my sympathy, but I held my peace, not wanting to intrude on their Mother's grief.

EPISODE II: FEBRUARY SADNESS

I was at the doctor's office with my parents for Dad's appointment on January 29th.

Dad had gotten very weak. Mom complained to the doctor that he wasn't eating or drinking water, and expressed her concern at how thin he had gotten. His diagnosis was Advanced Dementia and Alzheimer's. The Doctor explained that these patients normally forgot to eat and swallow. We got a prescription for appetite meds to increase his food consumption. Also, we were encouraged to get him some Ensure immediately after leaving. Mom and I were hurting, and we didn't have much conversation afterward. We just knew there was work ahead and I knew my mother would work tirelessly taking care of my father.

Dad had literally become skin and bones, and was practically bed-ridden. He never showed any pain except when we touched him to turn him over. I had made it a priority to stop by and help before and after work. As heartbreaking as it was to watch Dad's decline, I took every opportunity to massage his body and straighten his body out from its fetal position. His hands would lock up into a ball, so I would work to straighten his fingers out, as well as elongating his legs. I just couldn't bear the thought of letting him go. Mom had scheduled his next appointment, but when he started throwing up massive amounts of mucus discharge she called the doctor again. The doctor told her to check him into the emergency room on the following Monday and he would see him once he was admitted.

Lying next to my Dad, on Saturday, February the 7th I could have sworn he was taking his last breath. I could barely feel his heartbeat.

Scared, I screamed for Mom to come to his bedside because I didn't want her to miss Dad's transition. More than anything I wanted her to be able to say goodbye to the man she loved for over sixty-one-years. This was a beautiful moment because Dad was in no pain. Finally coming in, I told Mom what was happening. I told her not to fret with trying to get him to the doctor right now for help. Agreeing with me, she laid down next to her husband. We both showed him how much we loved him, and I keep repeating "Daddy" while Momma called him "Wilson". The two of us shared words of comfort about seeing *JESUS*, Big Momma, Mul. Kenny, Terry, Bo, Elbert, Sherrie…all the family who had gone to Heaven already.

Then, *GOD* had other plans as He spoke to me. The directions given left me confused, and all I could say was, "WHAT?" Spiritually, I knew *GOD* worked in mysterious ways and would step into situations as he deemed fit. Afraid, and astonished, I obediently began to massage my Dad. I told him we were going to stretch out and walk. When I got Dad to sit up comfortably, the spirit then instructed me to get him out of the bed. I did that by swiveling his legs out of the bed then I lifted him to a standing position. I told Mom that we were going to the kitchen. As surprised as she was by what was taking place she went to get his house shoes: She didn't want him to walk on the cold floor. This was funny to me, but I didn't laugh because I felt we were in the midst of a miracle, and time was of the essence. Daddy already had on socks so I told her, "No, not now, we're going to the kitchen", as Dad and I started for the hallway. It was so touching when he asked Mom a question. I didn't understand what he said, but I was sure she did.

Looking like Frankenstein, Dad was slipping and sliding with splayed legs as we made our way to the kitchen. Dad sat up in a chair with a dazed look on his face as I continued to massage and stretch his limbs, whispering "Breathe Daddy, inhale, exhale" the whole time. I was amazed when he had a moment of clarity. His eyes bucked wide open in recognition of himself while he smiled at me. He came back to consciousness just long enough to sit there and drink a little water with me. We made it back down the hallway to his bed, returning him to the loving care of his wife I was still whispering, "Breathe Daddy, inhale, exhale". Again, I was blessed to pray for my parents.

I had just witnessed a beautiful, breathtaking phenomenon. When I left I started feeling depleted and nauseous, with strange thoughts and memories crossing my mind. I thought about smoking a cigarette, but just the thought made me want to puke, and I got a sick feeling all over my body when I thought about all the times my Dad had tried to quit smoking. Now, Dad had only stopped smoking because he couldn't smoke any longer.

Then I thought about when Joshua was a baby, and I was weaning him off the pacifier. One Sunday at church we went to the altar for prayer, and Joshua threw his pacifier onto the altar. Surprised when he didn't cry I said, "Thank you *LORD*." Seconds later, back at our seat someone tapped me on the shoulder, saying "You lost this" giving me his pacifier. He grabbed it fast as I wanted to scream. Not many days later, I put my husband out of the house for the night. I wasn't ready for a divorce yet so I thought it best he didn't' see me take Joshua's pacifier for the last time because it was going to be a scene. My baby cried all night long, but by morning break, he never cried for that pacifier; never.

Then an unusual thought came as I pondered the story of the woman who touched *THE HEM OF JESUS'S ROBE* as he passed by. He didn't see her, but he felt the virtue flow from his body. I imagined with a hope that these ill feelings I was having could be some equivalent measure of lost virtue, though I was sure what *JESUS* felt was totally different in his pureness. To even consider any level of parallel with *JESUS* was an honor. I felt as if I'd come face to face with *GOD* earlier, and the devil didn't have anything to do with it. It was all positive, even the weird feel in my tummy. I even saw a beautiful sight of *JESUS* raising Lazarus from the dead, sure that event was much more eloquent than the drama that had just unfolded.

My mechanic called me three times very early on February 8th to bring *Taz* by so he could check a noise out. This was unusual, but I made tracks as I thought about Dad. I was full of excitement to see Daddy, believing a full miracle had continued into the night. When I opened the door I expected to see my parents at the table eating breakfast and sharing a cup of coffee. My Dad had not slipped away overnight. That morning he was laying in the bed, more alert, and complaining to Mom his leg hurt. Tickled at the irony of this situation I said to my mother, "Yes I did manipulate them. He hadn't been moving his joints laying down in a fetal position. So yes, he was going to hurt." And yes, my plans were to do the same thing again. Helping him to sit up on the side of the bed, Dad stretched his legs out off the floor, and he looked strong. A friend of his stopped by to see him, smiling Dad told him he hadn't been fishing. He even drank some coffee in the kitchen. This time he walked, leaning on his cane.

My legs were in pain, and Mom had been complaining about problems with her sciatic nerve. I thought maybe this could be my problem, but my symptoms were different. Both my legs hurt. The pain was something like what I would imagine Restless Leg Syndrome would feel like only more intensified. "*FATHER* anoint my prayers *IN JESUS NAME*. Take away this pain" I prayed. Flashing back to what Dr. Mike told me about blood clots forming, I began focusing on what I would do to lose the extra weight. This was my major problem I told myself. Also, I recommitted to take my blood pressure medicine consistently.

No matter what had happened over the weekend, Mom was insistent that we take Dad in to see the doctor on February 9th. When we pulled into the emergency room drive at the Veterans Hospital there was a man standing outside taking a break. I told him what the doctor had said about Dad being admitted to the emergency room. I explained Dad's weak condition, and how he would be unable to sit out in the waiting room. Unemotionally this man said, "Ma'am today is Monday, and the emergency room is full. You would do better taking him to LSU and let them airlift him back over here", as he turned his back to finish his break. Close to saying *Are you crazy?* to the man, I just stood there shocked as I peered into the backset to tell Mom what he said. I have a good **GOD**; within a few minutes this same man went inside and returned with a wheelchair for my Dad. He rolled him into an exam room, not even stopping at the admissions desk. It was amazing how smoothly everything went from that point. Dad was admitted to the VA hospital, which was within walking distance from my house, where he got preferential care.

On February 10th I met a man at the store who gave me a piece of paper with the words, ***GOD CAN, GOD CAN, GOD CAN***. These words were so true. When I went to visit Dad later, I was told that he'd sat up and also eaten. He'd even entertained a visit from my aunt Mary, his sister. ***GOD CAN, GOD CAN, GOD CAN***.

In January, I'd received a letter from the lawyer in reference to my fall at the store months earlier. He stated his office would be declining me as a client because they did not feel there was sufficient evidence that would ensure a win for them. I had accumulated bills from the chiropractor, and there was no way he wasn't going to be paid. Not only was he my doctor, but he was a very good friend. It became my mission to follow-up with this store. It turned out my paperwork had not gotten to the proper person who then contacted me. She informed me that her company was sorry for the incident, they had replaced the grease cover, and they would pay my doctor bills, and compensate me for the inconvenience.

At the hospital one day while visiting Dad, I called Dr. Mike excited because the check for his services had come in. He was very thankful to be paid. I shared with him about my new job, and the planned physical activities I was doing. He told me, "Wow, do something!" "*GOD CAN, GOD CAN, GOD CAN*," I said. Having shared my vision for **Can Do Enterprizes** with him on numerous occasions, I was not surprised when he asked me to share my vision with him in one sentence on the phone. Taking a moment, I said, "To see families come together as a unit working together in unity; spiritually, financially, and physically, combating challenges together. Everyone would have a part in the success of the family".

Dad was awake early on February 11th, and we talked on the phone. On February 13th, Dad rested, but he was getting weaker. "Happy Valentine's Day" was what the volunteers said as they entered Dad's room on the 14th. The little soldier on the greeting card was cute, but Dad didn't pay any attention. He had gotten much weaker; back to a very quiet state again.

I hadn't long left the hospital on February 16th when I received the text from my brother that dad was gone. Rushing back to the hospital, on the verge of a breakdown, I was pleasantly surprised when I arrived. From the first time Dad became bedridden at home, I spent time straightening, and stretching him from a fetal position, also making sure to un-ball his clenched fists. I had continued to do this in the hospital as he was reverting back to his fetal position.

This day I was happy and smiling looking down at my father. When my Daddy left this world, he was peaceful, and his crooked smile (I think he had a slight stroke when he was in the military) was upturned to a slight smirk. Dad was almost laying down straight in his bed with his hands open by his side. I could see he tried to straighten out, but he was just too weak. I felt consoled, believing Dad had left me a message of hope, and strength in his passing. His peace had transcended into a relaxed state, I felt was just for me. This was such an endearing sight because it took away most of my pain. And the *Angel Wing* I gained that day were the biggest ever. My sons took the news pretty hard. For their lifetime, my Father had been the constant man in their life.

February 18th, would have been my grandmother Ms. Charlsie's birthday. She loved my father as a son. I bet the whole family ran smiling when they looked across the way in Heaven and saw my Daddy grinning.

February 22nd, was Mr. B's birthday. I sent a birthday wish out to him in the wind praying *Please forgive me for the way I stopped Tae Kwon-Do, I was wrong. If I could have a redo, I never would have left your tutelage. GODBLESS Always.*

We were looking forward to saying our goodbyes to Daddy on February 23rd, but funeral services were postponed because of snow. Checking the forecast, we all prayed that within the next few days we could lay Dad to rest.

The sun came out on February 26th and there was no rain expected the next day. We had a nice family hour the next evening, and Dad looked as dapper as always. It was still hard for me to believe he was gone. Tears came when one of my classmates came up to read a proclamation in Dad's honor. I was so touched they cared, even though I had not really been a part of our alumni group.

It was a good day to say goodbye to my father on February 27th, though satan was up working early that morning. *Tae*, my explorer was still down, in need of a transmission, so the boys and I drove *Taz*. On the way to my parent's house, my car started making very loud noises. Initially I thought I had blown a tire, but I wrong. Refusing to get upset, the boys and I prayed as we made our way down the interstate. Making it to the house, I called my mechanic. *Taz* needed wheel bearings. *GODBLESS this man* I prayed, he was going to fix the problem while we were at the funeral.

While waiting on the family car, I went through one of my dad's drawers. He always kept a handkerchief, and I knew this was the perfect time. Collecting an assortment of Dad's best, and silkiest

233

handkerchiefs, I passed them out to the ladies of the family. They would need them, and it was a good memento. After the funeral service we came out into the cold. They had loaded Dad into a drop top limo, I was all smiles as I thought, **Goodbye my hero, this car is so fitting for an OG-old gangster like you.** He was a good gangster though, one that took care of his wife, made a home for his kids, worked hard for everyone's good. I was proud of his legacy, and hoped to live the better life he had prayed for me.

satan was still busy throughout the day. The Veterans cemetery had been backed up since the snow. Once they started burying again, every service thereafter was on strict timelines. Before we left the church, we found out that the limousine with our family in it needed air in its tire. "Why hadn't they checked this before, especially since we had a long way to go in a short time" I asked of no one in particular. Thank **GOD**, after a phone call, we were given a few more minutes.

I had never been to an actual military funeral. It was an impressive affair as the horn played *Taps*. I was close to losing it, until the folding of the flag from the coffin. This was a ceremony in itself. When the officer passed the flag to Mom I saw the tears in his eye. He was emotional, and I knew this was not for show. Even though he didn't know my Dad I sensed the comradery of military brothers. **Bless this man, LORD!** I prayed silently. Then they loaded the coffin into the convertible drop top hearse, what a sight. "**LORD**, bless our traveler" I whispered. Then I sang to myself as they drove away, "Diamond in the back, sunroof top, digging in the scene with the gangster lean, Ohho..." The man of my life had moved on to glory.

Our family gathering later was a celebration as everyone enjoyed each other. We all knew Daddy loved a great family get together.

Later, Mom gave me a couple of the house plants from the funeral service. I was afraid I might kill them, because I didn't have a green thumb, but I was willing to take the chance. I also got Dad's shoes he worked outside in, they were beat up, but were almost a perfect fit for my big feet. I wanted to walk in my Daddy's shoes. When I passed the Veteran's Hospital later it occurred to me that my Dad never returned home after he was admitted.

EPISODE III: NATURE OF THE BEAST

I was truly blessed at work. During my time of grief, I had been allowed to take necessary time for my family, without my job being jeopardized.

My legs were feeling better, as though sludge had left them. So much had already happened in this New Year. Jimmy had completed his training in North Carolina, and was now in Twenty-Nine Palms, California. If I had been a superstitious Christian, I would have been very mad at the Marines for putting my son on a flight on Friday the 13th. This old wives' tale about Friday the 13th being a day of bad luck had some of my friends out of sorts.

Putting every weight aside, I was very excited to be putting in full time hours at the recreation center. April 3rd-10th, schools was out for spring break, this meant I would be working full-time during spring camp. This would be the first time I had ever worked with a mass group of kids, over a hundred of them. I was sure I would be a positive influence in their lives.

There were campers, and more campers everywhere, boys and girls, ages six to seventeen. Things were going well initially as everyone was on their best behavior. By the middle of the week, some kid's personalities had changed, and I witnessed nastiness, meanness, and a disrespect I couldn't have imagined was so prevalent among our kids. Even as a Mother of four rowdy boys, I had never directly felt such a slap of dishonor from our future generation as I had from just this one week. I convinced myself this couldn't be real until I polled several teachers, and friends that worked with kids. They reassured me that this was how so many children acted. Not to be discouraged, I thought, ***This was just a week of Spring break. Surely during summer camp things will be different. I will do my part to effect change.*** It was a pleasure getting back to my small group of after-schoolers once spring break was over. We had established a respectful rapport with each other.

When D stopped by on tax day, April 15th, he told me he had been by several times, but kept missing me. I was really glad to see him, we had been friends for over ten years, and he'd never stopped expressing his desire to be closer to me.

When I first met this man, he was having some serious baby momma dramas behind his two daughters. And now here he was sharing his woes as a father because he was having baby dramas. His teenage daughter was a loose cannon, and he was having trouble disciplining her. This was hard on him because he didn't have a solution.

Many times over the years D would appear just when I needed help. This time, after a couple of weeks, we were spending a lot of time together. I started thinking that maybe I just hadn't given him a chance over the years. Shaking myself from all preconceived notions, I started dating D. It had been forever since a man treated me with such compassion, I knew he loved me, and I wanted to love him. I was pleasantly surprised that I could still feel shy, and coetish around a man.

One morning, just past midnight, D showed up at my door with a cute puppy named Jackson. He had rescued this dog from an abusive situation and thought my family would be a good fit. The puppy was a Goldador, a mix of Golden retriever and a Labrador. And he looked like Champion's little brother, even though Champ was a German Shepherd/Chow mix, and they were the same color. My friend apparently meant for him to stay, because he brought food and a kennel. Later that morning, it was puppy love at first sight. My sons were overjoyed playing with Jackson, asking over, and over again "Can we keep him?" With their kennels side by side in the house, the dogs were really enjoying each other, and I was almost convinced that we would keep Jackson. A couple of days passed, when I had an inkling to research the features of a Goldador. Looking at the picture I knew I couldn't keep him. This dog would grow tall with gangly legs. I didn't have the room or inclination for two big dogs. I told my friend what I had decided, and agreed to help find Jackson a good home.

Jordan, my neighbor was five. When I saw him walking down the street without his dog Misty, I called him over. Surprised when he told me Misty had died, I immediately asked him if he wanted another dog. "Yes" couldn't come out of his mouth quick enough. I let him see Jackson, and a bond was formed. I told Jordan to ask his Grandmother, if he could have a dog. A short time later his grandmother came down with Jordan. My heart warmed, and I knew this was divine when she said, "He wants a dog so bad, and this little five-year old boy has been on the internet trying to find him a dog." And so it was a perfect match as Jackson crossed the street to his new home with Jordan, and his Grandmother. Turned out Jackson brought much joy into the life of the Grandmother.

Having good friends was a great asset, but when you could be a good friend this was a true blessing. Being a friend even required quick thinking sometimes. My friend B called with an emergency. She was a new Mom raising her granddaughter. I thanked **GOD** for the Grandparent's that stepped in to raise their grandchildren, whose parents were absent or even deceased. B said, "Amari has a singing recital coming up, and she needs a dress". Both of our funds were low, so we explored ideas on how to get the dress.

The next day standing outside, I saw this guy named T-shirt coming down the street. He was the hustler in the neighborhood; he might come down the street with anything, you just never knew. People would give him their salvages, never anything new. Sometimes if I had a few extra dollars I would just buy something from him, especially since he was a veteran dealing with some mental issues. This day there he was with some old clothes in a bag. Since I had some free time, I entertained him by going through the bag. Most of the items were for a girl, so I politely told him no thanks. He knew I had boys. As he headed down the street I called him back, remembering my mission to help find a dress for Amari. I asked him to let me see the clothes again. There, in this bag was a beautiful satiny dress that would be perfect for Amari's recital. Giving him the few dollars I had in my wallet, I went inside to call my friend. The dress was perfect, right size, right style, and Amari even had the perfect accessories to match. I wasn't able to attend Amari's recital, but her Grandmother told be how beautiful she looked, and that she was very proud of her and thankful for me. Again **GOD** showed up on our behalf.

You can't help who you love. D and I had been kicking it strong, and he was a tremendous help to me spiritually, and lately financially. When my water heater went out, he took me to the store, purchased, delivered, and set it up a new one within a few hours. Our relationship was refreshing, but it didn't seem like we were destined to be a couple. Though we spent intimate times together, our conversations became strained as we looked for words to say to each other. As we drifted apart, I knew I was losing a very good friend again. I prayed for forgiveness for any wrongs I had done to my friend. I now understood how dynamics could change a friendship; some things were better left alone. When my *Grown Woman Crush* called and asked me to dinner I said "Yes". Whatever my heart knew, I had to find out. I still cared and still had a lingering hope for us. Reality set in: ***We were not destined to be a couple.***

EPISODE IV: PLEASE PRAY FOR ME

Holding out hope that I would get hired full-time on my job, I held my position.

Summer camp was fast approaching, which meant I would be working full-time for the next few months while school was out. On May 22nd I applied, then interviewed for a position at another center. Our new Mayoral administration had issued a freeze on city hiring which meant the job was in limbo. Everyone told me this was normal, and things would get back to normal soon. Still not discouraged, I determined that my *ain'ts* would not determine the *can'ts* in my life.

June 1st, was the first day of summer camp. The signs of relief showed on the faces of campers and their parents alike, summer was here. I kept my plaque close, the words read, ***GOD grant me the serenity to accept the things I can't change. The courage to change the things I can, and the wisdom to know the difference.*** I knew I would call upon these words frequently in the coming months.

My sons and I attended a picnic for all the city employees. I had never been a part of such an affair, but I was acquainted with some of the people there and some of them had waited on me from different city departments. Then there she was, our Mayor, smiling, assessable to me at only three feet away. Jumping in the receiving line to meet the Mayor, I was nervous when my turn came. The first thing I did was give her a hug, and tell her how happy I was that she had won the election. Introducing myself, and my sons, I quickly gave a quick elevator speech for ***Can Do Enterprizes***. Then I asked her if I could possibly sit down with her one day to further discuss my vision. She said "Yes, come see me. Call my office". These words were exactly what I wanted to hear. I had made the connection, even though I had no idea when I would make the call. After several more hugs, I moved on, happy that I had shared this personal moment with this phenomenal woman. I prayed for her success as the first African American Female Mayor of our city. My

239

sons were next up in the receiving line. They each proudly smiled as they shook her hand. Sitting down with my sons, we talked about some of the implications such a meeting could mean, and more, as we enjoyed our free lunches.

When I dropped my sons off for a Boy Scout lock-in on the night of June 19th, I headed over to a friend's house for a short visit. As I was pulling out to head home, my friend saw that I had a headlight out. It was after ten pm., and I couldn't get it fixed then, so I hurried home. Being very careful, I hoped I wouldn't be stopped by the police. I was happy because I was almost home, but my joy quickly changed when I turned the corner toward my house. Sitting at the stop sign on all sides of the street was about ten police cars with flashing lights. *What in the world?* I asked myself, thinking, *I came all the way across town without being stopped by a policeman, and now here three houses from my door is a fleet of police.* Whatever was going on, I knew I was a small fish in that pond. The officer standing in the middle of the street directed me to turn around, which I quickly did, thinking I still might get a ticket for my outed headlight. In doing so I made a block and came down my street. Turned out the situation was confined to just past my drive, which meant I had access to my home.

"Put your hands up you're under arrest", was what I heard when I got out of the car. Scared to death I hurried in the house. Peeping through the blinds I assessed what was going on outside. There was a flood light shining at the house catty-cornered from us. K-9 dogs were angrily barking. And there was a lot of shouting. Then "Where's the gun", "Hands up", apparently they had arrested someone. Feeling more confident about this situation I crept outside and sat on my front steps, out of sight. Saying a silent prayer, I watched the spectacle unfold before me. *Thank you LORD that I know where my black boys are in America. Three are at a Boy Scout sleepover, while my oldest was a Marine in California. Thank you LORD!* I silently prayed.

I actually thought this incident was over, then I heard more shouting, the police were now using bullhorns. "He's under the house", then, "We know you're in the house. Come out with your hands up. Hey, you know we are not going anywhere." This had become a standoff; it felt like I was watching an episode of *America's Most Wanted*. I didn't know these new neighbors. That house must have been haunted or something. There were child molestation accusations with the last family that lived there. The news guys found a spot in my front yard after eleven pm. Champ was tied up outside, and he was barking incessantly. Spectators were parked along the street listening to music. I went inside to go to bed about a quarter to midnight. The scene outside had gotten to be too much for me, and I was getting sleepy. Since I wasn't afraid, I really thought I'd be able to sleep, even though my bedroom faced the action, and my bed was right by the window. I heard a loud noise that sounded like a gunshot and my head went way under the covers.

It was 12:40 a.m. when the Megaphones blared, "You need to come outside. Hey (*they said a name? what did they say? I thought*), I know you can hear me. We need you to come outside so we can figure this out from here. Okay. We don't want anything else to happen. ... (*name?*) This is Rachel (*she must be a negotiator, like the ones on TV*, I thought). Talk to your Mom, son." They had the man's mom on the telephone. 1:00 a.m. "We keep trying. We would like to talk to you. We keep trying to call your cellphone, and you're not answering. We don't know if you have it or not. We're calling now. ... (*name*) answer the call so we can talk. We're not going away. We're getting a warrant to search the house. Tell your side of the story. So nobody gets hurt, come out, put your hands where they can be seen. We'd much rather the easy way, we just want to talk to you. These officers are real intimidating; I can assure you no one wants to hurt you. But we need your cooperation to make that happen". Yawning, as I drifted off, I wondered what had happened to start all of this, and what kind of person was in that house across the street. Were they scared, stubborn, or mentally disturbed?

I jumped out of my sleep when I heard someone outside in my yard. Dazed, I wondered, *how long had I been asleep?* Creeping in the dark, I took a look outside. The street was quite, so I assumed the police had gotten their man, while pondering what the noise was that woke me. Then, fear struck my heart, when I saw two men dressed in black crossing my yard. I screamed, "You need get away from here, I'm going to call the police!" I was disoriented, because a closer look revealed it was the police. I guess they were finalizing their details from earlier.

The first thing I did upon awaking, was to open my blinds to a beautiful morning. As I scanned my yard, the street, and the house across the way, there was no sign of the late night/early morning struggle. Streaming the TV, and the computer, I found several stories on the incident. *Man was robbed of his wallet and several belongings on his way home from work by several men brandishing a gun. Not stopping, moments later they robbed a second person just two blocks away. The suspects then fled into a house on ...Street as Shreveport police began to surround the area.* I thanked **GOD** again, *I knew where my Black Boys were in America.*

June 21st was my first Father's Day without Daddy. I was sad, but was not consumed; relishing in the fond blessing of memories I had.

EPISODE V: THE REALIST

I was not naive to believe my children were any different from the kids at summer camp, but there was no way I could believe they acted like some of the kids I worked with daily.

There was a number of kids who were good as gold. But my fascination was centered on the large percentage who were the opposite. Words like insolent and petulant came to mind, as I watched kids with bad tempers, rude behavior, and disrespectful ways. For the first three weeks, every day I wanted to quit at least three times a day. Having to repeat myself continuously had my voice hoarse, which caused me to eventually get laryngitis. I was then reduced to a whistle, and a pointed finger, like a mime directing traffic.

I hated the comparison, but I was feeling like a prison guard without a gun. I had to have a big voice dealing with my own kids, but at my job, I had to scale myself back to where I had to almost accept insults from small children. A six-year-old kicked me very hard and was dismissed from the camp. This was an angry child, like Joshua had been. This incident reminded of the time he kicked and bit his teacher. Finally regaining my voice, I was then rewarded with a summer cold. My body ached like crazy, and my ankles were making cracking noises. It had been about six months, and my legs were still throbbing, but they weren't necessarily hurting. I purchased a pair of compression socks, hoping this was the key. Then the soles of my feet starting feeling like what an injured dog paws might feel like, soft, fluffy, and hurting. It was suggested I might have plantar fasciitis, making a mental note, *If this persisted I would make appointment with a foot doctor*. Pains were also radiating down the left side of my leg. As soon as camp was over I would also make appointment with my regular doctor.

Discouragement was really setting in that summer. I even found myself asking Carl my mechanic to pray for me. This was a change because he was the one that often asked me to pray for him in his time of needs. One day we were together, and he told me that he was having chest pains that felt like a heart attack. Like a crazy woman I replied, "Let's go get some lunch," Him being as crazy as I was said, "Yes". When we got there I prayed a hard zealous prayer for the healing of his body, and the removal of his pain, *IN JESUS NAME*. Within minutes while we were still sitting in the car, he reported to me the pain was gone, and that he no longer felt the pain at all. Later that night I had a severe pain in my left chest that felt like I could be having a heart attack. As I thought about the earlier incident with my friend, I feverishly prayed for my own healing, **IN JESUS NAME**. The pain in my chest slowly subsided until it was gone.

Then I started changing, viewing the kids as just kids, young people filled with false bravado, and swelling from negative peer pressure, which when combined made some kids become monsters around their friends. I was reminded of the words from the Bible **The way of a child is foolishness**. And **Boy**, did I experience some foolishness, stomping, eye rolling, and ugly words spoken under breath. Then the words **but the rod of correction shall drive it out** came to mind. I couldn't use the rod, so I decided to use motivation and inspiration to show them I believed in them. As the summer brain drain was taking place, I worked hard to encourage their learning. My heart was humbled to the parents. And I committed to be a good help to the Moms and Dads, by standing in their stead in any way possible. It would take a village to raise our kids, and my kids were no exception. If I didn't do my part, then I'd be doing a great disservice to the kids. I couldn't give up.

My son Jimmy turned nineteen on the tenth. Nineteen was his favorite number, and the number of faith. I was proud to be a mother on June 27th when Jimmy sent me a lengthy text. This was the most important text of my life as a parent. Jimmy spoke about how proud he was of me, and how he now was beginning to understand my life as a single Mother. He said he didn't know how I did it. This scenario had been prompted by the responsibilities he now had as an adult. He had a car note, insurance, a full-time job, and now he was tripping over the traffic in California. This was a monumental day. After all; this was what it was all about, the day my child got "IT" (I Think) understanding, and was honest enough to share his revelations. My job as his Mother was not in vain.

One day while monitoring the restroom at work I overheard three young girls talk about what they wanted to be when they grow up. The three each had professional dreams; one to be a judge, another a pediatrician and the third wanted to be veterinarian. Overhearing this conversation among these girls was a saving grace to me for my work.

On Sunday, July 5th, my Mom shared some notes she'd taken on an envelope from the sermon. Her note read; **23rd Psalms. Victory In The Valley.** Then Pat (my sister) told me that morning on the way to church, **The word today is victory. The darkest hour is our first day of victory.** Their words escalated my hope and I was blessed with an even larger desire to be a difference.

Many times the campers would listen to music, singing loudly words of "Doing it for my fam", with no understanding what the words meant at that point in their life. In their minds they believed the hype that they would grow up, be famous then help their families. I wanted to get them to understand their families needed them to do good now, and mature into productive citizens. One day during a talent show for the kids, I was amazed. There was a lot of semi-twerking, silliness, and bashfulness, but then several of the kids got up to sing gospel songs. Wild eyes quickly became teary eyes as I listened to the **Voices Of Angels.** After my first thought of, *They are not demons after-all*, I began to praise *GOD* for the work *He* was doing in their lives, no matter how undercover it seemed.

Determined by now to do my best, I applied for the full time position that opened at my site, in spite of the drama, trauma, and the chaos of the summer I prayed for this job. I think the freeze had been lifted just to fill this vacancy, we were the largest site, and sufficient staffing was mandatory. I did not get the job, but it went to a nice young lady. On August 20th, when *GOD* told me, *You are released from the tears and confusion over your job*, I got very emotional. Joy overflowed my being at the idea of being released from the striving hurt down inside, and struggling in my mind. On August 27th, I had two job interviews that day. The first was for the exact position I'd been passed over for earlier, but at a different site. I assumed the freeze had been lifted. Familiar with the management there I was sure we'd be a good fit. Secondly, I interviewed as an Office Manager in an independent motor vehicle office. This would work for me, though I was not particularly ready to sit behind a desk in a small office.

Concerned that the pains in my legs had returned, one day I stopped by the quick care office on my way to work. When the doctor came in, I described what I had been going through. She prescribed me some pains killers, and told me to follow up with my primary doctor. I left, assuring the doctor I would set the appointment with my doctor. This office earned its name for quick care. I had seen the doctor, had my medicine in hand and was at work within one hour, making a mental note to set the appointment with the doctor. My primary doctor was at the huge public hospital. Making faces to myself, I knew it would probably be two months out.

Happy with my job progress, Champion and I took a short walk when I got home that evening. At 6:40 pm, Jayla, eight, and Jordan, seven, (the same kid I gave Jackson the dog to) had stopped by to say hi. Jayla was still in her school uniform skirt and white top with cute red sandals on, and Jordan had a bowl of popcorn and a Bible. When I walked out the door I saw these two small people sitting on my porch. Jayla was listening, while Jordan read St. John in the Bible to her. This was a beautiful sight.

The next morning Jaleen and I was off to the Fire Academy. He wanted to be a firefighter, and we were going to find out about the junior firefighter program. A tour of the facility meant that we got to meet several top personnel. It was a proud moment when I was introduced to one of the trainers. He was a young man that had grown up in our church. I was as proud of him as if he was my own. Seeing him made think of his mother, and most times when I would think of her I would pray for her. This woman had lost her only daughter and was now co-raising her daughter's daughter. When I gave this young man a hug, I just sensed his mother's pain. He was her only son, and I couldn't imagine this mother's sorrow.

Later that day at work, I met a recently published author named Brenda Saxton. Asking the price, without thought I quickly reached in my wallet to pay for my copy of her book. Once secured in my hands, I began a barrage of questions. Where, when, why, how, who, I asked, as I told her of my work in progress. We prayed together, then she invited me to a book signing she would be having the next month at the library. Her book of poetry was a short read that I finished before quitting work for the day. Inspired now by Brenda, I knew I had to complete *Relics of a Woman*. "After all, why not me? Jackie did it, Sand did it, and Terri did it. Why can't I be a published author?" I asked myself in a stern voice. After work, I was excited to get home. Driving in silence I kept hearing Diana Ross sing *It's my turn*. I reasoned that if the vision *Can Do Enterprizes* was a premonition for me, then the book *Relics Of A Woman* had to be a manifestation for me. As I considered my mental breakdown last summer, I wondered, *Would my heart stop beating if I didn't complete this book?* I didn't want to find out, so I started to prepare *Me, Myself, and I* for a new life change.

On August 30th, at 7:36 a.m., I shouted: "Thank you, *GOD!!!*" I had never felt this surge before while confirming my affirmations: This day I started again, committing myself to a promise that *Relics Of A Woman (ROAW)* would be completed soon. Then I affirmed; *Relics Of A Woman will be out for Christmas distribution, and ROAW will be a big success. And I will be standing in front of ladies at my book signing, animated, and laughing as I see the words on the pages.* I was enthusiastic about getting it done so I spent the day going through hundreds of sheets of paper and by 2:19 pm I had finished organizing my book by years. Proud I had done a really good job keeping the documents in chronological order, and the sixteen years it took to compile these pages was astounding. For so many years it really felt like I was just compiling one big diary that would be packed away. "Thank you **GOD**" I shouted, elated over the thought that **ROAW** was to be a reality. Still confirming my affirmations, I stated; *I WILL Enjoy this ride! And keep my eyes open. I WILL Feel this experience with all my being! And make it through to the next round! I WILL Be Lifted, as The Angels watch over ROAW and me!* It had been ten days since I was released from the tears and confusion over my job by **GOD**. The number ten meant testimony, law, and order. And that was exactly where my life needed to be.

Enjoying the movie, *Zorba the Greek* for the first time, I received new revelations. Zorba was a simple but wise man, and Anthony Quinn flawlessly played the part. His words left a great impression on me "A man needs madness, or he will never cut the rope and be free. Why do **GOD** give us hands to grab? Gifts put in your hands from paradise. Life is trouble, death is not. When a man is full, what can he do but burst". I could only pray that the words of **Relics Of A Woman** would be so profound.

On August 31st, my faith was increased. The supervisor called me in for an interview with the manager at the other center. *Let's see how this goes* I said myself.

Before leaving work that day I texted the twins, I knew they had a little money. I asked them each to save $2.00 for me to deposit in my checking account, saving me from an NSF charge of 35.00. I was broke to the negative degree that day until payday when I would be broke again.

As I was leaving work, pulling out of the parking lot, I saw my longtime friend Lisa. It had been many years since our paths had crossed. I thought about the way of the world. If I had not met Lisa who introduced me to her cousin B. who was Amari's grandmother, would Amari had needed a dress that I just so happened to get from a man walking down the street that fit her perfectly for her recital. Things that make you go **Hmmm**.

When I got home there was not one, but two checks in the mail;

$46.78, and $40.32, a total of $87.10 from some class action suit from a bank where I once was a customer. Funny thing was, it was for bad NSF practices on the part of the bank. This was a blessing because I was able to pay my nephew for a loan, and he really needed it because the waterman was there cutting off his water. And I didn't have to take my kid's money.

David, my kid's friend stopped by. I proposed to him a working partnership with me. He was seventeen and had created a YouTube channel that shared his life with his followers. Not to slight my sons, I knew I would need someone with David's skills. He was a photographer, and a videographer, willing to help me with book cover and book layout for pictures.

Gwendolyn Hampton

SEASON XVI

DARK

SHADOWS

EPISODE I: SEPTEMBER, OH SEPTEMBER, ART THOU FORSAKING ME?

September 2, 2015. I thought I should be used to weird dreams by now, but the one last night was still surprising me. In my dream, I was with a high school classmate, and a former co-worker that had given me a horrible time when I was her Manager. This was a very odd trio indeed. The three of us were thoroughly cleaning an apartment, making it ready for move in. The most amazing thing about this dream was that the entire apartment complex was black cast iron. *What did that mean?* I kept asking as I drifted in and out of sleep. One word came to mind when I finally got out of bed, *FORTIFIED*. Then as hard as I tried, I couldn't remember anything else about this dream.

My legs had stopped hurting, but I was still having occasional involuntary muscle spasms running down my legs. The bottom of my feet were still tender, but it felt like illness was leaving my body through my foot pads. And I didn't mind because the devil was under my feet.

What a morning September 4th was. Mom's car was down, and I got to chauffeur her around, running errands. This was one of the perks of my job, free hours in the morning. We got an early start, so we would get back in time to meet the tow truck for Momma's car. Our last stop was at the funeral home; we went there to pay our respects to Rickey. He was the childhood friend that had stood me up for the prom. On the way out of the building, I ran into my unfulfilled childhood crush, after a quick flash to age thirteen, I was quickly returned to the present. He was nothing like the boy from the past. And I no longer had the appetite of a thirteen-year-old and was glad for it. Just as we made it back to Mom's, the tow truck was driving up to take her car to the dealership.

On my way home I stopped to get me some chicken, and a drink, when I saw three men I knew. Each of them had some serious life issues going on. I came home feeling like a shining star, like the sun shining out. *Being single ain't so bad* I thought. Eating my chicken that day I had no guilt. I ate in honor of Rickey, because I knew he would be laughing right now.

After a few more stops, I made it home at 7:00 pm. When I got there all my sons were asleep. *What is this?* I wondered as I tried to image what happened today to knock everybody out. I came up with no answer, but I thanked them for saving me from *The Momma Nightmare*: The fear a Mother had when she nervously wondered where her children were on a Friday night. *THANK YOU GOD, IN JESUS NAME* I prayed. Feeling a little lonely, but thankful, I crawled into bed at ten. It was times like this that I couldn't help but think about having a special person in my life. I didn't want to walk alone anymore, even though I knew I was not alone with *JESUS* by my side. Often these times would evoke longings for someone to help along the way, someone to face things in life with combined courage, joy, and hope.

For years I planned on attending a Unity Church service, but things would always come up, preventing me from getting to their location on the other side of town. Earlier in the week, while driving, I noticed the sign under the tree in front of a small building, which read, *Unity Church of Shreveport* I couldn't believe it. There, just one mile down the street from my house sat the church. I had been in this neighborhood for almost twenty years; I asked myself, *How could I have missed this wealthy source of information?* Then I said, *Surely they just moved to the neighborhood. I couldn't have been that blind.* Feeling quite foolish, I could only surmise: *This is what happens when we live on auto-pilot, just going through the motions of our existence, seeing but not seeing.* As I reflected on the day I saw the church sign I remembered being aware of the funeral home which sat next door. Their huge sign for cremations under $1000 intrigued me as I thought about my death, and plans I had not made since my life insurance coverage had lapsed. Making a mental note to **Reinstate my coverage ASAP**. I had been careless by letting my life insurance lapse, but I was having trouble making the payments. And I knew I was **not exempt** from death.

I attended The Unity Church on September 6th alone, my sons chose not to attend. It had been almost thirty years since I attended a Unity Church service. Lately, I had been searching my mind as to how I could finally cross over to **GOD'S WAY** of being. I was looking forward to the service that morning because I thought I might get some answers to some of my questions. After the congregation enjoyed meditation moments; the spiritual leader, Ms. Judith did a superb job of allowing the spirit to speak through her, as she taught several enlightening lessons.

I would never forget the scenario given for guilt during the first service, **Wash, rinse, repeat. Wash, rinse, repeat.** So was my life. Then in the second service, my mind was impressed as I quickly took notes: *Outside the body is decoration. I can be peaceful, I don't have to internalize negatives, I am free.* **GOD** *is in me, and as me, he's at my total command. Not like a genie, but there to ensure I have a good experience as I participate in the ongoing good of* **GOD**. *Living every new now through the love of* **GOD**. *Don't worry about falling. Falling is a part of the process of growing. Like driving, you have to make sure you look in the direction you are going.* These words plus thousands more spoken that morning resonated within my soul in a wonderful eye opening fashion, as I made the short trip home.

On September 9th I was awakened by a dream that I couldn't remember the details. However, it was about Jackie, whose sister was Lo-Lo, my best friend from childhood. Jackie looked fabulous in the dream. These sister-friends of mine had lost their Mother over six years ago. Now, both their parents were gone. I took the dream as an excuse to catch up, so I called Jackie, and Lo-Lo later in the morning when I got up. Surprised by my call, we all agreed to stay in touch. I was so glad I made the calls. This joy was right in line with how I felt; **Renewed.** My life was being healed in all areas.

Flipping through the channels at 12:00 pm, I found a passionate movie about the mental anguish experienced by a widow whose wife was a victim of the 9-11 terrorist attack. It was a sad scenario. The man had lost his mental capacity to live his life. The movie unexpectedly sent me into a deep sadness, as it directed my thoughts to my Dad's upcoming birthday.

I was working hard on September 10th to keep my mind straight, praying to maintain and hold on. I had to believe change was coming, even though the job freeze was still on.

September 11th would have been my Father's 82nd birthday. He wasn't here, but his spirit would forever live with me. And his **Angel Wing** on my back would help carry me through life. **I LOVED MY DADDY.** And I missed his crooked smile. I thanked **GOD** for the memories, because the mental pictures of my father were very clear. I would always have a reason to smile and be thankful for my wonderful Father.

At 7:08 a.m., my spirit was quickened as Champion and I headed down the street. I had challenged myself to walk the two-mile round trip to and from The Unity Church. Revived with each block, I arrived back home feeling like a new creature. Taking the time to luxuriate in a nice bath, I even washed my hair. I wanted to be pristine, as I would be headed to the cemetery shortly with Mom and Jerry to visit Daddy's gravesite.

Before leaving home, I heard my spirit speak: **No more posting.** I accepted this word to mean that I was now released to finish my book of recollections. This day was the sixteenth year since I started the journey called **Relics of a Woman.** Signing off to my readers in my journal I wrote, **I am logging out till we meet again. Bye for now.** I was going to just live fully for each day, and enjoy **IN JESUS NAME.** And I would no longer track my life in journals.

I looked flawless after a quick check in the mirror. My hair had cooperated that day, and there was not a strand out of place. And, my makeup was perfect. Before heading out the door, I blew myself a kiss in the mirror, saying "You look good Lady". This was a very special day; I had even taken the time to put in my contact lens. Before pulling out of the drive, my last thought before leaving home was, *The Power Of Life And Death Is In The Tongue*. Unsure what those words had to do with the day, I threw my sunglasses on as I headed out to see my Daddy.

At the cemetery, I didn't find sadness, but a word from on high. I clearly heard *GOD* say to me, *You have a new name now*. This was interesting to me since I had so many names, Momma, Ms. Gwen, Ms. Hampton, Gen G, Lady Gwendolyn, some folks even still called me by my maiden name, Bradford, and some not so nice names. *Your new name is Baby G* I heard *GOD* say. This made me smile as I made my way back home. While pondering the implications of the name *Baby G*, I realized it meant that I could start over from where I was. The mistakes were the past, and I had *a clean slate*.

I had a great joy sweep over me when I got home. Not only did I have a new name, but a new opportunity to complete a wonderful history book entitled *Relics of a Woman*. Cleansing my room later, I removed all the ten books I had been reading from my room. Not to blaspheme I even took my Bible to the bookshelf. It didn't take long though before my Bible was right back by my bedside. I was determined that no matter what, I would get published, believing I would be a top rated author, whose story would encourage millions. *I will not read another book till I have read my first copy of Relics Of A Woman* I told myself. The acronym for *Relics Of A Woman* was *ROAW* (row), and that was exactly what I had to learn to do, so many times when my ship was sinking. My oars went from 2x4 planks to pencils, at my weakest times. Had I not kept *ROAWn* (rowing) my ship, or learned to **ROAW** with the punches, I would have drowned. Depending on what day it was, **ROAW** would sound like (rawl) in my best southern accent. **Rawl** would be a combination of the roar of a lion, the growl of a mad bear, and the howl of a hurt wolf. Had I not been up for the journey, I would have gotten **ROAWed** (rowed) over, shipwrecked at sea or **TKO'ed** into eternity

From that day forward I started feeling like a new woman. It had been sixteen years since I had just lived, without journaling. I sniffed the air like Champion would have. The days were brighter as I bounced around like a teenager. Even the kids were in my good graces. I heartily smiled at my neighbors, and work was a breeze. I even took a turnaround trip to Baton Rouge with my friend Denise. It was a weird sensation, but I was getting my stride. Settling down, I laid the groundwork for order. It took me a long time, but I finally chronologically re-organized years of notes and manuscript for the book. I was knee-deep in pieces of paper as I purged, thrilled at where I'd come from and where I was going, **UNTIL....**

EPISODE II: THE DAY THE WORLD STOOD STILL

I was awakened by the quiet voice at 4: 00 a.m., on September 24, 2015.

It said *Get up and take three blood pressure pills, and a swig of apple cider vinegar.* Laying there, thinking about this odd request, drifting in and out of sleep, I saw my cousin Sharon. She was a woman who truly believed apple cider vinegar was a cure-all for many ailments. Finally, feeling urgency in these words, I obediently took three blood pressure pills and a big swig of apple cider vinegar.

I was awakened again at 6:00 a.m. This time with a repeating singsong of *Yea, though I walk through the valley of the shadow of death, I will fear no evil. Thy rod and thy staff they comfort me.* Over and over, and over again this mantra played in my head. When I noticed a heaviness in my left thigh, it never occurred to me that something was wrong. I just assumed I'd slept on it wrong, and again I snoozed off to sleep.

At 7:15 a.m. the alarm went off. The twins were now in high school and Jaleen had a make-up test that morning. He didn't want to miss his test, so he had asked me to drive him to school. Back at home, I took a luxuriating bath, knowing I had a busy day ahead. There would be no mid-morning nap for me today since I had promised to take Ms. Jai to the bank, and then we planned to have lunch at her church. I figured I could get everything accomplished before I had to be at work for three.

I had a strange feeling in my face at 10:30 a.m. While getting dressed, I even noticed that my face looked strange. And my left arm felt heavy and my left hand was weak. There was a slight lag in my walk, and when I tested my speech, the words sounded funny. My thought ran across the word **STROKE**, but I just knew I couldn't be having one of those. Adamantly, I believed there was no way possible I was having a stroke, but just in case I started praying for my healing **IN *JESUS* NAME**.

All the way down the interstate to Ms. Jai's, my body was changing even more. As I signaled to turn into the driveway at her apartment, I saw that I wouldn't be able to make the turn into the complex. The driveway had been taped off to prevent entrance, and workers were there repairing the concrete drive. However, just as I got to the driveway, I stopped. A worker had removed the tape and began waving his hands. I thought he had done this for me to enter, but at the same time, I wondered at the oddness of this man allowing me to enter the torn up driveway. As I began to execute my turn, the man frantically motioned for me to stop, screaming, "Ma'am, you have to go the route!" Looking past where he was standing, I realized he had been flagging a go-ahead to the cement truck behind him, it was not for me to proceed. Strangely ringing in my ear was this man's words, "Ma'am, you have to go the route". This was so strange to me because normally a man working on the street would say something like, "Ma'am you gotta go around", not the proper way this man had spoken. Instinctively, as a divine revelation, I knew exactly what he meant as I went around to the other entrance. Sitting in the parking lot, waiting for my friend to come down, I understood my predicament. Still thinking about what the man had said, "Ma'am you have to go the route", I accepted my reality. Realizing that whatever I was going through, would not end with the instantaneous healing I'd been praying for, but instead, this would be a process, a route.

When Ms. Jai got in the car, she was alarmed as I detailed my morning to her, then she looked at me closely, seeing that things were not normal. She asked, "Do you need to go to the hospital?" I said, "No, let's pray", and she was a breath behind my last word. Vehemently we prayed in that parking lot before leaving. This friend had always believed in my strength, and this day she put her life in my hands as I pulled out of the drive. Headed down the street, I looked again at the man and heard his words once more, *Ma'am you have to go the route*. I knew he had no idea what had just happened, and I was saddened by the fact that I would never see this man again. When we got to the bank, I dropped Ms. Jai off in front. There were no open parking spaces, so I parked on the side of the street. Slowly, with a droopy face, a hanging left arm, a lax hand, and a dragging leg I sauntered into the bank. As we were leaving, out of sympathy or fear, Ms. Jai purchased a beautiful butterfly earring, necklace combo for me. Putting it on me as armor, we found our way to the church for lunch, where her daughter joined us.

It was 1:00 pm when we finished lunch; not a pretty sight it was. Ms. Jai was alarmed by my slurred speech, the way I could barely use my hand, or even raise my arm, and my dragging leg as I walked out of the dining hall. This time she told me, "I'm going to take you to the hospital!", and I told her "No, I'm going home. The guys will be home soon". Pulling out of the parking lot, I glimpsed her frightened face as she sat in her daughter's car. For some reason, I just couldn't fathom my kids coming home from school, and getting the news I was in the hospital. It didn't even cross my mind that they could have come home and I was dead because I had refused to go to the hospital. There was no way I could make it to work that day, so I called the Manager and told her "I have a virus, and won't be in". She squealed, "Oh *LORD*, don't bring no virus here!" I smiled, as a part of me still hoped this would pass. I prayed while I rested, waiting for my kids to get in.

My sons got home from school at 4:20 pm. By then my speech was garbled, I barely had any use of my left hand or arm, my walk had gotten really bad by now, and I was having trouble getting out of bed. They were immediately concerned, but like Ms. Jai, my sons believed in my strength and my belief that I would be alright. Jaleen was so sweet, as he exercised my barely functioning legs and arms. Loudly we prayed, vehemently *REBUKING THE devil*. I was very sad at Joshua and Jeremy's indifference about what was going on in my bedroom.

Finally, at 5:30 pm, I told Jaleen, "Son, this is not going to pass, and it's time for me to go to the hospital". I tried calling my nephew Kel, and after several attempts, he eventually answered his phone. I said, "I think I'm having a stroke, and I need to go to the hospital". For what seemed like the longest time I waited, as anxiety, and fear began to creep inside of me. *What does this mean? Will I be irreversibly affected for life? Why didn't I call 911, even up to this point? w*ere the questions I keep asking over, and over again, as I rebuked myself for being an irrational fool, and not loving myself enough to pick up the phone to dial 911. Then I remembered I didn't even have any life insurance. Silently I prayed, *LORD, I know this could be my last day on earth, but LORD, please keep me here until I can work things out. I don't want to leave my family with the burden of trying to find funds to bury me, and LORD, let me stay till my kids are grown*. My Dad's face flashed across my mind. It had been seven months since we'd said goodbye, and I was glad he wasn't here to see me like this. He would have been brokenhearted.

While waiting on my nephew, Jeremy asked "Can I go to our football game? It's against our archrival". Not to be outdone, Joshua said, "I'm going to stay home and study", I thought, *For real Joshua, RIGHT!* Too far gone to argue, I agreed to their requests. Feeling betrayed by them both, I was deeply hurt by their selfishness; especially after all I had done for them. Everything was more important than me. All I wanted was a little sympathy, not a pity party. *How audacious can you be Gwen? You have a lot of nerve getting mad at them for not caring, when you just spent this entire day not caring your damned self* I thought to myself. Jaleen quickly spoke up, "I'm going with you Mom." Kel did come, and I was so thankful to him. Again, stuck in stupid, I thought to myself, *Why didn't you just call the ambulance? They would have come much quicker.* After Jaleen, and I loaded into the car, Kel stood at the car door waiting for Joshua and Jeremy to get in. I told him I had given them permission to go to the game, and stay home and study. Like a bull that had seen red, he glared at the two, and it felt like he told them, *I will kill you both, if you don't get in this car, right this minute.* He then told Jeremy, "There will be other games".

It was 7:05 pm on September 24th, 2015 when I checked myself into the University Health emergency room, while Kel parked the car.

University Health was a special place to me because my mother had retired from there when it was named LSU Medical Center and my grandmother retired from there when it was named Confederate Memorial Hospital. I felt safe there because this was the hospital where I was born. And practically every time I received treatment there I'd had a positive experience, but the long waits could be tiring.

Sitting there waiting to be called, I found myself being embarrassed by my disposition. The man next to me started talking to me. Preparing me for the worse, he told me he had been there for seven hours. I really got upset at myself, again asking, *Why didn't you call 911?* Kel flew in the door, and zeroing in on me he asked,

"Do they know you are having a stroke?" Quickly turning, he walked to the admitting window, I don't know what he said, but the clerk said, "She will be next". It wasn't long before I was stretched out on a bed, waiting for the doctor.

This scene reminded me of months ago when **GOD** had shown favor to Dad, when he had been given preferential treatment in the emergency room at the VA. While lying there I looked over at the *FAST* PSA poster on the wall. Reading the words made me want to cry, but not one tear fell. F-face drooping, A-arm weakness, S-speech difficulty. I had these three symptoms of a stroke. The last letter T-time to call 911 pierced me as a dagger into my soul. Again I asked myself, *Why didn't you call 911?* I had been in no pain, but I guess if I had been in pain I would have rushed to the hospital. For the concern I had for my life, I thanked **GOD**: *He pitied me the fool*.

When the doctor came, I cleared my mind, because I wanted to understand everything he said to me. Sorrowful for my actions, I recalled my day to the Doctor, telling him how I just couldn't find my way to the hospital. He consoled me somewhat by telling me, "Your brain has been affected, and you probably couldn't think clearly". I didn't understand much of the medical terminology spoken, but best I could understand was that; *I had a blood clot that had blocked the oxygen, and blood flow to my brain on the right side. The part on the right side of my brain controlled the movements of my entire left side. Part of my brain had died because it had not received the necessary blood, and oxygen needed to keep the cells alive. This caused a disconnect in the circuitry of my muscle, and nerve operations.* So, this explained my inability to control my left leg, to lift my left arm, or even straighten my fingers from their locked down position.

Cringing, I visualized how I must have looked to Ms. Jai, and my sons; what a sight I must have been. My left leg dragged, then

261

splayed out to my side, and didn't want to flex or bend. I couldn't control the popping and buckling at the back of my leg as I attempted to walk. My face was twisted, and my speech sounded like a new foreign language. My left arm and hand just swung loosely by my side, like the useless limb it had become.

I used an analogy to explain this complex situation to myself, *A protected child had gotten lost in a dense forest in the dark. She'd never had to do anything for herself, and she became consumed by fear. Blinded by the darkness, she bumped into trees, tripped over branches, and lost her sense of direction. In search of her protector, she stumbled deeper into the forest, getting totally lost. After a long day's travel, the child reached a clearing. Here she found her protector. The Protector had been injured, some "thing" had tried to murder her protector. Reunited again, The Protector vowed to the child to forever take care of her, but since the injury of The Protector, the child's ability would be limited. Life for the child would never be the same as she had to learn to live with new limitations.* This was a sad rendition of what was happening to me. My brain had protected things I took for granted. Now it had been afflicted with a *Stroke*, or in terms, the doctor used, "Brain Attack". My health, mobility, and speech had lost their protection in a critical area, and I would now have to learn life in a whole new way. For *GOD'S PURPOSES* though, he allowed me to keep my reasoning faculties. I had heard the saying before, "Man only uses 10% of his brain", for me this was a good thing. If the stroke took 10% of my brain power, and I was only using 10 %, then I still had 80% available for new understanding. I was elated as I started to believe that *GOD* still had work for me to do, like completing my book, *Relics Of A Woman* (ROAW). The story of *ROAW* continued as I now had a new episode to share.

No one would give me a straightforward answer as I continuously asked the questions. "What does this mean for my future?" then "Am I destined for life to look, and live like this?"

Later, someone told me about a pill that could have dissolved the clot had I called 911 in time. I cried to myself, *I didn't know about the pill*. Then, I thought about Dr. Mike's warning nine months earlier, "Gwen, I feel a blood clot forming". I was amazed when I suddenly realized that I was no longer experiencing the pain sensations in my legs I'd been having for months. I guessed the blood clot had completed its course. "What have I done to myself?" I cried out. After a thorough physical examination, I was transferred to room 7-K-11. My thought, *Thank you, GOD, seven for divine completion. A completion of so much*. Again I thought about the words of the man working in the parking lot, "Ma'am, you have to go the route". It was then I gave into reality, saying "Yes *LORD*." I wasn't angry or depressed, but immediately I started focusing on *GOD'S WORDS* that had replayed in my mind that morning, *Yea though I walk through the valley of the shadow of death, I will fear no evil. Thou rod and thy staff they comfort me.*

Settling in for the night, I finally stopped asking questions, as I reflected on the events of my day. I was still alive as my sons returned home alone, leaving me in the darkness. As I started to drift off to sleep I bolted upright in my bed, actually in my mind, because my body was not responding to that thought. Laying there I remembered. Just two weeks ago, on September 11th, *GOD* had given me a new name, *Baby G*. According to what I visualized, my *Baby G* persona would get a fresh, new start. I had been so excited about the future possibilities, and joys I would be experiencing.

I had to talk to the *LORD; LORD have mercy! Why didn't You tell me that Baby G meant exactly that? Baby G, Gwen would become a babe and have to relearn to talk and walk again. I can't even comb my own hair anymore.* If I had known what *Baby G* would be going through two weeks later, I'm sure I would have asked *GOD* to let this tragic malady pass me by. The decree had been given however, my name was to be *Baby G*, and there was nothing I could do to change this present situation. I refused to wallow in despair, so

263

I girded myself in prayer.

When I closed my eyes, I went to sleep, only to be awakened throughout the night for continuous checks by the nurses and aides. As nice as they were, I wanted to escape, but I couldn't even make it to the bathroom ten feet away without assistance. I realized that rock bottom was not a place of residency for me, but it was a place I had visited many times throughout my life. What I was going through was just another rock bottom, one that didn't kill me. Therefore, I must be here for **GOD'S PURPOSES**. ***LORD, you know everything. Only I can't see now. This is going to be a real fight for me, but you GOD win wars. This Battle is not mine, but I will continue to walk IN JESUS NAME and this is my prayer LORD***.

The next day my sister Pat, and my cousin Sharon came to visit me. I told them not to call Momma. She was on vacation in Arkansas. The next day when it was no longer made sense to not share the news that I had had a stroke, I called my son Jimmy and my brother Jerry. Jimmy was very upset as he tried to figure out how to come home. I told him I was getting the best care, and if he had to come home then I would let him know. Before I got off the phone with Jerry, I asked him to call Mom. When Mom called, I told her that Pat and Sharon were with me, and that I was being watched carefully. I also implored her to finish her vacation because I was being well cared for in the hospital for now.

EPISODE III:

ROCK BOTTOM

BY

JOHNNY PRESTON

It's a long way to Rock Bottom

Past Straight and Narrow Trail

Past safe confines of Shelter Street

Past stable Financial Status Road

Past Any Kind of Employment Blvd.

Proceed all the way down (Worst) Bad Choice Hwy.

Upon approaching Rock Bottom, follow these directions

First, throw the sensible morality map out the window

Then make a left at One Way To Hell Hwy.

If you feel lost, but haven't made a U-turn by now, you're almost there

Now make every green light, never yield, run all red lights and barrel over all stop signs full-speed down the muddy hill.

When you feel the thud, you've arrived

The sign reads "*WELCOME TO ROCK BOTTOM. ONE WAY IN-ONE WAY OUT*"

The first people you meet are,

The Mayor, SkidRow Bum and his wife, Fallen Angel

His button reads, "Elect a Derelict"

They wear dirty clothes and tattered dreams

Her old ribbons read, "Prom Queen"

He goes into his well-rehearsed, worn out speech

"Welcome to Rock Bottom,

Come one, come all

There's always a vacancy

Our motto is "There's always room for more."

You start to see new signs that read

"Too Late", "No Way Out", "Dead End", or "Next Stop To Nowhere".

One really peculiar sign reads" Next ***Town-Rest In Peace"***

But no one lives there.

There are no street lights, no street signs, no nice scenery, just grimy sidewalks. No pretty houses, just rotting slums.

There are no jobs, only handouts. To get daily rations of misery. You don't even have to stand I line.

Welcome to Rock Bottom

The place where life goes on, but time stands still

Every choice there is a bad one

Some are satisfied to live in Rock Bottom

Those who leave either formulate or stumble across someone else's discarded plan that shined right through the lid of a strategy stuffed trash can.

Many surrender without ever trying to find the one-way out.

There are no Counselors or Guides.

The best advice to follow is your own

You use your head to follow your heart.

Go quickly while there's still time.

Proceed. Back up the long steep muddy hill

Keep moving. If you hesitate you'll fail.

Go back past all the signs that read, *"Quit Now", "Why Try", "You'll Never Make It", "Life's Sweeter On The Bottom", "Why Dare The Impossible", "You'll Be Back", "Pessimism Is The Key",* or *"Just Surrender"*.

Go until you see the sign at the top of the hill

"NOW LEAVING ROCK BOTTOM. ONE WAY IN-ONE WAY OUT"

Many never find the way.

Gwendolyn Hampton

SEASON XVII

GWEN'S HOPE

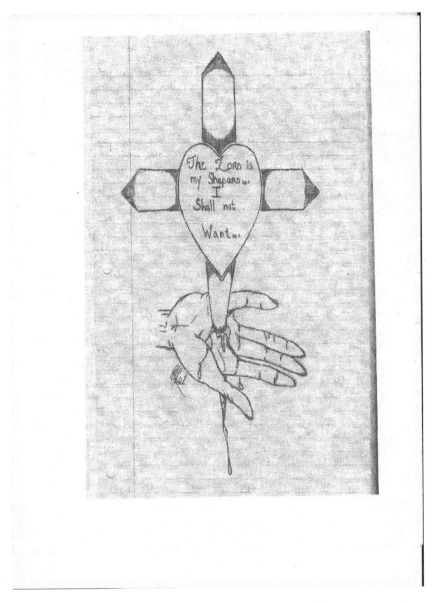

This is an original illustration by Mr. Markus A. Reed, and it was done twenty-five years ago. Thank you Markus for your contribution to ROAW!

EPISODE I: PSALMS 23

<u>*THE LORD IS MY SHEPHERD*</u>- my *Guide*, my *Supporter*, and my *Provision*. <u>*I shall not want*</u>- my *Shepherd* always make sure I get what I need, always leaning in my favor for some of what I want. *GOD* is good. <u>*He maketh me to lie down in green Pastures*</u>- Green pastures of vitality and vigor, and good health. *GOD* could have allowed me to lie down in a barren desert, instead I am in a green place to grow and blossom. *He* has taken me down to bring me up for his purposes. Since you have chosen me *LORD*, I agree to go forward as your mouthpiece. <u>*He leadeth me beside the still waters*</u>- After this storm I will need a place to recoup. *He* gives me a refuge of peace in the midst of the storm. *He* guides me to this place. <u>*He restores my Soul*</u>- *He* allows me to believe a new me is possible. I CAN. *He* restoreth my body, my temple. By *His* stripes I am healed. <u>*He leadeth me in the path of righteousness for his name sake*</u>- My testimony will count for someone else's victory. I am strengthened for *His* purpose to strengthen others. <u>*Yea though I walk through the valley of the shadow of death I will fear no Evil*</u>- Even though I walk through an entire valley covered with the spirit of death, I will not be afraid. Even if death is lurking, waiting for weaknesses, a chance to devour, destroy, frighten, confuse, and bring doubt, I won't be afraid. My mantra, *You gone go through trials, challenges, and dead situations, and in everything you have to see life, and believe all is well.* <u>*Thy rod and thy staff, they comfort Me*</u>- I don't care if I am toddler with a Hemi-Walker, or little girl that can't clap my hands, or even if a wheelchair has been my mode of transportation, my strength comes from on high. My *Papa* is strong, and *His* strength strengthens me. <u>*Thou prepareth a table before me in the presence of my enemies*</u>- Oh *LORD*, you have set before me a beautiful five-star table, your beautiful Mother Earth with delicacies fit for a Queen. My enemies, fear, envy, strife, anger, bitterness, plus a whole entourage of demonic personalities, sat down with thoughts that they would be indulging on me. <u>*Thou anointed my head with oil*</u>- while the enemies were preparing to feast on me, my *GOD* anointed me with oil. My protection. Like a boxer's Manager would grease his

face to prevent the hits from sticking, my **Holy Father** has slathered **His** protection all over me, to protect me from the hits of these enemies. <u>*My cup runneth over*</u>- After battling with these enemies I am restored for another fight, and given strength to help others in their fight. I am given more than enough for the fight. This ain't no pity party, it's a victory party. <u>***Surely, goodness and mercy shall follow me all the days of my life***</u>- And **GOD'S BLESSINGS** shall overtake me, and follow me till I die…

EPISODE II: A WEEKEND TO REMEMBER

I had been transferred to a Christus Schumpert Highland rehabilitation center after a week in the hospital. The rehab center was located in the hospital where my father had retired, and this was where I worked my first job. This knowledge comforted me as I made great strides in getting my strength.

When the nurse walked into my room one evening she was hysterical when she saw me sideways in the bed with my legs up the wall. She thought I had gotten contorted some kind of way in my bed and I was in distress. Quickly, I told her that I was alright. She finally calmed down when I explained, "My computer tablet had died, so I decided to make some phone calls. I wanted to stretch my legs so I found a way to get them both up on the wall" I said that, but I didn't share the great effort and time it took me to get them up there. Actually, I had been contemplating how to get them down without a big bang just before she walked in. The nurse didn't yell, but she did get her point across as I twisted into position with my legs on the bed.

The outpouring of love from family and friends was overwhelming. But, I thought I might have a **HEARTATTACK** when my sons' father Jimmy peeked his head inside the door of my room. When he stepped in, I had a five second moment of repulsion.

This emotion was very intense until it was replaced with a peaceful calm. A part of me tried to hold on to the negative energy that had washed over me just a few seconds before. But that was not to be so.

Jimmy and I was able to talk to each other like adults. We talked about my health. He asked about the kids, and we even laughed when a funny memory was brought up. When he left me I felt cleansed from the near hatred I felt for him. The feeling was renewed daily because Jimmy started watching over his kids. He checked in on them every day, since they were home alone. He made sure they were fed and got whatever they needed. I was proud that he finally took his role as a father seriously in this time of need.

Days before my release from rehab, I received an invite from Ms. Dorothy: There was a paid reservation for a women's retreat in Tyler, TX that had come available because the participant was unable to go. Without thinking; I said "Yes! I want to go." Then I remembered: *This was the same retreat I had been invited to by event co- promoter Sharon; the prior year to be a presenter for my Forgive Me Body segment (she was the same Sistafriend who had invited me for two years to her women's conferences). But because I would have had to pay my own way then to the retreat, I declined the offer because I couldn't afford to go.* I hugged Dorothy tightly because I immediately knew **GOD** was calling me to this woman's retreat in Tyler in the woods by the lake. This time my singsong mantra became: ***He leadeth me beside the still waters***. I knew **GOD** wanted to talk to me. And this trip would be a saving grace for me.

On October 16th I was released from the rehabilitation center. It was hard saying goodbye to the great staff that had worked diligently to save my life. Mom and my friend Carl came to pick me up. On the way home, we picked up my sons who were walking on their way to the hospital.

At 3:00 pm, my good lady Dorothy arrived at the house to pick me up. My neighbors came down to assist getting me to the car.

Dorothy and I were on our way to a women's retreat in Tyler, TX. Some of my family members were horrified that I had chosen to go directly from rehab in a wheelchair to a two-hour bus ride with my monster assistant, called *The Hemi-Walker*.

We made it to the bus, with time to spare before departure. There were several things however that I had failed to consider. These questions never crossed my mind: *1) How would I get on the bus with The Hemi Walker? 2) How would I use the restroom?*

I was blessed with above and beyond genuine kindness. The retreat promoter had assigned me the front seat next to her. There is a saying: You never know who you might meet, in this case; it was, who you might know. My Sistafriend Sharon was still a co-promoter for the event. And the promoter was Mrs. Prelow. Mrs. Prelow was the Mother of a young lady I managed many years ago. Her daughter Faith was a sixteen-year-old whiz kid working her first job back then.

Dorothy and I were separated when I sat down on the front seat, but she was assured that I would be okay. Sitting there waiting to leave I got in a tight and had to use the restroom really bad; even though I had used the restroom before I left home. Since the stroke, I was subject to frequent trips to the restroom. I knew I couldn't make it to Tyler without going. So I got past my fears, stood up, and ambled down the aisle, where Dorothy meet me halfway. The uncomfortable looks of sympathy from the others passengers inspired me to stand taller. I had to use the toilet, so I slowly made it to the small cubicle at the back of the bus. Once inside behind the closed door, I gazed into the mirror with misty eyes, proud that I had made it.

I guess some of the ladies had a sigh of relief for me because when I started back down the aisle to my seat, it seemed the air had gotten lighter. I was smiling. Getting back to my seat, someone came over and started talking. I laughed as she told me how she never traveled without wearing a disposable adult pull-up, for those tense moments of need. This made so much sense because that would have relieved a lot of stress off my brain.

It was dusk by the time we got to Tyler and dinnertime at the retreat. Unloading off the bus, in the dim light, I immediately got a sense of the maneuvering I would be subject to during the weekend. My heart froze when I looked at the winding trails leading into the woods to the cabins. Wondering *How in Heaven's name I would get around these graveled trails, especially this night in the dark with this huge monster, The Hemi-walker.*

I was blessed to get a ride to the cabin on a golf cart. I waited on the cart while our bags were deposited to our room. The driver agreed to drop me off at the dining room because there was minimal lighting along the trail leading from the cabin to the dining room. In turn, Dorothy and her sister-in-law decided to walk over to the dining room.

During dinner, I received word that my bags had been moved to a cabin up front near the promoter's cabins. Compliments of the promoters, my sleeping arrangements had been upgraded.

There was a night service after dinner, and I courageously made my way to the meeting room with my partner *The Hemi-Walker* aided by Dorothy.

During the session, single ladies were separated from the married ones. Dorothy went one way while I stayed where I was.

The topics were very personal to me. One speaker talked about the necessity to be your best woman to yourself. She stressed the point; *A woman should be the woman she wants to be before she becomes a woman a man wants her to be.* Her words were so true. This raised a question for me; *Do you want a husband?* I was almost afraid to answer this question as I thought, *With three marriages under my belt, could GOD be so gracious as to ever allow me to have another husband.* That night I decided to pray for what I wanted. In my mind I confirmed what I wanted from a man, and then on my notepad, I listed what I would do for such a blessing. I remembered a Bible verse *We have not because we ask not, and when we ask we ask amiss.* This verse was heavy on my mind as I prayed: *LORD I don't want to ask wrongly for anything in my life. Teach me what to ask for, then LORD guide me in right thinking that I may come to you in the right way. Yes, I do want a companion to share my life with, especially since my sons are swiftly growing up, and will soon be on their own.*

The next powerful speaker agreed with the first. She elevated the meeting with a spoken word of prophecy. The hope given was inspiring; she even told me later "You will be walking tomorrow without your walker." This was a good word for me, as she came over an anointed my leg, and deemed it so.

At the end of the first session, I was pleasantly surprised when Faith, Mrs. Prelow's daughter arrived at the retreat from Houston. She'd hardly aged, even though it had been over twenty years since I'd last seen her. She treated me with such compassion. When I needed to go to the restroom, she drove me to the dining hall facility to use the one there. She didn't want me to have to walk down the steep steps at the meeting facility. At the end of the final session Faith and Dorothy assisted me to my room. Again surprised, I was blessed with a room alone, while Faith and her sisters lodged upstairs. Over into the night my leg seemed to be limbering up, in bed I could move it up, down, and higher than before.

On October 17th I woke to a magnificent morning. And I was able to take three steps without my walker. Since I hadn't lost my mind, I did know to keep my walker close though. *How phenomenal is GOD, look at me* I said to myself smiling.

After a delicious breakfast, we convened in the same meeting room from the night before. Faith's good friend, Dr. Jones who had driven down with her from Houston, gave a touching presentation. She started her talk with; "I want to talk to the girl behind the door". I related to her analogy of how we hide behind doors looking out at the world.

Everyone was full as a tick after a delicious lunch. Assembling on the veranda outside the dining room after lunch, the ladies lined up for pictures by the lake. I passed on picture taking that beautiful afternoon, as I settled into a huge red rocking chair. Rocking back and forth I was at perfect peace. I could only compare the feeling to what I imagined Heaven must feel like. Even the insects stayed away.

The looks of hope on each woman's face confirmed that she had come seeking something special from **GOD** at the retreat, and so far **GOD** had not let any us down. I got to meet so many ladies from different backgrounds. And the encouragement given to me was very inspirational.

Later, while fellowshipping before the last session of the evening, I proudly listened as Faith shared stories of me as her Manager at her first job. Laughing as she talked about how mean I was. She made me smile when she talked about how I pushed everyone hard though. Strolling in my mind back to those times, I remembered that most of my crew was young people. Though I was only about fifteen years older than the youngest, I was determined back then to teach them positive work habits, and responsibility. I was truly moved to tears as Faith thanked me for being a good Manager. Then a huge question popped into my head; ***What if I had left a negative impression of bitterness on this young lady?*** I was thankful as I considered how this could have been a spoiled weekend for everyone, instead of the blessing it was.

I declined to go to the evening service. Not only was I tired, but I didn't want to be a hindrance to Faith in the dark again. There was no TV in the room, but I was totally entertained as I viewed pictures and videos on my camera. Memories of my Father and my sons took me back. I was touched to my core: I realized how rich my life was. Remembering again that there was no phone signal in those woods, I prayed that no one at home was worried because I was doing great.

While alone, I practiced walking without *The Hemi-Walker*, and getting up and down off the bed and the low couch.

Again, Faith showered me with love when she brought my dinner to the room that evening. Unintentionally, I got a frightening reaction from Faith and her Mother when they returned to check on me later. I was sitting on a stool with my feet dangling in a dresser drawer eating dinner. Awkwardly I explained how I'd gotten up on that stool. They had no idea how much it took for me to get up there but I had been confident that *GOD* was with me when I did it. With a sense of relief, they both smiled. Faith was so tickled; she even went and got her friend Dr. Jones to come see me. Smiling, all Dr. Jones could say was "Go girl!" In return, I said, "Having a date with *JESUS*".

Faith and her four sisters were at my service the entire weekend. They were so kind, helping me at every chance. Like their Mother, they each had a good and pure servant spirit. My friend Dorothy was relieved by the help given.

We headed to church on October 18ᵗ after a delicious breakfast. Everyone there was so kind. The Minister's sermon was on point. It was as though he had a personal message from *GOD* to me as he preached. He stirred the audience with his words: "The opportunity of a lifetime must be seized within the lifetime of the opportunity. It's *GOD'S AGENDA*, and my assignment is from creation to death. The establishment of *GOD'S KINGDOM* rests upon each of us, and we are each unique pieces to the puzzle. Hide *Jehovah's* word in your heart, so you don't lose **GOD'S WORD** in your consciousness. When **GOD** arises in your life, enemies abound, moving in and out, seeking where they might find weakness. When **GOD** manifests himself, **He** shows up. Time makes a change. The love of money hides **GOD** *f*rom our view, we can't see him as our provision". This was a timely message.

The last leg of the weekend included a nice lunch.

Rolling down the highway headed home, I closed my eyes and meditated on the past weekend. The closer I got to home, doubts, and fears of the unknown began to creep in. When I got off the bus, suddenly my hands, my walk, and my mind, all seemed confused and afraid. It was as though all of me had been blinded during this trip.

When I settled in that evening, the true reality of having a stroke set in: *My life would never be the same*.

EPISODE III: A LONG ROAD FORWARD

Adrenaline and endorphins were in full effect at the retreat the past weekend. But on Monday morning October 19, my world was in focus. I had a doctor's appointment that morning, and Mom had agreed to take me.

My hair has taken on a life of its own by now. I was a mirror image of Wild Woman, Cali's doll. This doll had the craziest hair, hence my name for her Wild Woman. What a mess my hair was.

It was a good thing I started super early getting ready for my doctors visit. Enlisting the support of my twins, I cracked up when they tried to comb my hair; it had gotten very thick, and long, and huge, huge, huge. They brushed my hair at least a hundred strokes; what they really did was brush the top of my hair. They tried to put it up in a rubber scrunchy. Then, three, two, one, **POP!** The scrunchy flew across the room. Heartily laughing, I called Mom to tell her what happened. I was blessed with another great laugh when she showed up with hats. As funny as this was, my heart sank as I thought about what my future looked like.

I asked questions of the doctor again; "Will I recover? How long before I will be better?" She didn't have an answer. This upset me, as I silently prayed, **_LORD please, I want my strength restored._**

After the doctor's appointment, Mom and I discussed with Jeremy and Jaleen the incident with my hair that morning. We all thought it best I should move in with Mom. The fact was that she could help me in ways my sons couldn't.

At night it was almost impossible to sleep, whether it was acid reflux, breathing issues, the inability to find a sleep position, or just random thoughts, a good night's sleep was hard to find. Getting out of bed would call for a see-saw rocking giddy up and go motion that sometimes catapulted me to the floor. From reclining to crawling, everything was very difficult. Finding myself in the exact spot in my parent's bed where my Dad spent his last days at home was unnerving. This was emotionally hard for me as I recalled the day not too long ago when I got him out of bed to walk, and helped him do a Frankenstein stroll down the hall that day. Now, however, here I was looking like Frankenstein myself. My stroll was assisted with the huge monstrosity **_The Hemi Walker_**. That walker was a terrible reminder of my disability, but I desperately needed it.

The pressure from use of the walker caused me to get carpal tunnel syndrome in my right hand. Carpal tunnel was a whole new set of confusion for me, as painful spasms would attack me during the day, but mostly during the night. Now I had another reason for a sleepless night. I cried so much. However, as much as possible, I managed to hold back the tears around my Mother. I didn't want to make her sadder than she already was. I felt hopeless being there with Mom. I had lost my strength, and I couldn't help her if she needed me.

My days turned into weeks, which turned into months. They were filled with rehab sessions, bouts of depression, anger, and sadness as my recovery took on a snail's pace. A fight brewed within, as my soul and body fought for victory and freedom. I keep asking myself, *How could I have avoided this stroke?* While admonishing myself for not taking care of myself, I realized that something was bound to happen to me after the wild and crazy fifty-five-year ride my life had been. I forgave myself once again for living a fool's life.

Finally, deciding to stop beating myself down, I started heading to the mirror daily with a, *Hello Lovely* to myself, determined to live my *GOD-GIVEN PURPOSE* and fulfill his vision for my life. My daily challenge was to keep an upbeat positive outlook on life. I couldn't give up, but I did understand how easy quitting could be. The me that was left behind after the stroke was not a lovely sight, but I was determined to fight to the end, till death would part me from this life. I would live the rest of my life disabled if that was what *GOD* said, but I chose to believe *HIS WORD* as I daily prayed, *BY THE STRIPES OF JESUS, I AM HEALED*. I even had a funny laugh in the kitchen one day, after I spilled everything on my plate onto the floor. If Gordon Ramsey had been listening, I would have told him *"Gordon I know you think its hell in a kitchen with you, but you should consider doing a show called: It's hell in this kitchen being handicapped."*

EPISODE IV: BRAVE NEW WORLD

When I turned fifty-six, my Mother gave me a really wonderful birthday gift when she told me, "When we had you, we were so happy." Just hearing those words made me happy, as I reminisced about the picture of Dad holding me as a baby.

During the Christmas holidays, I fought a bout of depression. Feeling an impending doom, as in a *Twilight Zone* moment, I jettisoned out of 2015. I was sure if I had not clicked, then I would have been stuck forever in depression's grip. The word of my stroke got around, family and friends rang the doorbell or rang my phone in a great show of love and support. Friends would bring lunch, text daily words of encouragement, or even pick me up for social moments. I truly appreciated everyone, and as I pondered how to change things in my life, my decision became clear. There was no way I could just let my sons slip away, I had worked hard to provide a good life for them. I moved back home in January of 2016.

Initially, I felt like a stranger in my own home, surprised at how the boys had grown and matured. Stunned when Jaleen jokingly told me, "Go to your room!" I knew I had to take back my life, even in my limited capacity. I prayed to be a better parent, and was forever grateful that I was having the opportunities to talk to my sons about their future plans. We even celebrated Champion's sixth birthday. Still a beast, he got out the other day, terrorizing the cats in the neighborhood. Jeremy said, "Champ was so fast that he looked like a lion chasing a gazelle".

Waking each day gave me new rays of hope that I might get through this challenge. I knew a change was near. And even though I was proud of myself for changing, I still had many occasions to fight back tears. Every day there was a reason to cry, I was always just a blink away from a huge pity party. When I couldn't move my fingers that looked like stuffed sausage, or when I had to get up off the floor after a great fall, or when I was unable to take care of some personal needs without great struggle, or even when my knee would pop so hard as I walked that I felt my knee would break, I fought through with watery eyes. These were alarming situations. One of my sons even told me, "You should go back to grandmothers!" I had taken for granted the simplicity of just opening my hand. Having a stroke caused me to evaluate the simplest things, I never realized the importance of my wrist. I couldn't bear any weight on my hand because my wrist was locked, I couldn't even rest my hand on my bed or a table. My hand would float away into space, sometimes I

281

would sit on my hand to remember what it felt being stabilized.

Combing my hair was still an issue when I called my hair stylist Mr. Lee. Finally, ready for something new, I gave him permission to do the big chop. Tearfully, I sat as gobs of hair fell around me, grabbing some of my hair before it hit the floor, I stroked it like it was a pet. I had intended to take a clump of my hair as a keepsake, but the floor had been cleaned while I was getting my hair washed. Gasping, I realized my beautiful salt-n-pepper hair was forever gone. Mr. Lee calmly told me, "Let it go, let it go. You have a new life now. This is what you need for the next phase of your life". Anyway, I had always told him I would go natural when I got tired of combing my hair, but now I had given in because now I was going natural because I couldn't comb my hair. I couldn't comb it. Taking a deep breath, I told Mr. Lee, "Now you get your wish. I'm going natural, so you might as well go ahead and color it like you want to". Mom had taken me to the shop that day. The look of surprise on her face was exactly what I was thinking. I didn't like it, but for now, that was it. They say, "Blondes have more fun". Well, I was about to find out.

I was in shock, and unable to wrap my head around this new diva look. One week after the coloring I called Mr. Lee saying, "Can you please just change the color? Maybe make it all silver, that would be good". He replied, "Going natural is a process, it takes time. Your hair is beautiful, and so are you. Give it some time." What he said made sense, and I just commented, "Yes."

Exactly one week later, overtaken by remorse still, I called Mr. Lee again. This time he cut me off before I could start complaining. He said, "I have a customer now and can't talk", then he hung up the phone. Feeing bad, I sucked up my feelings.

By the third week in, I knew this color had to go. Bracing myself, I dialed Mr. Lee's number. This time he cut me off with a question. He said, "Have you met the man?" Confused, I said, "What man?" "The man" he said. Even more confused now, again I said, "What man?" "The man. When I was coloring your hair I prayed that **God** would send a man in your life that would understand what you were going through, and he would take care of you." Stunned, I repeated what he had said, "You mean to tell me you prayed Mr. Lee that **God** would send me a man to take care of me? You anointed my hair?" The love I felt at that moment from my hair stylist superseded any thoughts I had about being a blonde. All I could say was, "Dang Mr. Lee, I guess I have to keep this color". Thus began my life as a real blonde, proud that he loved me so. As best I could, I walked under the sun, my hair, like a Queen, then under **THE SON**, MY **SAVIOR JESUS CHRIST** as a child of **GOD**.

Joshua turned eighteen on July 15th 2016. He had finished his Eagle Scout requirements on time. I remember when Josh took a stand after Jimmy didn't finish his criteria. He said, "I will be better than Jimmy. I am going to be an Eagle Scout". I smiled so wide when I opened the envelope containing Joshua's Eagle Scout certificate.

My heart continued to long for the fruition of **Relics Of A Woman** and **Can Do Enterprizes**. When I turned my computer on one day while watching TV, I was surprised that I remembered the keyboard. Before long I was pecking away at my computer typing **Relics Of A Woman** with one hand. Then another day as I watched about fifteen kids play down the street, I tried to figure out how I could start helping the kids on my street. Later, I talked to them about my vision of **Egan Street Youth Services (ESYS)**. The kids loved the ideas I presented to them. Calling in the help of my friend, Dr. H, I began to put a plan of action together. Before long I was engrossed, trying to figure out how to make things happen for the kids, and complete the first draft of my book all while being handicapped.

EPISODE V: WISHFUL REFLECTIONS

The New Year came in. I wasn't invited by the church to be a 2017 self-defense presenter for the conference. It seemed **GOD'S HAND** was in the mix. We buried my cousin Stan that weekend. This man was the only person in the whole wide world that called me **Gwendolyn Sue** every time he saw me, and I in turn called him **Stanley Ray**. He was a character and I would forever miss him.

On February, 2017 **Happy Valentine's Day** words filled my inbox. They were only niceties, because no one loved me as their Valentine. My son Jimmy's text did however make me happy, **Happy Valentine's Day Beautiful**. When we talked later, he was at a glitzy holiday affair for the Marines at the Ritz Carlton. President Obama was out playing golf with a group of Asian delegates, and he hoped his group would get a chance to meet the President. I prayed he would.

The next day started with stormy weather and hail that passed to a beautiful sunny morning. I guess the gloom outside earlier triggered something on the inside of me. When Jaleen broke my favorite candle holder, I was sad. When I saw the broken pieces, I started screaming, "You don't care because it's mine and not yours!" Then a tear fell, which led to a deluge; a flood of tears rained. I became very emotional, then I realized I was not angry at Jaleen, but sad about my Father. The next day would be two years since his death, and he had been heavy on my mind earlier. Looking at his pictures, I realized how much I missed and loved him. It had been a very long time since I cried like this for my Dad. Thank **GOD** Jerry was at home with Mom. **Surely, If I was grieving, she must be as well**, I thought. My friend Donald called, he listened as I boo-hooed, consoling me till I felt better. After I apologized to Jaleen, I was able to get past the moment, realizing my Dad rose in my heart each day.

February 16th, 2017. This day was off to a good start. I had rehab and my physical therapy appointments that day. Remembering the words of several therapist and doctors "Most of what you get back will come back within six-months of the stroke", I was petrified because I was within 30 days of six-months. I wanted to scream when Stan, my physical therapist said, "You have what you need with the brace. You're doing good and I am releasing you today". Maybe he didn't want to hurt my feelings by telling me this was as good as my walk would get. I wanted to shout at Stan and say, *No, you can't let me go, this brace hurts my foot.* Without complaint I left thinking, *Is this a Medicaid issue, my public insurance won't take me all the way?* A part of me felt like Stan had just said; *Go in faith and by faith good woman, be thankful, you are still here.* I would be sure to ask my occupational therapist her thoughts about this at my next appointment.

When I left Stan, I was feeling unsure whether I could go the distance in my rehabilitation alone. I found myself ambling upstairs to the inpatient rehab floor. I wasn't sure why I was there, but when I got to the floor I quickly found out. Dr. Henderson was there as I turned the corner, crying out when she saw me; "Gwen! I was just talking about you. I want you to meet someone". She introduced me to a fifty-two-year-old woman who had a stroke two weeks prior. She looked good but was very sad. By sharing my story, I was able to encourage and pray for her.

Just a few doors down was the grandmother of twins I had worked with at the recreation center. This lady had been so nice to the staff after camp. My heart overflowed with compassion when I found out that she was not only dealing with health issues, but she had concerns at her job. Spending time with her, I was able to express my heartfelt appreciation for her kindness. After praying with her, I offered her my phone number and told her to please call.

By the time I made rounds on the floor, thanking all the caregivers who had been there for me, I was tired. What seemed like a roundtrip mile long walk had been worth the effort. Spending time with everyone made me want to be a peace instigator and a joy deliverer. Feeling better about my predicament, knowing things could be worse, I prayed that **GOD** would work all things out as I waited for the transportation bus to pick me up.

Later that day Mom, Jerry and I went to visit Dad. The Veteran's Memorial Cemetery was pristine as always, beautiful. Dad was okay, Mom and Jerry were good, and I was ready for my next round at life.

Finding daily inspiration was getting easier, as I began hearing more stories of people having strokes. The people now were family, friends, and even local celebrities who had had a stroke, or died from one. These incidents were just a small number of the many people afflicted by this deadly killer. Just to think, I thought I was exempt from such a tragedy. But, ***Time and chance happens to us all***, according to the Bible. And that meant even me.

SEASON XVIII

THE

EDGE OF

LIGHTS

&

GOLDEN

PATHWAYS

EPISODE I: RELIC OF A WOMAN

I am a relic of a woman, my mother. This lady means the world to me. Having witnessed her strength on so many occasions, I had huge respect for her. It had been two years since my Dad passed, and I felt his absence, but I was able to smile as I reminisced.

February 24th marked the seventeenth month since my stroke. Again the 24th of each month reminded me of that day.

My Mom had a bout of illness a few months back. The source of her sickness was never discovered, as she recovered. Her symptoms returned with a vengeance in February. She had been vomiting, with diarrhea and nausea and hurting in her side for about a week. A colonoscopy and other tests only revealed results in normal limits and no explanations as to her pain. Late morning on the 24th my mother called, saying, "I am going to the emergency, what time are you coming over?" "Now" was all I said, but I thought to myself, ***Please GOD, not my Mom***.

By the time my sister and I got Mom to the emergency room, she was very weak, and nervously shaking. It had been fifty-five years since she'd been admitted to a hospital, and that was for the birth of my sister. I had never seen my Mom look so fragile, she even looked afraid. I wished I was strong physically, but I was determined to do everything possible to stand strong for her now though. She was admitted to the hospital where tests were run. Sitting there awaiting test results, looking over at Mom, I saw myself. This woman had held her resolve for as long as she could until the pain was unbearable. Seventeen months ago I had done the same; held out till the end.

Thank ***GOD*** nothing as traumatic as a stroke happened to Mother. She had gallstones and needed surgery. After the operation, the Doctor said, "Surgery usually doesn't take so long, but your Mom apparently had this issue before and it resolved itself leaving scarring…" Now the mystery was solved, it was undetected gallstones that had caused her illness earlier. Amazingly, this woman had fought through her severe pain. I guess she was so strong that the pain gave in and healed itself. The operation was a success, and she healed beautifully.

On March 1, Dr. Henderson referred me to a surgeon to schedule surgery for carpal tunnel in my right hand. The thrill of the thought of freedom from this pain was short lived when I realized that having this surgery would render me totally helpless: 1) I wouldn't be able to use my right hand for about a month, and 2) My left arm and hand were of no help. I visualized myself as a helpless walrus wallowing around to and fro. Sadly, after many weeks, I canceled the appointment for surgery. My sons had been helpful, but I knew that if I went through with the surgery, I would experience some serious stress.

GOD showed up in his providential way when he sent Anita my way. She was a volunteer with my sons Boy Scout troop. She brought me over two massagers, one for my chair, and the other a nice handheld for my overall body. I thanked *GOD* for good people. A few days after, Ms. Anita returned with her son. This time she brought a huge stair master machine for me. I couldn't even raise my left foot up high enough to even get on the machine properly. But I accepted with hopes that one day soon, I would excel on this machine, and do fifteen jumping jacks.

EPISODE II: MOTHER NATURE

The first day of spring was a few weeks away. I started considering who I could get to help me with spring cleaning chores.

At the store one day, a man stopped me with, "Oh, you don't remember me?" Confused I said "No." Introducing himself as Andrew, he explained that I had agreed before to let him wash my car. Instantly my mind snapped to *Egan Street Youth Services (ESYS)* and the kids I had just left on the street playing basketball. Giving a quick explanation to Andrew about my plans for *ESYS* I then asked him, "Would you come over to my house, and show my kids how to detail my truck. This will be important when they make money cleaning cars. Give me a few minutes before you come so I can share with the kids what you are going to do." Andrew did an excellent job instructing the kids on intricate details of cleaning a vehicle, they even used cotton swabs for tight areas.

I got more than I bargained for when I offered Andrew some dinner. When I found out that he was homeless sleeping on porches, in abandon houses, or occasionally with a family member, I thought about the spring cleaning chores on my to-do list. Going one step further, I explained to him that I had an old garage out back, and he could stay there, but Champion would be his roommate. I shared with him my needs and told him he could eat meals with us if he would choose to help out. So many times I was charged with being too friendly by family and friends, and allowing Andrew full access to my house could have been a terrible situation.

A few weeks in, I just had to call Mr. Lee. I shared with him everything Andrew was doing to take care of me. Then we laughed when I said, "Mr. Lee, I know you anointed my hair and prayed for *GOD* to send a man who would understand what I was going through and want to help me. Well, that's what *GOD* did." Then I ended our conversation with, "The next time you pray for a man for me, would you specify, maybe a husband for me."

Andrew became a valuable member of our household. He cooked, cleaned, washed clothes, mopped floors, and fixed the plumbing. I was quickly spoiled, but I took his presence as a gift from *GOD* because I was freed to devote more time to completing my book. My poor Mother had sleepless nights worrying about us in the house with the homeless man Andrew.

It was the first day of spring. I took a nap on April 20th, and was awakened by a dream. In the dream, I was healed and fully restored with no deficits.

Sitting outside about 7:00 pm that night I was admiring the beautiful evening as I stretched my left arm and leg with my right hand. Watching a worm in the dirt, I wondered, *Where is his family?* The worm was writhing, twisting, turning, coiling and stretching over and over again, as though in rhythm with me. Suddenly I felt something on my right arm. Quickly I moved my arm, sending a flying moth to the ground about two feet away. Amazed, I watched this moth turn toward me. Crawling over leaves and dirt as it started my way. A shiver ran up my spine as the moth found its way to my left shoe, making a straight line up my leg. My hand was resting on my leg, which the moth used as a bridge to go up my arm, where it traveled to a resting place just below my arm socket.

A moment of fear was washed away when the moth and I looked at each other. I then knew this was all *GOD*, I believed he had sent me an *Angel Of Reassurance*. This was my left side that had been debilitated by the stroke. I watched this moth for a long time. Curious as to what would happen next, I reached over with my right hand, and the moth transferred from my left arm to my right hand. When I raised my hand to the sky, the moth flew to the ground, landing on its back in the same spot as before. Around it went in circles, then it zigzagged its way back to my left foot. My heart raced as I watched this moth move toward me again, this time stopping just above my ankle. Unmoving for the longest time, this moth became *The Patient One*. After a while, I headed inside, with the *Angel Moth* still in tow on my leg. Once I stepped inside, I became emotional as the *Angel* flew away.

Feeling inspired, I recommitted myself to all that I believed *GOD* was. As I sat at my computer later that evening to write the last chapter of *ROAW* a fierce rage against satan, all his demons, and all the evil he had done to me, and the world seemed to take over me.

I had too much going on in my head, and I was becoming stressed, so I called Dr. H and informed him that I would take on one challenge at a time, and that **ROAW** would be my number one priority. I also told him that **Egan Street Youth Services** was next up on my agenda, and that when the time came, I hoped he'd continue to be my mentor.

EPISODE III: EXPOSE'

As I live my life, I make concerted efforts to always remember that I am forever satan's enemy, yesterday, today, and tomorrow. As a **Child of GOD**, I know satan hates me because I love **GOD, MY CREATOR**. The following words express what I was feel toward satan. I believed this was to be the last chapter of **Relics Of A Woman**.

God created **Angels** to worship and serve **Him**. Through infinite love, **He** bestowed the qualities of understanding, free will, might and power upon each of them. The free will choice **GOD** gave to **His Angels** allowed for the potential to sin. satan was the most esteemed and beautiful angel in the **Kingdom Of Heaven**. satan began to think of himself as comparable to **God**, and was not satisfied to just worship and serve his almighty creator. Mad, and unhappy, satan was defiled with jealousy and pride, which ultimately consumed him. he led a rebellion amongst likeminded angels for the ruler ship of Heaven. he truly believed he could usurp **GOD'S AUTHORITY**, and match **The Omnipotent, Omniscient, and Omnipresent Powers of God.** An **All-Knowing God** was not surprised by the actions of **HIS CREATION**, satan. **GOD** was not one to commit or tolerate sin, thus **He** cast satan, and his followers from heaven as fallen angels. These angels now demons of darkness were forever enemies of all of **GOD'S CREATION**. **Other Angels** still in heaven were now on alert for a pending battle with this ousted evil one.

GOD was a **Beautiful Heaven** and created a **Beautiful Earth**.

He created the first human, a man named *Adam*, and as a gift to him, *GOD* made him a beautiful woman named *Eve*. Their job was to care for *God's Paradise, The Garden of Eden* and to be fruitful and multiply. Since being banished from heaven to earth, satan had sworn to steal, kill, and destroy any, and everything he could from humans for all generations. He lay in wait for an opportunity to tempt and deceive Adam and Eve to commit sin against their creator, their *FATHER GOD*. satan finally got his chance to put his scheme of deceit into action. Beguiling Eve, satan persuaded her to eat of *The Tree Of Knowledge Of Good And Evil*. This was the same tree *GOD* had commanded Adam not to eat of because he would surely die if he did. In his sly way satan convinced Eve that *GOD* didn't want their eyes to be opened to know good and evil because they would become gods like *HIM*. Eve then convinced Adam to disobey the command given to him by *GOD*. As he gave into this sin against *His Father*, satan watched in delight as our first father committed the greatest sin ever against humanity. Adam and Eve were then banished from paradise, eliminating any chance that they might eat of *The Tree Of Life*, and live forever. *GOD* then placed Cherubims and a flaming sword which turned every way to guard *The Tree Of Life.* Man was now separated by sin from *GOD,* like satan was from heaven. The shame man had before *GOD*, convinced satan he could win. And Adam was no longer happy as he had to toil the now cursed fallow ground he had been taken from to work hard until his dying days.

GOD created Man for *HIS DIVINE PURPOSES*. *HE* created *HIS* earthly family with love. Even though *HE* knew satan was roaming the earth seeking to devour all, *GOD* did not abort *HIS* plans for *HIS* chosen people. Our *ALL-KNOWING GOD* knew from the beginning what ravages satan would wreck on the lives of mankind. From the beginning, our *LOVING GOD* predestined a *Plan Of Salvation* for *His Children. HIS NAME WAS JESUS*

CHRIST!!! *The Bible*, a historical, **GOD** inspired account of humanity prophesied of the coming of **CHRIST**. **CHRIST THE MESSIAH** would be *Mankind's Savior*. Only a **Human Death** could pay for the **Sins Of Humanity**, and the human death of **Christ** would signify *The Ultimate Sacrifice* for the *Atonement* of the sins of man.

When time came, **GOD** incarnated **HIMSELF** into human form, as *JESUS CHRIST, SON OF GOD*. **HE** was born to a virgin named **Mary** and his father was **Joseph**. For **thirty-three years HE** experienced humanity which in turn lead to **His** paying **The Ultimate Price** for the **Sins Of Man**. **HE** suffered, bleed, and was crucified on a cross at **Calvary**. This was a **Voluntary Act Of Love** on **JESUS'S** PART. **His** sacrifice was an example of the voluntary, willful love that **GOD** wants from us. satan trembled that day, because **JESUS** had carried **Our Sins** to the cross before **GOD**. satan knew his days were numbered. The sins of man were **Nailed To The Cross**, and man did not have to bear them anymore. Three days later, victory was perfected when **JESUS CHRIST** arose with **All Power In His Hand**. **The Price For Sin** had been **Paid In Full**, and mankind had been **Reconciled With GOD** by the death, burial, and resurrection of **JESUS CHRIST**. Mankind had to believe that **JESUS WAS THE SON OF GOD**, he had been sent to save the world, and only because of **His Death, Burial, And Resurrection** would they have the **Power To Stand** against the devil. They would have to call upon the mighty name of **JESUS CHRIST** in the midst of their trials, and thank **JESUS CHRIST** for their triumphs. When **JESUS** died mankind was left with a **HOLY SPIRIT** guide within, an **All Knowing Link** to **OUR FATHER-GOD**. **GOD** also ensured **Earthly Protection** from satan and his demons till their time on earth would be no more, by sending **Angels from Heaven** to watch over **His** people.

Freely **GOD** created all things, freely **GOD** loves all things, I declared on May 1st, 2017. Even though eons of time have passed, satan is still **Mad**. he still to this day has never created, or originated anything. he has never done anything authentic. Always the bridesmaid and never the bride, satan is still intent on stealing, killing, and destroying humanity. his place in history is sealed and he will always be a **hater** *Of GOD*, and in turn he would seek to make fake replicas that will pollute, pervert, corrode, and spoil the good *GOD* has set forward for Man in nature. Then he would flip things on us by making us our own worst enemies by using our *Insatiable Appetites* for food, money and excessive cravings in our lives to make us sick, and obese.

At the end of the day, no matter what, *GOD Is The Creator* of all things. satan has been deemed to have some *Powers On Earth*, but *JESUS CHRIST* through *GOD* has won the *Victory For Mankind*, specifically for *me*. I am not defenseless against the *Arrows Of Darkness* shot at me continuously throughout my days. I am not defenseless, as I sojourn through this life. I welcome each new day with a song on my lips and a prayer in my heart, *Praising GOD For JESUS* as I rebuke satan *IN THE MIGHTY NAME OF JESUS CHRIST*. I am not separated from *GOD* anymore, and my greatest desire is to help others FIND *RECONCILIATION WITH GOD THROUGH CHRIST JESUS*. As you have read *Relics Of A Woman* I pray you will never forget this: *No matter what you go through, satan can only do what GOD allows. There will be times GOD will operate for our good by allowing dark events to happen, like my having a stroke, to have a talk with us, to teach us a lesson, or give us a needed rest.*

EPISODE IV: THE GREAT CONDUCTOR

May 5th, 2017 was Joshua's last day of school.

When Cowboy stopped by to see Andrew, he had puppies in his truck bed. I choose the deep black stocky one for Joshua, calling him Jinxy. No one liked the name I chose, so I decided to let Joshua name him. I knew Joshua would love this little dog as a graduation gift. And I also knew I'd have to fight with him to take charge of the dog's care.

When Joshua came home, I was happy that he liked Jinxy. He told me he would have to think about his name. The seniors had gotten out early that day and Josh had come home to change cars with me. He didn't want to drive Taz to the park where he was meeting his friends. I didn't mind but was surprised when he came back in an hour to get ready for work. Before he left, I asked him to sit down for a minute. I sensed something was very wrong: Joshua had no joy. This was very odd for a kid who had just finished high school, and would be graduating the next week. I asked him, "Son, are you alright?" "Yes ma'am," he said. We talked for a few minutes and Joshua assured me he was okay before leaving for work. I was still concerned.

That evening at 9:48 pm my phone rang. Joshua was calling; maybe he just wanted to let me know he was on his way home. On the other line was a woman instead. She asked me, "Is this Joshua's Mother?" "Yes. Who is this?" I said. "You don't know me, but your son has been in a car accident...." she said. Dizzily I bombarded her with questions. And I panicked trying to find my walker.

The twins weren't home and I knew I shouldn't be alone. Outside I didn't see anyone but just started calling my neighbor Johnny's name. Out of nowhere, he responded. When I told him what happened he jumped in my car and made the three-minute trip around the corner with me. I thought about a defensive driving class I had once where the instructor quoted the statistic that most accidents happen close to home. Josh was only about seven blocks from home.

When we pulled alongside the road, I tried to get out, but Johnny held me back. He went to the police and ambulance workers seeking information. I cried when I saw *Taz* had been destroyed; she had given her life for Joshua. I didn't know the severity of Joshua's condition when he was removed from the car onto a stretcher. Panicked, I thought about Josh's behavior earlier. I had heard before that some people know when they are going to die and they might say or do something strange before death. *Is this what was happening today? Is my son going to die?* I asked myself. Then I saw Josh's arm move on the stretcher. Like a sign from heaven, I was *Reassured*, like Joshua's middle name. We followed the ambulance to University Health. I was grateful he was going to this renowned trauma center because I knew he would receive excellent treatment there. This was the same hospital that took care of me after my stroke, and I had received stellar care there throughout my stay.

A call that lasted one minute and one second began a nightmare straight from hell. I was living every parent's nightmare that had a teenage driver in their home.

I called the twins, and they were devastated when they got to the hospital. Word had gotten around quickly, as the waiting room filled with grieving teenagers. The Chaplain sat next to me in the waiting room. He tried to console me as he explained the severity of my son's condition. When the Chaplain said, "Pressure and bleeding on the brain. Threatening a possible stroke" my heart stopped. As he continued, I tried to understand what he was saying, "He has a fracture on the bone in his neck, which could cause paralysis. His pelvis is fractured. Also, his urethra, the tube that connects to his bladder that allows him to urinate has separated. He needs surgery. You can see him after they complete their assessment." Nothing, not nothing had ever affected me like this. *Oh GOD, not my son* I silently prayed. The Chaplain prayed with us before leaving.

The clock ticked slowly as we waited for a word. Finally, the Chaplain came back with amazing news. *GOD* had begun to orchestrate a symphonic situation that superseded everything. The Chaplain said, "The head doctor was heading out with his bag on his shoulder when he passed by Joshua on the table. Stopping, he immediately began to give orders. I have never in all my years in this position seen anything like it." Rejoicing, he told us Josh had been moved to ICU, and that we should head up to see him. As we walked down the hall, doors swung open. Then the Chaplain exclaimed, "That's the head doctor!" I stopped the doctor and poured out my thankfulness. Then the Doctor did something I had never seen before, he prayed for my family. As he moved to leave I grabbed him and prayed for him and his works.

When we got to see Joshua he looked like a little boy, badly bruised, with a neck brace on. The Doctor explained the surgical procedure and complications the might occur during and after the surgery. I thought, *satan, you have been after My Joshua since he was a child*. Rebuking him *IN JESUS'S NAME*, I spoke, "You can't have him!"

When Joshua was taken into surgery, we went home. I prayed and believed that **GOD** was in charge as we left. I actually fell asleep once I hit the bed, then I was awakened by the ringing phone. I understood most of what the doctor was explaining. It went like this: The orthopedic and urology surgeons had worked together to correct the damage done to Joshua's pelvis and bladder. A successful surgery was performed on his pelvis, but because of swelling, they were unable to repair his bladder and urethra. A catheter was put in place till the swelling healed. Joshua had stabilized and was back in ICU.

Comforted, I knew **GOD** was in control so I stayed away from the hospital that day. Besides, there were so **MANY** kids at Joshua's bedside and he was in the best of care.

With this great news from the doctor, I finally called my son Jimmy in Twentynine Palms, Ca. on Saturday, May 6th. He couldn't talk because he was at work, so he demanded I text him. Immediately Jimmy called with great concern in his voice. He wanted to come home but wasn't sure he could since he was scheduled for a thirty-day leave in about three weeks. After several texts, he found out that the Red Cross could help in a situation like ours. He asked me to send a message to the Red Cross so he could come home. Agreeing, I found the number but didn't get an answer. Then I texted him that they were closed until Monday. Adamantly he told me to call the hospital for info about help from the Red Cross, but they had no information. Not even a minute later he texted me the website and toll-free number for the Red Cross. Within four hours my son texted me his itinerary. The Marines and the Red Cross had worked out the details, and he was scheduled to fly out the next day.

Midnight on Sunday night, the twins and I waited in the corridor for Jimmy to embark off the plane. We were excited because we hadn't seen each other since December. As I watched the passengers walk by, I got excited when I recognized one of them. It was our school board superintendent, Dr. Goree. Shocked to see him, I rushed over, introduced myself, and told him what had happened to Joshua, and that he was supposed to graduate the next Saturday. Dr. Goree was so kind, and ended our conversation with, "Call me if you need anything". Then, Jimmy came down the hallway, I cried as I watched my sons hug. We were so happy to see each other, even on this tragic occasion. Leaving the airport, we headed straight for the hospital.

The twins made it to school the following day. I was surprised when their Dad called asking to speak to Jimmy. Apparently, he'd found out about Joshua. When I took the phone to Jimmy he was in a deep sleep. When he finally woke up, I told him his Dad wanted to talk to him. Groggily he told me, "Tell him I'll come by and see him later". I told Jimmy what our son said, and we disconnected. Not long after that, the phone rang, it was their Dad again. He was outside and wanted to see Jimmy. This man was very sick and could barely walk. When I went to wake my son again, I told him, "Your Daddy is very sick and can barely walk, but he drove over here to see you." Nudging him, I implored my son to go outside. Staying inside

I watched through the blinds as their Dad slowly made his way to the back of his car, where he waited. Jimmy talked to his Dad for a while, then he came inside to tell me he was heading out, his Dad had insisted he take him somewhere and he would be back soon. Worried, I followed him to the porch, watching as he drove his Dad away. Later I found out that their Dad had very few words to say about Joshua.

On May 9th Joshua had a second surgery. He had been in and out of consciousness after surgery, and someone was always there.

Throughout this process, **GOD** had given me amazing peace, increased faith, and a powerful strength. Since the stroke, I normally would cry at the slightest thing. Though I was a frantic mess on Friday night, I had only shed tears once since then.

Later that night, Joshua asked a young lady visiting him, to call me. When he asked, "Can you come and get me?" I couldn't hold back the tears as I tried to explain to him why he couldn't come home. He didn't even remember the accident. All I knew at that moment was to talk to him about **GOD'S PLAN** for his life, and **GOD'S PLAN** for satan. Understanding his pain, I got off the phone.

Joshua was moved from ICU to the orthopedic care unit. Continued grace and mercy preceded us as Joshua was transferred to the floor supervised by a family friend, Mrs. Green. He was receiving supreme care from the staff as family, friends, and Josh's coworkers managed around the clock watch. We had to because Josh was angry about being there, and his neck collar was uncomfortable, so he would try to take it off. I had been told the importance of him keeping the brace on. From what I understood: Joshua had fractured the bone that connects the skull and the spinal column. Without the brace, one wrong move could render him paralyzed. I was so afraid because I knew how strong he was. When the physical therapist started working with him, he was difficult. Things changed when I was able to tell him that he would be graduating on the 12th at the hospital.

GOD sped the process. The school board superintendent, the principal, and counselor from Byrd High School got everything in order. We were blessed when the hospital administration agreed to allow us the use of the hallway outside of Josh's room for graduation.

Things with Andrew at home was getting stressed, even though he took great care of the household and me, it was time for him to leave. This man was not my husband or boyfriend, and our friendship could only be saved if he left. The week before, I'd called a hotel that was designed to help the homeless. I called the motel again that morning to see if they had an opening. The director told me, "Yes, we do. As a matter of fact, Andrew was on our list to call today for an intake appointment." They couldn't get him in before Monday though. Satisfied that things would be good for Andrew, my sons and I left for the hospital.

On Friday, May 12th, friends, family, and staff filled the space awaiting the graduation ceremony. I was saddened that my son Jeremy had to take a final exam and couldn't attend the ceremony. Dr. Goree and Principal Badgley dressed in their graduation robes and caps welcomed the crowd. The school counselor Mrs. Byrd was also there in an official capacity. Cordarius, Josh's Manager was amazing as the videographer, he filmed the graduation and even set the mood by playing the graduation march.

Tears and cheers flowed as Joshua dressed in his cap and gown walked out of his room, using his walker he was assisted by his therapist. We had been told he wouldn't be able to bear weight on his pelvis for weeks, but after moving speeches by Dr. Goree, and Mr. Badgley, my son with walker in tow, stepped up to receive his diploma, without the assistance of the therapist. This was so like Josh, he had something to prove by taking that walk alone. This was the most awesome graduation I'd ever attended. Josh was very happy as he returned to his bed. I was eternally grateful to everyone who

301

had made this happen, and all the support from everyone throughout this ordeal.

Our enjoyment of the day's activity was interrupted later that night. Jimmy had gotten a call from his father's family. Their Dad had been taken to the emergency room at another hospital and things didn't look good for him. Without hesitation, Jimmy asked for the car keys, and my sons quickly left Joshua and I to be there for him.

I had never had a week of turmoil like this before in my life. I spent the night with Josh, and while he slept I tried to cleanse the clotted blood from his matted hair. He had been the hairstyle trendsetter for the family, sporting waves, mohawks, even braids, and dreads. I wanted him to feel good when he looked in the mirror, getting past the scars on his face. GOD had shown much mercy on that handsome face.

I didn't get much sleep, and I was restless when I considered my life with and without their father Jimmy and the parts we both played in raising the kids. I even thought about the paradox of this situation with Josh and his Dad, and I was taken to a place long ago when Jimmy was arrested with Joshua in tow. A twinge of resentment crossed my mind, but I swiftly rebuked the thought. My sons didn't stay the night at the hospital with their Dad, but early the next morning till late afternoon they tended their Father's bedside.

On May 13th I received a call from my son at 3:33 pm. He told me that their Dad had been moved to ICU and the doctors had given him three to six months to live. Jimmy had also been informed by the doctor that as the oldest son, he would be responsible for making the decision to pull the plug if necessary.

Jimmy came back to Josh's room later to trade places with me. He stayed with Josh while I went home. Before stopping to rest, I checked on Champion and Jinxy. Andrew was taking care of those two, but I had really forgotten about the puppy till I heard him yelping. Within a few days, Jinxy was dead. I was told he had died of the puppy disease PARVO he probably had since his birth. It was sad to see Champion sniffing around for his new friend, and I had no way to tell him Jinxy was gone. As we honored his death with a burial in the backyard, I could only wonder, ***Did I bring this on by naming him Jinxy***. Up to that moment it had never occurred to me what his name meant. It just seemed to be the perfect name. I shed a few tears when I realized Joshua never got to see his puppy again.

Shuffling between hospital runs, exhaustion was taking its toll on everyone. We were blessed when Josh's friend agreed to spend the night with him. We all crashed as soon as we got home.

On Mother's Day, May 14th Jimmy was in a rush to get out the door. He asked me what my plans were. I told him "While you go see your Dad, I'll go be with Joshua." As though I had turned around in a circle, I surprised myself by then saying "I'm going with you son."

Their father's family was already there at 11:10 am when we arrived.

The doctor came in to report that his time was near, and we were allowed to visit. He was staring ahead, and when I looked into his eyes, he seemed so sad, unable to express any emotions. I was humbled as I looked into this dying man's eyes.

It was the strangest thing when suddenly the room felt like we were the only ones there. I was standing at his bedside holding his hand when I started to speak. His heart rate jumped to 43 and he appeared to be listening to me. I said; "Jimmy, Joshua is going to be alright. We did good thing together, and our sons are good. It's okay to go ***Home***, you can let go now". Slowly his eyelids fluttered as his heart rate fluctuated from 43 to 2 then back to 38.

Standing there, I was suddenly reminded of the great care and consideration my family had been given at the hospital University

Health (UH), and also about the Chaplain at UH where Joshua was. Then I remembered the great care I had received at the same hospital after suffering from my stroke. This seemed like an odd time for these thoughts until I realized there was no Chaplain on duty at this hospital.

Since there wasn't a Chaplain in the room, I waited, expecting one of Jimmy's family members to pray. In a moment of silence, the purpose of my being there was revealed to me. I just couldn't believe that *GOD* had chosen me to be what I called *The Minister In Charge* of my ex-husbands transition to *The Other Side*. I was honored to be a part of this rite of passage. Looking around at his family, I then started to pray. This was the hardest prayer of my life because I had held so many resentments toward this man for a long time. As in a flash, I was then released from all the resentments I held against him. Truth was, I no longer had a reason to be resentful. Then, while walking between his nieces, I started to sing "When we all get to heaven, what a day of rejoicing that will be. When we all see *JESUS*…we'll shout Victory." That day, I had no shame in the fact that I couldn't sang. My niece said "Aunt Gwen I am so glad you're here" as I held her in my arms. Solemnly we all watched as the heart monitor ticked from 20 to 7. Then, the doctor came in and said, "It's over". I looked up at the clock and it was 12:01 pm. Smiling, I thought *What a fitting time to go Home for a Desperado like Jimmy!* My vision was an old cowboy in a western taking his last breath after he'd fought his last fight at high noon at the OK Corral.

Later, I shared this testimony with a friend. Ashamed, I held back a smile as she said, "At least you got the last word".

Josh was transferred to Christus Schumpert Highland hospital rehabilitation facility. This was the same rehab place I was transferred to after the stroke, and the place where my son's father had died. He was cared for by the same professional and caring crew that took care of me. Everyone on the floor was very kind, but Josh was mean as a firecracker. One night he literally took off his neck brace. As a strong young man, he scared the nurse, and she called me in a panic. While rushing to the hospital with my sons in tow I called Josh's friend and manager Cordarius on the way. He arrived before us and was able to convince Joshua to put the brace back on. With constant prodding and pleadings, Joshua finally understood the consequences of taking off the brace.

The doctor allowed Joshua a release from rehab a day before his father's funeral for a chance to say goodbye. At the funeral home, I got a surprise when I learned that Jaleen and Jimmy had stepped up to help pay for their Dad's funeral. I was very proud of them. Jimmy was unable to stay for his Dad's funeral due to military obligations, but he was alright because he had been there for him. The twins did go to the funeral, and they were able to reconnect with their father's family.

When Joshua was released, he was delivered into my care. I continued to pray for his healing, but he would have to wait six months before surgery could be done on his bladder and urethra. Like a Champ, Joshua went through his day with humility. I was surprised when he would wear short pants with his catheter exposed.

University Health once again became a primary in our life as Joshua was scheduled for ongoing visits to the orthopedic and urology clinics. It was nice to know that we received the same quality of care and service as before. When we got to the six-month period to schedule surgery, we were told that the tearing of his urethra was extensive and the surgery would have to be done by an outside specialist. UH was a student teaching hospital, and I laughed at the vision of interns looking at each other saying "I'm not going to be responsible."

As we searched for an outside specialist; Joshua continued his care at the clinics. The devil must have been smiling because from the start it became apparent that we might not find a surgeon who would accept Medicaid. With each call, I'd get sick to my stomach at the thought that my son might not be able to get the surgery he needed because I couldn't afford to pay for this out of pocket expense.

Like trillions of times before, **GOD PREVAILED**. The Medicaid offices of Texas and Louisiana coordinated everything for Josh to be able to visit a specialist in Longview, TX. And his surgery was on May 9th, almost a year to date since the accident: **SUCCESS**.

Today, all my sons are still maturing into great men. Neither of them is a father and I have never been to the jailhouse to pick them up. Jimmy is a Sergeant in the USMC stationed in Pittsburg, PA. Joshua works now as an over the road truck driver. (This is amazing for someone injured in a terrible accident, and he still has no recollections of it). Jaleen and Jeremy have graduated in high school and completed their Eagle Scout requirements. Now, I can proudly say my sons finished the Boy Scouts program; one a Life Scout, and three Eagle Scouts. Jaleen works and has interviewed to be a Firefighter, we're awaiting word. Jeremy works full-time in telecommunications, exploring his vast interests from fashion designing, owning a clothing boutique to being a success in the foreign exchange market. Jeremy seems to be so much of me.

I am still challenged by my stroke condition. Though I have moments of regret about my actions on the day of the stroke, I am sure **GOD** chose for me to stay and tell this story *Relics Of A Woman (ROAW)*. I thank **GOD** for rescuing me, and because of **Him**, I move forward in my newness and completeness daily. I'm still here, still striving for my goals, and still encountering demons along the way.

During the completion of my first draft of **ROAW**, a family member playing the devil's advocate asked me "Why you want to write a book?" I told him, "I don't want to write a book, but I am writing a book because **GOD** has commanded me to do so." As the conversation continued I was close to crying when he said: "People want to read about triumph." I couldn't believe what he said because without a shadow of a doubt I knew my life's story was filled with triumph, even though sometimes it didn't seem like it.

Many years ago someone told me, "You always searching for the diamond on top of the garbage heap. Yo' problem is that all you had to do was reach up and take the diamond."

No longer searching, it took me a long time to learn that:

::: *I AM THE DIAMOND!!!*

I AM

THE DIAMOND!!!

I

AM

THE

DIAMOND...

Gwendolyn Hampton

GOD SAID SO!!!

Please let my weaknesses inspire you for your journey,
and let my strengths be stepping stones on your path.
Life is good if you're still alive.

Relics Of A Woman may be ordered through Amazon.com
or
Gwendolyn may be personally contacted for autographed copy at

Relicsofawoman18@gmail.com
or
paypal.me/ROAWFamilyFranchise
or
@Facebook /Messenger – Gwendolyn Hampton

Gwendolyn Hampton

Made in the USA
Columbia, SC
16 December 2024

49414203R00174